Praise for MUSICPRENEUR

"Next time you are deep into the 345th game of Angry Birds while sitting in your un-air-conditioned tour (mini)-van, feel guilty ... feel very guilty because you are wasting your talent and squandering your career if you aren't reading this book. Knowledge is power and Aaron's book is powerful!"

DAVID HAYMAN
Music Supervisor

"Well written and accurate."

PELLE LIDELL
European A&R Executive, Universal Music Publishing Group

"This book is a must-read for any emerging artist who wants to be able to understand and navigate the ever-changing landscape of the music business. Aaron shares knowledge within these pages that it took most of us years to learn on our own."

CHRIS KEATON
Nashville Songplugger (Reba McEntire, Brooks & Dunn, Martina McBride, George Strait ...)

more praise ...

"Personal and authentic, and chock full of useful advice. The chapter on social media marketing is worth the price of the book."

MARTY NEUMEIER
Author of *The Brand Gap, Zag* and *Metaskills*

"A great guide for musicians who need to master the sometimes daunting aspects of branding and marketing. Musicians all over will thank you for sharing your experience, practical advice and resources. ... Your chapter on branding is wonderful."

KAREN KANG
Author of *BrandingPays*

"In his book, Aaron adeptly discusses complex social media and brand management. His personable and knowledgeable writing style guides readers through the multifaceted new music industry, allowing them to benefit from his genuine expertise. In today's world of disruptive technology and big ideas, Aaron's book is an invaluable resource for any artist in the industry."

ROB FEDUK
HootSuite

"In the wake of technological disruption, a new music industry is emerging, and with it, the rise of the 'musicpreneur': those dedicated to craft and artistry, but also to entrepreneurial innovation and the DIY ethos. In *Musicpreneur*, Aaron explores the various components of a music 'start-up' and offers the reader practical tips for building a business. From profiling fans and creating a brand to managing social media and generating revenue, *Musicpreneur* offers you an inside look into what it takes to succeed in today's music market."

STEVE KELLER
CEO/Strategist, iV Audio Branding

"Musicians: Ignore this book at your peril. Here is a complete road map to career success, broken down for even the most novice of artists. If you are wondering why your music career hasn't taken off yet, here are the answers and the solutions to getting you on track. If you are looking for a solid sustainable career playing music, *Musicpreneur* takes a fresh look at what it means to be successful and provides a solid road map of getting there. Every musician needs to read this book right now."

LEE PARSONS
Co-founder, Ditto Music

Resources

THE FOLLOWING LINK WILL TAKE YOU TO AN ONLINE
RESOURCE COMPANION FOR THE BOOK:

ATNMUSI.CA/MUSICPRENEUR

FOR ANY QUESTIONS, SUGGESTIONS OR OBSERVATIONS,
INCLUDING LINK UPDATES, PLEASE CONTACT:

RESOURCE@MUSICPRENEUR.CA

MUSICPRENEUR

The Creative Approach
to Making Money in Music

By Aaron Bethune

Published by Above the Noise
abovethenoise.ca

Published in Canada by Above the Noise, Victoria, BC
www.abovethenoise.ca

Quantity sales: special discounts are available on quantity purchases by corporations, associations and others. For details, contact the publisher at the address above.

Printed in Canada

ISBN 978-0-9936367-0-7 (Print Version)
ISBN 978-0-9936367-1-4 (Ebook)

First Edition

Edited by Cheryl Cohen
www.cherylcohen.ca

Cover and interior designed by Josh Nychuk
www.nychukdesign.com

Foreword by Martin F. Frascogna
www.musicglobalization.com

For more information on the book and author please visit www.musicpreneur.ca

Library and Archives Canada Cataloguing in Publication

Bethune, Aaron, 1980-, author
    Musicpreneur : the creative approach to making money in music / by Aaron
Bethune ; edited by Cheryl Cohen ; designed by Josh Nychuk ; foreword by
Martin F. Frascogna.

Issued in print and electronic formats.
ISBN 978-0-9936367-0-7 (pbk.).—ISBN 978-0-9936367-1-4 (pdf)

1. Music entrepreneurship. 2. Music trade—Vocational guidance. I. Title.

ML3795.B563 2013   780.23   C2013-908584-X
                                      C2013-908585-8

FOR LAURA AND OLIVER

Contents

Foreword

BY MARTIN F. FRASCOGNA

We all have a passion for music. Oddly enough, we all interpret music differently. Music is beautiful because it's left up to the subjective process—and I'm not just talking about songs. Artists focus on chord progression, labels fixate on sales, managers drum up popularity, publishers focus on commercial appeal and lawyers care about contractual language.

One decade ago the music business was a marvellous yet predictable three-ring circus; now it's a chaotic free-for-all given the new outlets, fan interaction and do-it-yourself tactics within every professional avenue. One area has become immune to DIY, though, and regardless of time, it can never be duplicated by apps, seminars or blog postings: information about the "international music economy" is now a kind of holy grail, but unless you have practical experience navigating the global music market, it can't be acquired. Just like the subjective process of music, depending on the geographical region, the global market can be interpreted as either a glorious opportunity for expansion or a scary fast track to unemployment. As a result, it's essential to gather tools for expansion in all areas of music, and this book—envisioned through the eyes of practical experience and incorporating up-to-date knowledge—delivers those tools.

I first had the pleasure of meeting Aaron Bethune as an interviewee on his podcast *Above the Noise*. During the interview, Aaron asked me several questions that forced a level of self-assessment. My legal practice revolves purely around international expansion for artists, labels and publishers, but I had never thought about how I ended up here. "International expansion" is an extremely niche area of the music industry—more so, within the legal aspects of the music business—so I was somewhat shocked when Aaron explored the depths of my answers on his blog. It wasn't until months later that I realized Aaron possibly possessed more "global" music experience than anyone else I've been in contact with. This revelation came through the form of a modern-day version of Seven Degrees of Aaron Bethune. While I was speaking with a client in Nashville, the band referenced a producer who worked with Aaron in Canada. Later, during a conference call with a client in Dublin, they too referenced Aaron. Weeks later, during contract discussions with a manager in Stockholm, the manager directed me to information found on Aaron's blog. At that moment I realized Aaron not only understood every aspect of music, but he was globally respected for his view and, more importantly, understood that music works differently in different places, with different contexts. Promotional tactics being used in Sydney don't work in the same way for an artist in Los Angeles. Booking agents don't approach venues the same way in Finland and China, nor do labels and artists engage fans with the same social media strategies in Asia as those used in Europe. The music world is vast and filled with opportunity, but the music world is fragmented and different.

What is this book? This book is *un-ordinary*. Unlike most books, *Musicpreneur* can be read from middle to end, backwards to foreword, Chapter 3 to Chapter 5. Just like music, the book will work differently for different people, different professions, different regions with different objectives. However, one thing is consistent: the information is more practical and far superior to any other industry reads. Regardless of your music industry knowledge, *Musicpreneur* will educate and force you to re-evaluate your approach from both a social media and global perspective.

—December 2, 2013

International entertainment lawyer Martin F. Frascogna has Grammy Award-winning clients, is a published author on touring in Europe and is known for his blog (www.musicglobalization.com). In recent years, Billboard *has ranked his lectures as a top attraction at the annual Midem music event in Cannes.*

Prologue

I have been struggling with the idea of the so-called middle-class musician and what success means in today's music industry. Making music is still a long way from being a selectable option as a full-time career. I can't say that I really believe the middle-class musician currently exists. You're on your way up or on your way down in this industry. Sensational success stories of independent artists like crowdfunding record-breaker Amanda Palmer and chart-topping rapper Macklemore are the anomaly, and certainly Palmer and Macklemore were not overnight successes. They are entrepreneurial, independent grassroots performers who have built their careers by connecting directly with fans and without needing labels. But the fact that they are not the norm is why we hear about them.

When something is "different" we pay attention and, if all the right ingredients are there, we may see a recipe for success. However, trying to replicate the recipe will always miss the key ingredient "difference," because what originally made us pay attention will have already been done before. The more people imitate others the less engaging their work becomes, because a pattern starts to form. And to engage a potential audience's mind you need to break the patterns and create novelty. The exciting thing is that now is the perfect time to be novel, to get creative. We have all the tools available and no one telling us what to do. The most talented, creative, committed, connected and daring individuals stand the best chance of success.

I have come to believe that Talent + Experience + Knowledge = Ability to see opportunity; how you react to the opportunities you are given is the true test of commitment and dedication. Major factors in how you will react include the moments that lead up to the opportunity that turns into the "overnight success"; the environment you have been in; and the support you have around you.

I truly believe that knowledge is a powerful tool. The more knowledge you have, the more ability you will have to see opportunities clearly and make better choices. My hope is that the contents of this book can help to build your knowledge and that you can take action on some of the ideas to build your own experiences. The best thing you could possibly do is take the information and turn it on its head to find new ways of using it.

Albert Einstein said: "No problem can be solved from the same level of consciousness that created it." In order to solve a problem you cannot do it from within the problem; you have to be outside it. For this reason I believe that the music industry is not necessarily the place to look for answers to help you build your career, but rather that those outside the industry may provide more insight into creative ideas that you can apply back to your career. So read books about other industries, talk to people in car sales and in hospitality, find the light that will allow you to shine in completely new ways, because if you can interrupt the patterns people will pay attention.

We are living in an exciting time in the music industry. It is a time of great opportunity and creativity. We get to be confidently ourselves and to celebrate our difference, and for the first time we have all the tools at our fingertips to let the world know we exist! We can create and at the click of a button share it with the world. How cool is that? But, as Eleanor Roosevelt said, "With freedom comes responsibility": with the middleman gone we need to know how to do it all ourselves.

I remember being told that before you can run a company you need to know how to do everyone's job. When it comes to promoting yourself in the music industry you certainly need to know how to do it all, at least until you build a team. I will, however, emphasize that it is impossible to "do it all" and that nobody with a high level of success does, which is why it is imperative to build a team. People in this industry want to work with artists who are talented and who understand the bigger picture. You would be amazed at how many people will give you their time if they believe in you. Studios, managers, lawyers, agents—they all have stories to tell of artists they have helped pro bono because they believed in them. This book will give you the skills to do it all and attract a team along the way.

At first it might seem surprising that with all the free information, platforms and resources available at our fingertips, and with all the millions of talented musicians out there, there aren't more making a full-time living from music. But is it really that surprising? The truth is that as musicians we love the music but not the business. Many musicians dream of making a living from performing and recording original music exclusively. We want the music to be enough. And the fact that the resources are available doesn't mean that they are being taken advantage of. Chances are that 99 percent of the people who read this book will never put a significant portion of the contents to use. And if they do, their efforts will be short-lived and lack consistency in application. Probably 99 percent of all musicians in general will never approach a career in music as a business. Business simply does not interest them.

So who are the 1 percent? Who achieves success? Who makes money in music and builds a lasting career? Who makes music their business? My answer is the highly talented, creative, laser-focused and dedicated entrepreneurial musician. The musicpreneur.

Perspective is everything. You are already an entrepreneur:

> "Entrepreneur ... a person who starts or organizes a commercial enterprise, esp. one involving financial risk."
> —The Canadian Oxford Dictionary

Just think of the work you have already put in, the risks you have already taken, the money you have already invested in gear, travel, lessons, recording, marketing and so on. Your business is your music, your band, your career. You were immersed in musicprenuership a long time ago.

What's exciting is that your only real competition in the musical workplace is the 1 percent—people like you, I hope, who are willing to read this book and make the commitment to apply its contents.

Once you look at things from this new perspective, you'll realize that getting heard above the noise is easier than you might have thought.

I began writing *Musicpreneur* while I was preparing to teach a course on the music industry. My focus was as much on mindset as it was on the hands-on tools that musicians can put to use immediately. Mindset takes a little more practice!

Since picking up my first instrument at the age of four and my second at the age of seven, I have had the opportunity to record albums, play studio sessions, perform live, study music at university, manage artists, book international tours, place music in film and TV, market projects and brand careers, as well as consult for labels, publishers and other businesses. I have had what feels like a unique opportunity to see many angles of the industry. Even so it took a while for me to feel I could write this book. But, of all the things I have done so far, this labour of love has felt most authentically me. I simply had to write it.

I've called it *Musicpreneur: The Creative Approach to Making Money in Music* because it is meant as a resource, a source of inspiration and a practical guide not only to help develop your artistic career but also to make you more money. It can be read from beginning to end or by jumping from chapter to chapter.

After condensing my experiences in both the music business and music performance for a series of workshops and a full-length course, I had a ton of notes that really needed to be in the hands of musicians while the information was still relevant. I was especially happy when two people I really respect, graphic designer Josh Nychuk and editor Cheryl Cohen, agreed to join forces with me to present this in the form of a book.

Keep asking questions, keep sight of your goals, keep going and always enjoy the ride. Music should first and foremost be fun. When you have fun, so does everybody else and it becomes contagious.

I want you to be successful because I know you can be.

Before reading any further … **Step 1: Make incredible music.**

Introduction

THE WISDOM OF A MOUNTAIN

An Eye- and Mind-Opening Experience

Dreams become reality when you stop seeing them as dreams.

In late January 2000, just a few weeks after my nineteenth birthday, I stood looking up at the summit of Cerro Aconcagua. I was 200 metres from the top of one of the world's Seven Summits, the highest peak in the world outside of Asia. I was so close to reaching the goal I had set and had spent seven intense months preparing for physically and mentally. I was so close, so close, and yet I decided to turn back!

The decision to turn back and the sequence of events that unravelled afterwards have been some of my biggest life lessons. I apply these lessons to music, business and life on a daily basis. If I didn't tell this story I would be leaving out a major factor in the driving force behind what I do and how I do it. You see, it is not what we do that makes us successful but rather how we do it.

There and back

On the eve of our Argentine summit bid, as I lay in my tent contemplating the fourteen-hour climb ahead, I heard someone calling out "Mike, Mike, Mike … " The same American voice started asking "Does anyone have a radio?" Nobody answered. At over 6,000 metres and well after 10 p.m., most climbers would have been sleeping. What could be wrong? I stuck my head out of my tent and called "Over here." The others in the encampment were Swiss, Polish, German, Chilean or Argentine and not about to try to communicate with the American who had called out into the night. I was the only other native English speaker in our high-altitude camp.

It turned out that "Mike" had left for the summit at 1 a.m. and still had not returned.

A seasoned climber who had previously summited Everest, Mike had felt confident he could make the Andes summit bid alone. It was his climbing partner who was calling out for Mike and somebody with a radio. Mike's partner had stayed behind because he was not feeling prepared to attempt the summit due to trouble acclimatizing (later he was evacuated by helicopter due to a cerebral edema).

The fact that Mike had not returned was concerning because some of the world's worst storms are known to cover the Cerro Aconcagua summit after midday. No living person was likely to be descending the mountain after ten o'clock at night!

Climbing Cerro Aconcagua is said to be comparable to climbing an 8,000-metre-high Himalayan mountain. In the Himalayas the treeline reaches around the 5,000-metre level, and in the Andes the treeline ends 3,000 or so metres up, suggesting comparable conditions in terms of oxygen. For this reason there is a a school of thought that says the Cerro Aconcagua might have a "death zone," where the oxygen level is below 50 percent of that available at sea level and is not enough to sustain life.

The possibility that Mike was still wandering in the death zone on a storm-beaten mountainside was unlikely. The possibility that he would make it through the night was even more unlikely.

At the time, I was sharing a tent with Christian—our team leader and a native of Chile. He had climbed some of the world's highest mountains and later that year would accompany his sister to the top of Mount Everest, making her the first South American woman to set foot on the summit.

Christian had participated in many successful high-altitude rescues and seen his fair share of death too. He knew how to lower a living body down a mountain and he also knew the techniques for getting a corpse down.

It was Christian who radioed base camp to pass on word of Mike's disappearance. We were told that an Argentine army rescue party would leave in the morning and that there was nothing that could be done until then.

With my lack of experience in high-altitude rescues, and the enthusiasm of a nineteen-year-old, I felt concerned that we should leave immediately to search for Mike ourselves. Christian assured me that we would be risking our own lives and that we were highly unlikely to find Mike until sunlight. So instead we told Mike's climbing partner to have soup, other liquids and food on hand in case Mike should return that night. It was going to be a matter of hurry up and wait.

That night all I could think about was the possibility of having to step over Mike's dead body the next day. What would I feel if I saw Mike lying lifeless in front of me, having failed at what I myself was about to attempt? Did I really want it that bad? Was I like Mike, ready to give my life for a dream? I couldn't stop thinking about it and the questions spun in my oxygen-deprived brain until it was time to get up.

We had decided to leave for the summit at 4 a.m. Due to the fact that we had carelessly melted ice with our Coleman stove next to the tent opening, the condensation from the steam had frozen to the inside of our tent during the night. So between the thoughts of finding Mike's corpse and the subzero temperatures of our tent-turned-igloo, it had not been a restful night to say the least. In the neighbouring tent I could hear another member of our team throwing up his breakfast in a struggle with altitude sickness. It was the start of a day to remember.

When you climb in high altitude, everything is slow-moving—including your thoughts. The lack of oxygen gives you just enough of a high to let you feel somewhat detached from the rest of your body. Everything becomes rhythmical: ten steps, stop, breathe, ten steps, stop, breathe. The interesting thing is that you realize the true test is more about the mind than the body. You are so alone. You can hear your every breath and every heartbeat. Even if you can see other climbers, you feel isolated and alone inside your own body, left to your thoughts and mental stamina. With all the physical and mental discomforts that go with high-altitude climbing, it is a wonder people keep doing it.

Because of the conditions your body is under it is important to stop frequently to hydrate and consume calories. Having enough provisions for the climb requires multiple portering trips up the mountain. For our trip to base camp we had used mules to porter everything. From there on out we were our own porters. From base camp we portered up half our equipment and provisions to "Cambio de Pendiente" (also known as Camp Alaska), roughly 1,000 vertical metres above base camp. After dropping off the material we headed back down to base camp. We would continue up the mountain in this way. The additional benefit of going up and down the mountain portering is that it allows you to acclimatize.

We were also applying a technique called "climb high sleep low." The idea is that you take your body to a new altitude, forcing it to adapt and acclimatize, and then you descend to a lower altitude to sleep. This way the lower altitude feels more comfortable as your body has been pushed to new extremes. For example, you might climb to 3,500 metres and sleep at 3,000 metres, then climb the next day to 4,500 metres and sleep at 4,000 metres, and so on.

A person suffering from the effects of high altitude can be put into a special bag that gets pumped full of air to increase the air pressure and recreate the effect of descending to a lower altitude. We had a bag with us and I wondered if we would be putting it to use.

I had been experiencing pain in my hands that had started shortly after leaving the tent in the morning. The pain had grown consistently worse as the morning progressed. It got to the point where it felt like knives were being stuck into my hands and I was having trouble moving them. Finally I could take it no longer and Christian helped warm my hands with friction. They had begun to get frostbitten due

4

to my gloves being too tight and cutting off the circulation. I could only imagine the pain that Mike must have experienced being lost on the mountain for more than twenty-four hours.

As I rested on a rock in the morning, the sun emerged over the horizon, casting a giant shadow of the Aconcagua over the surrounding mountains. I distinctly remember it because it looked like a giant pyramid with the sun directly at its peak. At that moment I remember feeling totally insignificant in the grand scheme of things. Material objects had absolutely no importance. I felt small and the world felt immense. I was grateful for the oxygen I was breathing and became acutely aware of what was truly valuable. It was perhaps the closest to a religious experience I had ever been. I felt truly humbled at the enormity of the world and of life. I was a small being among massive and majestic mountains.

The climb toward the summit was slow but sure—a consistent combination of climbing and resting to regain energy. The higher we climbed the tougher it became. It was by far the most physical and mentally challenging experience of my life.

In the hour before I decided to turn back I had started to think about the trip so far. I was living in Spain at the time, and had missed my flight from Bilbao to London, England due to unexpected circumstances. I had got to the Bilbao airport extra early to check in, only to discover that no one could find my reservation until five minutes after the plane took off. I asked them to check that my flight from London to Santiago, Chile the next day wasn't going to give me any problems. The lady at the British Airways desk told me, "I'm afraid, sir, we have you going to San Diego in California … " My trip to the Andes had started on an unexpected footing. I was put up in a five-star hotel in front of the Guggenheim Museum Bilbao, driven to and from the airport in a Mercedes, wined and dined, and had my ticket changed from San Diego to Santiago free of charge, resulting in my ticket costing half the price it would have cost had they not made the mistake. As I thought about the process I realized everything had felt natural—nothing was forced. I had enjoyed every step of the way, but now my thoughts were interrupted; I had begun to realize that I had trained only to get to the top and had never visualized my descent. I started to doubt myself, and I wasn't sure I was supposed to continue. The lack of sleep and the physical exhaustion were taking their toll. I remember distinctly feeling like I could make it to the top but uncertain I would have the energy to make it down.

The hardest part of the decision to turn back was imagining what people back home would think. While I thought about these things I continued putting one foot in front of the other. Finally as the summit appeared I heard the voice of my grandmother, who had recently passed away. "Don't worry about other people," she said. "Making the decision to turn back is harder than deciding to continue. Your friends and family will be proud." At that moment I decided that I was not going to continue. It was such a difficult thing to do, yet my gut told me it was the right thing to do. I told Christian my intentions and he said he and the other climbers could always help me down if need be. I told him that I had enjoyed every step of the way so far but didn't feel I would enjoy the rest. I certainly didn't want to rely on others to get down.

I knew I could descend alone and assured Christian I'd be okay. We hugged and I gave him my camera to take photos from the summit.

As I started down the mountain I became aware that I was alone. At that time of day climbers were either getting to the summit or had already turned back. I enjoyed the beauty of the mountain and sat for a moment contemplating the experience. I don't remember feeling for one moment that I had made the wrong decision to turn back. I got up and kept going down the mountain.

After about an hour into my descent I started to notice my body feeling the benefits of a lower altitude. As I came around a large rock I noticed what appeared to be a person wearing a red and black mountaineering suit lying on a glacier in the distance. As I got closer I could see one of this person's arms moving in an attempt to put snow into his mouth. Nobody would be attempting to head up the mountain at that time of day and neither would anyone normally be trying to "drink" snow. Could it be Mike?

"*Eres* Mike?" I called out in Spanish.

No response.

"Are you Mike?" I called out in English.

"Yes."

Mike had reached the summit the day before, around 1 p.m. He had got lost on the way down and ended up on the wrong side of the mountain, dangerously close to the south face, a 3,000-metre vertical drop. In the Southern Hemisphere the south face is always the most treacherous; of course in the Northern Hemisphere it is the north face that is always the hardest.

Mike had ended up sleeping a short distance from a high-altitude makeshift shelter used by many climbers in similar situations. Sleeping in the shelter would have saved him from being exposed to the subzero temperatures and gale-force winds. The extreme cold had frostbitten Mike's fingers and his toes on both feet (something we discovered later after cutting his boots off).

When I found Mike he was still heading in the wrong direction and in bad condition. I helped him sit up and gave him some of my juice and chocolate energy bars. He started telling me what had happened but was making little sense. After what seemed like fifteen minutes I helped him stand up, but he lost his balance and fell. He could not put any weight on his right foot (it had suffered the worst frostbite). I helped him up again, this time putting his arm around my neck so I could help take some of the weight off his foot.

We started down the mountain. Once again it became a rhythm—we would go a few steps, stop, start again. Mike was a big guy, my build but about a head taller. Surprisingly, all my own feelings of fatigue and mental stamina had been replaced with wanting to get Mike down to the last high-altitude camp.

The process of starting and stopping for air as well as needing longer breaks to drink and consume calories made our descent extremely slow. Surprisingly nobody passed us. We were still "alone together."

After five hours some brightly coloured spots appeared below us in the distance. It was the camp where we had spent the night and where Mike's partner would be waiting for Mike's return.

Mike and I continued to slowly make our way down. Seeing the tents was both an encouragement and a challenge as I knew we would not be there for hours at the pace we were going. Once we got closer I estimated that, if I left Mike, I could be back at the camp in under an hour and notify people to get help. We could go back up and bring Mike down more efficiently. I told Mike my plan. I told him I would leave him my supplies and be back to get him. He agreed to stay put and wait.

I couldn't get down fast enough. I wanted to be able to tell Mike's partner that Mike was okay, I wanted to get help, I wanted to let the rescue team know where Mike was ... but at high altitude things take a long time—it's hard to be fast.

Close to an hour later I was walking into camp. It was like a ghost town: the tents were empty and nobody was there. Then I saw Mike's climbing partner. He was talking to a Japanese climber and they appeared to be the only people in camp. As I got closer I could hear Mike's partner telling the other climber about Mike, what he looked like, when he had left. They hadn't noticed my arrival and continued to talk until I came right up to them. Mike's partner didn't recognize me and I had to recount our interaction from the night before. Then I told him that I had found Mike. He physically dropped to his knees. He started to say "What will I tell his wife, what will I tell his children ... ?" It suddenly occurred to me that, because I'd said I had found Mike but he was not with me, he had assumed I'd found Mike's body. I quickly told him that Mike was alive, that I had had to leave him in order to come for help. The look of joy the man had was contagious; you could see the weight come off his shoulders as he realized his friend was alive and that he wouldn't have bad news to deliver.

After explaining the situation to Mike's partner and the Japanese climber, they convinced me to stay in camp and rest while they went to get Mike. Technically Mike was close by and as soon as they got just above the camp they would see him where I had left him waiting.

I went to my tent and collapsed inside from exhaustion. I have no idea how much time transpired—it felt like only a minute but it was probably hours … I awoke to a familiar voice outside my tent: it was Mike's partner. They had found Mike but not where I had left him, because he had managed to continue lowering himself down the mountain but once again in the wrong direction. Still, they had finally managed to get him down to camp. His boots had to be cut off due to the swelling and frostbite. Mike's partner had come to me to ask what to do. I realized later that because of our interactions he had come to believe I was an experienced climber in high-altitude search and rescue, which I was not. I knew there was a rescue party somewhere but had no way of communicating with them. Christian had our only radio and he was still coming down from the summit (that day Christian summited Cerro Aconcagua for the thirteenth time).

Outside my tent the camp had started to come to life with people coming back from the summit and new climbers arriving to spend the night before their own summit bid.

I got out of my tent and began to search for a radio, but couldn't find a single person who had one. I asked other climbers for help to get Mike down to base camp, but none of them were about to change plans or leave their groups.

In the process of looking for a radio I met a climber from Whistler in British Columbia, Canada. You never know where you are going to run into a fellow Canadian!

After a while I saw somebody getting into camp. I approached him to ask if he had a radio. He did. He was an Argentine who worked as a park warden down the mountain and he was on the way back from climbing to the summit for the first time himself.

The park warden radioed down to let base camp know that Mike had been found and to inform the rescue team where he was. Once he got word of where the rescue team was we realized we needed to get Mike down ourselves, at least part of the way. Mike's partner was too weak to be of use and said he would stay to pack up their gear. The Asian climber was part of a team on their way up not down.

The warden and I decided that the best way to help Mike was to hold two ski poles between us, with the warden at the front, Mike in the middle and me at the back. We had taped Mike's boots onto his frostbitten feet so he would still be able to have them protected from the ground and the cold. We were going to be carrying most of his weight with the ski poles, but he still had to take some of his own weight.

Before leaving I had packed up half the tent and supplies so that Christian could rest when he got back from the summit and yet not have to carry everything. We had given our soups to Mike's partner the night before and I had given my remaining food and drinks to Mike as we came down together. At this point I was oblivious to my own dehydration.

The three of us started our descent, from the high-altitude camp at 6,000 metres toward base camp at 4,500 metres. Carrying Mike on ski poles had seemed like a good idea but was easier said than done. Finding footing was treacherous and the three of us had to work at it together. We took a while to find a rhythm. I remember that at one point we reached an especially steep section of scree and snow, at the bottom of which was a cliff with an almost 2,000-metre fall. In the heat of the moment we decided to go down the scree without rope and hope we would be able to stop ourselves before the cliff. The warden told Mike to put his arms around us and just try and walk forward; meanwhile, the warden and I were going to brace ourselves together physically to slow down the descent. Our technique worked and resulted in a controlled descent of skidding and sliding down.

What had taken eight hours to climb up the day before took twenty minutes to descend!

Moving in a rhythm and making good time, we arrived at the Nido de Condores camp at 5,500 metres. We stopped for a break and the warden said I should wait with Mike for the rescue team. He told me they would be there shortly and would take over.

Mike and I waited for more than an hour. The little break finally gave the two of us a chance to chat. We talked about his climb and the series of events that had taken place. We talked about previous climbs, including his time spent on Everest. At times Mike's sentences made little sense, which gave me an idea of his mental condition.

When Mike heard about my own frostbite due to my gloves, he tried to offer me his as a gift for helping him. He told me I had saved his life. We also talked about having a beer at base camp and celebrating, not only the climb but the safe return.

Finally eight climbers appeared. It was the Argentine army, the rescue team. We were very happy to see them—we had been looking forward to this moment all day!

What should have been the end of our worries was not. It turned out the rescue team had not acclimatized and were suffering from altitude sickness. The warden appeared from wherever he had been just in time for the army team to ask if the two of us were okay to continue carrying Mike. Of course it was not what we had expected, but we were not about to leave Mike with a sick and fatigued army rescue team that needed rest themselves.

Mike, the warden, eight soldiers and I continued down the mountain. The warden and I continued carrying Mike as the soldiers walked ahead. After probably no more than twenty minutes into our descent there was a loud flapping behind us and then a large thud. We all turned and there, not even 100 metres behind us, was a combination of ropes and colourful material flapping in the wind, covering what appeared to be a man.

Believe it or not a man had attempted a world record by jumping off the summit of Cerro Aconcagua with a paraglider. His attempt had ended abruptly when he fell from the sky and crashed behind us. At this point the Argentine soldiers left us so they could rescue the paraglider. Once again Mike, the warden and I were heading down the mountain alone.

It was at Cambio de Pendiente, the first camp, at the top of the 1,000-vertical-metre slope directly above base camp, that Mike, the warden and I were finally met by six acclimatized climbers, including wardens from base camp.

We had been watching the party of six make their way toward us for some time. The warden had recognized the group and signalled to let them know it was us. They took Mike in a quick changeover. The warden went with them, leaving me to retrieve some gear I had left hidden close to the camp at Cambio de Pendiente.

I was alone again. It was surreal, as there was no longer another person to be worrying about and no distractions from my own thoughts of exhaustion. I started to realize how thirsty I was and that I had given all my drinks and food to Mike.

Just as I started to think about where I would find something to drink, I heard a familiar voice say "Aaron! *Aqui!* [Here!]" It was Christian and was I ever happy to see him again—the last time had been when we hugged 200 metres from the summit, and that felt like a long time ago because so much had happened since.

Christian told me that he had been looking for me and that he was afraid I had gotten lost.

The warden, Mike and I had completed in one day what usually is a two- or three-day descent from the summit. We were in view of base camp. Although far below us it felt so tauntingly close! Christian had given me the last bit of his water, but I still felt thirsty. It was getting dark and I wanted more than anything to get back to base camp.

We started down the scree slope. Since my mind was no longer on getting Mike down, but rather on getting myself down, I started to feel extremely tired. I was dehydrated and burning my last calories. I was thankful to have Christian with me and to know he would get us to base camp. It looked like I would still be getting his help down even if it wasn't from the summit.

Two and a half hours later we entered the maze of snow and ice formations at the bottom of the scree. We had to wind and squeeze our way through the remarkable formations that towered above our heads.

When you come out of the ice maze you are so close to base camp that you can hear people talking as well as smell fires burning and food cooking.

I remember stumbling into base camp, getting to the mess tent and taking the largest swig of orange-powder drink of my life. It was so satisfying that I still remember the feeling to this day. I felt exhausted but with an adrenalin rush that wasn't about to let me sleep.

Down at base camp they had been following the events and cheered us in as heroes. Although taking credit doesn't come easily to me, I certainly was made to feel like a hero for one day.

That night the whole team gathered for dinner. We all had reasons to celebrate—the mountain had given us each an individual experience. At base camp they had champagne for us, and Hans, our German team member, had brought a bottle of Ballantine's eighteen-year-old whisky.

By the time we finished dinner we were all happy and feeling the benefits of warmth, food and good company. Some of us had made a circle and were using the massive water barrels as drums; some barrels were empty and some were full, and so the sound was quite musical. Someone played the mouth harp and another person danced like it was some kind of ritual. We played until a neighbouring team, I believe the Germans, asked us to stop. What a party, but we were all happy to call it a night. Our tents and sleeping bags were waiting for us.

I had had only a glass of champagne and a sip of whisky, but at high altitude your body reacts differently from usual and in my case that meant I was more than a few sheets to the wind.

Outside a storm was blowing something fierce. I made my way to my tent and crawled in. As I lay on my back I couldn't help but hear the storm, which was blowing my tent so hard that it was folding right over and the sides were touching my face. In a haze of exhaustion, alcohol and a full stomach, I fell asleep feeling more comfortable in my sleeping bag than I had ever felt at a five-star hotel.

I have never seen Mike since. We never got to have that beer or get each other's information to stay in touch—he was flown out before we had a chance.

Personal realizations

"Only those who will risk going too far can possibly find out how far one can go."—T.S. Eliot

Extremes give us the ability to learn about ourselves, about the way we react, the decisions we make, and how perspective is everything. You never truly know what you are capable of until you push yourself to your limit. Always challenge yourself because life really does begin at the end of your comfort zone.

Successful businessman-turned-actor Rick Wells once told me that he had got into acting to "feel uncomfortable." He had been highly successful at everything he had done and it was because he was able to grow from the experience of being outside of his comfort zone. The fact is that success stories all seem to involve challenge.

It's the people who not only endure the journey but find ways to enjoy every step of the way that make it to the destination. You can't climb the highest mountain without ever losing your breath, but you can't deplete your energy on the first hill—you have to be ready for all weather conditions, and you can't depend on anyone else to get you to the top. Success in music certainly isn't a sprint, it's a marathon.

With great success often comes great risk. The greater the risk, the greater the reward. In climbing, the person taking the lead has the farthest to fall but also enjoys the first view from the summit.

Sitting on the side of a mountain in high altitude gave me a vision of the world and a new view on life. We really are not as important as we think we are. We are a piece of the bigger whole. Perspective is everything. No matter how big a deal something may feel to you, it really is a minute piece of the big picture.

CHAPTER ONE

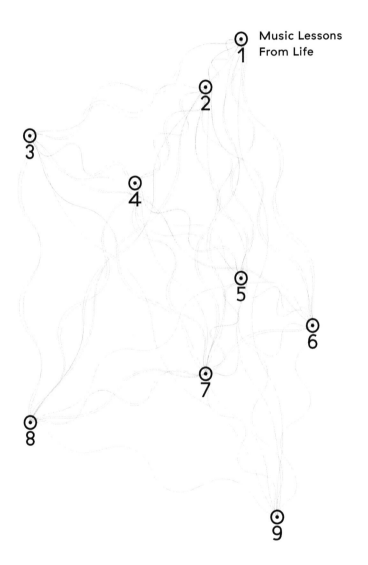

1 Music Lessons
From Life

2

3

4

5

6

7

8

9

Music Lessons from Life

Mountaineering taught me that the importance of life is in every breath I take and in the experiences that come with the moments that take my breath away. There is nothing a BMW or Mercedes is going to do that would be more important than my next breath. I realized that my life could affect others. I realized that life doesn't always go as we expect but that if we trust our gut and let life guide our decisions the outcome can be better than our expectations.

Are things meant to be?

In my late teens, during a high-altitude climb in the Andes, I saved a climber's life (see Introduction). The idea that I trained seven months to overlap with another person's life at a crucial moment is an interesting thought. I can't help but think that it was meant to be. So the question is: Do we have any control or is everything just meant to be?

Are successful musicians meant to be? Are they born to be stars? Are they handed more opportunities?

I believe we are put in the path of opportunity constantly. But we have to recognize opportunity when it presents itself. And for that we need experience and knowledge. Success is not an overnight event; it comes about through developing talent, building knowledge through experience, meeting the right people, making good decisions and knowing how to act when opportunity presents itself.

When opportunity does present itself, how we act on it is based on a combination of our experience, our ability to take risks, our commitment and dedication, our drive, our passion … And when we are given an opportunity to shine, we have to believe we are worthy to take it.

This idea that people are born with talent or that success is something that happens to a select lucky few is hotly debated. Recent research has perhaps come up with an answer; it was led by Fred Travis, PhD, director of the Center for the Brain, Consciousness, and Cognition at Maharishi University of Management in Fairfield, Iowa, and Harald Harung, PhD, of the Oslo and Akershus University College of Applied Sciences in Norway.

"There must be some common inner attributes and processes that make top performers able to deliver at the top level, regardless of profession or activity," Travis was quoted as saying in a recent article on the Psych Central website. "We found this common inner dimension to be what we called higher mind-brain development."

The study examined top performers in management, sports and music and found they also had "peak" experiences that featured such qualities as inner calm, maximum wakefulness, happiness and transcendence of ordinary time and space.

The article said the research has brought up questions such as "Is there a way to develop one's brain to have more of these characteristics and perform at a higher level?" and "Can measuring a person's brain predict the potential for someone to be a world-class performer?"

As a musician, I have had peak experiences while performing and in business I have had peak experiences when making critical decisions. These peak experiences have been directly connected to my confidence. This confidence comes from the knowledge, talent and ability that I have developed over my lifetime involvement in music and its business. With knowledge and experience, over time I have become a master at my craft.

I don't believe that we are born successful or exceptionally talented, but rather that we have the ability to develop and cultivate our bodies and minds through practice over time. The environment that surrounds us hugely affects our success. To use the mountain analogy, I believe that with the right amount of training and preparation anyone can climb a mountain; however, the environment—in particular the weather—will affect the outcome. Many factors contribute to success and how it is obtained. Did your family teach you to expect great things? Or were you told that life would be a struggle and that success only comes to a select few? It all plays a part!

10,000 hours

Over the years more than one of my teachers and mentors has told me that in order to become an expert, a master, at something you need to spend ten thousand hours working on your craft. Whether it is business or performance, you have to put the time in. Practise enough scales, chords, motifs, licks and riffs for long enough and they'll find their way into your playing without your even having to think about it. With time you'll identify chord qualities, progressions, harmonies and so on. Your knowledge will expand so that you can write for orchestras and big bands or produce commercial tracks for radio. But it doesn't happen overnight. The greatest players will always tell you that they are not thinking about what they are playing when they play, but rather that they are just letting it come out. They are in the moment. With ten thousand hours of practice you don't need to think; you just react and can "let it come out." You can be "in the moment."

Malcolm Gladwell, in his book *Outliers*, makes a great case that ten thousand hours is the key to success in any field. He states that achievement is talent plus preparation. Especially interesting is one particular example in the book that I feel musicians reading this will relate to. It's a study that was conducted in the early 1900s by the psychologist K. Anders Ericsson and two colleagues at Berlin's elite Academy of Music.

The academy's professors helped divide the school's violinists into three groups: (1) students who had the potential to be world-class soloists, (2) the "merely good," and (3) students who were unlikely to ever play professionally and were more likely to become teachers in the public school system. The focus of the study was to determine how many hours of practice the students had put in over the course of their career.

The results were remarkable. Although all the students had started playing at about the same age (at age five), and put in a similar amount of practice over the first few years, by the time they were twenty they had put in vastly different hours of practice: well over ten thousand hours each for those in the elite group; about eight thousand hours each for those in group 2; and about four thousand hours each for those in group 3.

Of particular note in Ericsson's study is that, as quoted from Gladwell's *Outliers*:

> He and his colleagues couldn't find any "naturals," musicians who floated effortlessly to the top. ... Nor could they find any "grinds," people who worked harder than everyone else, yet just didn't have what it took to break the top ranks. Their research suggests that once a musician has enough ability to get into a top music school, the thing that distinguishes one performer from another is how hard he or she works. That's it. And ... the people at the very top don't work just harder or even much harder than everyone else. They work much, much harder. (p. 39)

Gladwell uses examples of the ten-thousand-hour rule with the careers of the likes of Bill Gates and The Beatles. He explains that it takes ten years, four hours a day, to accumulate ten thousand hours of focused practice.

The more I have researched, the more examples I have found of the ten-thousand-hour rule in action. Ed Viesturs, the first American high-altitude mountaineer to climb the world's fourteen highest peaks and the fifth person to do so without supplemental oxygen, made his first attempt to climb Mount Everest in 1987, exactly ten years into his climbing career. People in Nashville say it is a "ten-year town."

Is the problem that we are too impatient when it comes to finding success? It seems to me that with time everything is possible. You just need to be consistent!

Consistency

My experience while mountaineering made it excruciatingly obvious to me that success and reaching my goals had no fast track—it was going to be a slow burn to the top. More importantly, I learned that by putting one foot in front of the other and not losing sight of my goals anything was possible no matter how great the challenge.

The same is true with anything. If you want to learn a new language, it is not going to happen overnight—you're going to have to stick with it. You can't get frustrated and decide to try and learn an "easier" language halfway through; there is no easy way, you have to be committed. If you want to make changes to your body by going to the gym, you can't expect it to happen overnight. You have to stick to a routine and hold yourself responsible to follow through. If you want to get a degree, you have to take all the courses and pass the exams.

The difference with a career in music is that you have to have more drive, persistence, consistency and self-belief than most people. Unlike being encouraged to keep learning French, to stay with your workout schedule or to keep studying for your exams, as a musician you are likely going to be told to give up considering a career in music and, even worse, your failures are often celebrated more than your successes just to make the point that you should get a "real job."

When you aim for a college degree, you know what it will take to get it, how long you'll be in school, the required courses, the papers, the projects, the exams ... A career in music isn't laid out so clearly. Unlike a college education, where friends and family can encourage you and support you in your last semester, knowing how close you are to a degree, a career in music doesn't come with a universal understanding of what it will take to "graduate." Even when working at a company, it is common knowledge how to get promoted. Musicians get frustrated and lose hope and the people around them don't encourage them because they have no concept as to how close they are to succeeding.

Think about your music career like any of the above examples— learning a language, going to the gym, getting a degree ... You need to stick with it and work hard at it. You need to be consistent and persistent. You have to set your own exams and benchmarks to ensure you are improving, and you need to know that you are not stagnant and that you are on your way to getting that "promotion." You might play in many bands before you succeed—it's all part of developing your talent, building experience, and gaining knowledge. That way when the right opportunity appears, you can recognize it and act accordingly. If you don't work hard at your career and give yourself time to develop your talent and knowledge through experience, you wouldn't know when an opportunity was staring you in the face. When you buy something you know is a good deal, you know it is a good deal because your own knowledge and experience give you something to compare it to. If every day were sunny, how would you know it was good weather? Experiencing a storm helps to educate you.

The combination of consistency, developing your talent, gaining knowledge through experience and recognizing and acting on opportunities is the key to a successful career in music. Follow this advice and you will have a career in music—it's that simple!

Believe

Most successful musicians have an extraordinary drive and self-belief. This often comes from a good support system around them. With the amount of failure and rejection that musicians experience on a daily basis, a strong belief in oneself and the will to persevere are requisites.

You have got to believe in yourself,
because if you don't nobody else will.

How many times has somebody told you how great you sounded after you played a show and you told them "It wasn't that good, I wish I had played better" or you tell others you are "not that great." By saying these things you obviously don't believe in yourself, but more importantly you are not valuing yourself for what you are truly worth. How are you ever going to accept success when it comes your way if you don't believe you are worth it? How are you going to make the money you want if you actively are telling people you are not worth it?

You will never cut a deal that gives you the value you are worth until you accept how valuable you really are. A friend told me once that "you can have a million jobs but only one life. When you work for somebody else you are selling them time out of your life. Make sure you are giving value to that time because you won't get it back." Successful people understand their value. Successful musicians do not undervalue themselves. Amanda Palmer would never have raised over a million dollars if she hadn't truly believed that what she was doing was worth it. She knew the value that her music and performances gave her audience; what she could do for them was just as valuable as what her audience could do for her financially, so it was a fair exchange. She believed she was worth it, and she was comfortable accepting it through crowdfunding.

Getting 200 metres within reach of one of the world's highest summits and then choosing to turn back was an experience that made me realize I wasn't ready for a dream to become a reality. Or at least so I thought for some time. I even came up with the concept of "fear of the summit"—the idea that, when a dream is within reach or success stares us in the face, we can experience fear of realizing it. This might sound ridiculous, but it is widely the case that people sabotage their own success out of fear. Under closer examination I realize that the only true fear is of not being worthy. Am I worthy of living my dream? Am I worthy of reaching success? And the answer is yes, you need to value yourself for your true worth, otherwise success will stare you in the face and you will cower in its shadow.

If you want your dreams to come true you have to stop seeing them as dreams and start seeing them as the natural result of your actions. If you are great then great things will come to you.

Visualization: Creating the future with our thoughts

When I trained for the climbing expedition to the Andes in my late teens, I always visualized reaching the top. I envisioned the summit as success. What I had never given any thought to was the descent. By the time I made my decision to turn back, I had become aware that I had visualized only half my goal. The complete goal, and a truly successful journey, should have included the return.

Descending the mountain, and still above 6,500 metres, I found a climber lying helpless in the snow. Mike had been lost for more than twenty-four hours in high altitude and was frostbitten, disoriented and suffering from altitude sickness. The chance encounter was the start of a life-changing journey. From the moment I began to help Mike descend the mountain I always visualized a successful return to base camp. I was able to visualize it clearly. There was no doubt in my mind that we would succeed in reaching safety. Knowing that gave me confidence in the decisions I made on the journey.

My father is the master of visualization, especially when it comes to financial success. He is in the world of fine art and antiques. Each item has a different cost and estimated value, but what he receives ultimately depends on what the client is willing to pay. This makes predicting how much he will make in sales on a given day next to impossible.

Every time I have been with him when he sells, he tells me the night before how much he "needs" to make in sales with exact dollar amounts. He has told me "I have to make $90,000 this weekend," and by the end of the weekend he has made exactly $90,000. This doesn't happen sometimes—it happens always! The best example is the time he told me he had to make $20,000 over three days. The first day he made $8,000 and was off to a good start. I of course had learned to expect he would reach the goal he had set; however, on this occasion he had an unexpected setback. He dropped his wallet, with all of his cheques and more than $4,000 in cash, when he went to the washroom. His wallet was later returned empty. At the end of the weekend he reached his goal even after having an unlucky experience along the way. I asked him how he did it and he told me he always visualized money going from a client's pocket to his. He told me he had not given a second thought to the stolen wallet—he wasn't going to spend negative energy—but he just hoped the person who took it needed the money. His ability to visualize a desired outcome and materialize it has fascinated me my whole life.

Visualization is mentally rehearsing for success. You visualize the outcome you want and you envision yourself already accomplishing it. You become your thoughts.

There are many scientific studies that confirm that visualization and mental imagery enhance physical performance. The imagination and our perception of the real world are closely linked, since both functions engage the same neural circuitry. For this reason the brain doesn't always clearly differentiate between something real and something imagined.

Part of visualization is focusing on "feeling" the way you will feel when achieving the goals you set. For example, when I taught guitar and my students played perfectly something I had just shown them, I would immediately stop them and ask them: "Did you feel how that just felt? You just played it perfectly and that is what playing it perfectly feels like." I would then tell them to focus on the feeling and try and repeat the "feeling." If you have a great night onstage, then I suggest remembering what it felt like to play perfectly and strive to internally replicate the feeling before you go onstage the next time. The result will be another great night. If you do a radio interview, focus on how it will feel to do it perfectly before you start. I used to go to bed at night visualizing my hands gliding over the fretboard of my guitar and creating the feeling in my mind of what it would feel like. The next day I would pick up my guitar and replicate the feeling of the night before.

Don't visualize reaching your goal as the end of the journey; just visualize goals as something you get to along the way. I made the mistake of visualizing reaching the summit of Cerro Aconcagua as the end of the journey when it was only partway, not the finish line. Martial artists visualize punching through targets, not just hitting them. Olympic athletes use visualization in their training to push their physical limits beyond their current ability. You need to visualize from day one and, like everything else, it takes practice. But visualization has the power to make you reach your goals and go beyond. You can live the way you want: you just have to visualize it.

Start out by writing on paper what you want. Dream big. Get into enough detail that you can really envision what reaching your goal will look and feel like. Don't limit yourself, as you will only ever be as big as you can dream.

Setting a goal: 1,000 true fans and the Dunbar number

Before you even begin, you need to have an idea of where you are going. You've got to know your goals in order to visualize them. Don't be random. Enjoying the journey requires having a destination, otherwise you're just floating along without a sense of direction. And it's hard to feel like you are getting anywhere if you don't know where you're headed.

Start with little goals that can become milestones. Reach one and then aim for the next. It's like a to-do list: don't overwhelm yourself with a hundred things to do in a day when one task alone could take you a week. Set goals that you can achieve and allow yourself to feel the success of reaching them.

Use viral blogger Kevin Kelly's concept of one thousand true fans — or brand ambassadors (more at atnmusi.ca/ch1h1). Work toward having one thousand people who each spend $100 a year on your music, shows, merch and so on. This is a lot easier than worrying about a million people buying your latest album. Perspective is everything. Knowing that you don't need to have millions of fans to build a sustainable career in music should make "starting" a lot easier. Don't get overwhelmed with a rock-star dream!

It is, however, impossible to have more than 150 close social connections. This number is referred to as the Dunbar number, which suggests that 150 is the cognitive limit to the number of people we can maintain a stable social relationship with. As Malcolm Gladwell puts it in his book *The Tipping Point*, "these are relationships in which an individual knows who each person is, and how each person relates to every other person."

The fact of the matter is that even for you to maintain a stable social relationship with 150 people, there needs to be an active, engaging reason to stay so closely connected. British anthropologist Robin Dunbar has pointed out that actively maintaining those relationships would take 42 percent of your time. Groups of people who are physically closer are more likely to maintain a closer social connection. And it's not hard to find studies online that show people are more engaged in smaller groups than they can possibly be in larger numbers.

What does this all mean? For one thing, it means be realistic. In today's cyber world we get carried away with "adding" and "following" so-called friends. The truth is we are buying into the idea of social status being tied to the amount of online "friends" we have. The reality is that they are just numbers, as we will never truly know most of those "friends."

Dunbar's number doesn't include past relationships or people you used to know even if you could easily rekindle the friendships; the number refers only to the people you currently engage with. I take the perspective of attempting to be connected to people who are good at keeping close relationships within their network. You may only be able to maintain 150 relationships, if that, but you can certainly spread your good name to the networks of others, through the people they trust and have a close social connection to.

Look to make connections with people from completely different social groups, industries and so on, so as to penetrate as many different networks as possible. Your name is likely to spread a lot further than it would if it just rotated around the same network.

Consider 150 close relationships as your way of reaching 1,000-plus second-generation fans. Let the 150 be the ones to introduce you, your music and your brand to their networks. One thousand true fans come about not only when you provide amazing experiences and follow up in person, at concerts and online, but when you maintain as close to 150 real relationships as you can.

Find ways to monitor your progress
To reach any goal you set, you truly have to believe you are going to reach it, and you have to have the drive, passion, consistency and

persistence to reach it. You need to have ways to monitor your progress along the way. So with this in mind, **I challenge you to set yourself physical goals that are parallel to your musical/entrepreneurial goals**. If you plan to go for a run every day, or hit the gym three times a week, train to climb a mountain or run a marathon, you're going to need to demonstrate drive, passion, consistency and persistence. If you give up on your physical goal—missing a run or not going to the gym, for example—chances are you're demonstrating the same lack of discipline in working toward your career goals.

Set your physical goals as a barometer for your overall success. You will cross the finish line with all the goals you set!

Keep a list of all the things you accomplish. Try writing five a day. Celebrate the little things as well as the big ones.

The Rule of Reciprocity: The Golden Rule!

Who you know is a big part of this industry, but those willing to help you are the most important of all connections. The rule of reciprocity is the idea of a kind action being returned with another kind action. It's a big part of social psychology. We are likely to help out somebody who has already done something for us in the past. It's a form of social obligation. A favour feels like it should be returned. For this reason, no matter who you know or who you are trying to meet, consider what you can do for them before you ask them to do something for you. This perspective should give you creative ways to meet and engage with new connections and to make an impact on people who will help you progress in your career. You need to understand that the first move in the rule of reciprocity comes from *you!*

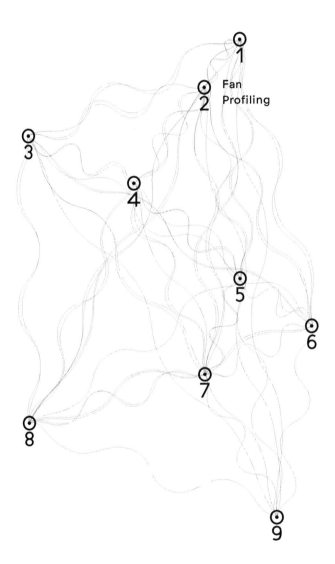

CHAPTER TWO

Fan
Profiling

Fan Profiling

Fans are the single most important element of a professional and satisfying career in music. Without fans you're an amateur!

Two things I have noticed in successful musicians are that (1) their goals are clearly defined, and (2) their audiences are even more clearly defined. If you don't know your fans, how are you going to market your music to them?

In this chapter I have put together links to free tools, with suggestions of ways to use them for developing the profile of your "Super Fan." And by Super Fan I mean the fan who is going to buy all your music and merch products, attend as many shows as he or she can, rave about you to friends, join your street team, call in to the radio to request your song, leave reviews, talk about you online, blog about you, contribute to crowdfunding campaigns, and so on.

Start by identifying at least five bands that are embodying the goals you have set for yourself. Don't pick big household names, because they will have too many fans who are not exclusive to their band. Start by picking local acts you like who have a good following both off- and online.

If you don't know who you sound like, start off by asking other people. If you find categorizing and comparing your music to that of others to be difficult, you can also use the tools in this chapter to help you search for similar bands.

A good way to begin to know the profile of your Super Fan is to consider what you already know about your existing fans, find out more about the fans of artists who are similar to you, and then look for overlaps. More established artists will have a clearer understanding of their fan base and you can use the available tools to tap into that information. I suggest that you write out a profile of your Super Fan, using as much information as you can acquire.

My descriptions below may not provide sufficient information on their own, especially if you do not have prior knowledge of how the platforms involved work. But I have listed links to all the sites mentioned so that you can educate yourself as well as start accounts and put them to use. The most important thing is to get your mind working on these kinds of concepts and ideas and how they can be used to serve a specific purpose. Of course, there are countless websites that can help you profile your fan, and I suggest you look further than just the ones listed in this segment. Note that this way of doing things may not be to every musician's taste, but it's always better to know what's out there than not to know.

Here are some of those tools:

Next Big Sound
atnmusi.ca/ch2h1

Next Big Sound conveniently takes stats from twenty-seven social platforms and gives you feedback about your fan base. This information includes gender, location, preferred social platforms and even which songs and videos are most popular. One of my favourite features is being able to cross-check which events directly impacted the number of views of videos and plays of songs and got your fans buzzing about you online. If you create an account with Last.fm (atnmusi.ca/ch2h2), you can see suggested "similar artists." If you know of artists you sound like, you can get all the same information on them. Knowing more about their fan base and what type of events created spikes in fan engagement can be a great way to learn more about your potential Super Fan and about ways to create better fan engagement.

Music Metric
atnmusi.ca/ch2h3

Use Music Metric to search for artists who sound similar to you and to get insight into which social sites generate their fans, where their downloads are happening geographically, and the buzz and overall online sentiment that surrounds them. This gives you a ton of leads as to where to focus your own fan-building attention.

When you research fan bases, it's a good idea to keep in mind that fans of bands that are household names are usually not exclusive to those artists, because such fans can be more affected than others by passing trends and what's "hot." They are likely fans of songs, not artists. This is in great part because of how they discover and experience music. Because you want to build a fan base of Super Fans, I highly recommend focusing on artists who are less well known but who still have strong followings. Focusing on regional and national artists, rather than international names, will make it easier to engage their fans and build stronger relationships, as you will be able to tour in their markets. Touring and face-to-face interaction is still, by far, the most effective way to engage and develop Super Fans. Nothing can replace a live experience!

If you are unaware of less well-known artists you might sound like, you can start by searching Music Metric for well-known artists who sound similar to you. Once you are on their Music Metric profile page, Music Metric will give you a list of similar-sounding artists, some of whom will be less well known. You can then use Music Metric to find out more about them.

Essentially, Music Metric tells you about similar-sounding artists and their fans. Knowing which social media sites generate their fans and have the most fan interaction gives you insight into where to focus your own online attention. Study the fan profile of others and start building your own!

Hype Machine
atnmusi.ca/ch2h4

> *"Every day, thousands of people around the world write about music they love—and it all ends up here."* —Hype Machine

Hype Machine scans blogs across the internet and finds the music that is being featured. Once you find a blog that is featuring music by an artist who sounds similar to you, you have the option to see other tracks or artists those blogs play. This has two great functions: (1) it helps you find artists who sound like you and tap into their fan bases on social networks (e.g., follow and interact with their fans on Twitter), and (2) it gives you a great way of knowing which blogs to approach with your own music. Being featured on blogs is a huge source of exposure today. I have spoken to countless industry folk, including label representatives and music supervisors, who discover artists on blogs.

Obviously you can use Hype Machine to find similar-sounding artists to you and then use Music Metric to get more information on them. Just saying …

Followerwonk
atnmusi.ca/ch2h5

Followerwonk is an amazing analytical tool. It gives in-depth analysis and profiling of your followers and those you follow. Knowing the gender, age, location and so on of your followers gives you insight into your fan demographic. This in turn tells you how, where and when best to market to them. The best part is that not only can you use it with your own Twitter handle, but you can enter the Twitter handles of similar artists and get the same in-depth stats on them.

From the perspective of profiling your fan, this has two benefits: (1) it gives you an idea of what type of followers/fans you have, and (2) it analyzes the same information of like-sounding bands' followers to determine if those fans will match your fan profile. If they do, then start following and engaging with those fans online and soon enough they will be your fans too!

Wolfram Alpha
atnmusi.ca/ch2h6

This computational knowledge engine is a great resource for all kinds of calculations. However, in the case of profiling your fan, I recommend typing "Facebook Profile" in the search box. This will provide a detailed analysis of your Facebook profile. You will find stats on people's ages, genders, geographical location, who "likes" and "shares" your posts the most (this give you an insight into who your existing Super Fans are), which posts and photos generate the most interaction (this gives you an idea of what to post more of!) and so on.

You might just find that your biggest fans are not the age, gender or nationality that you thought!

Also keep in mind that targeting friends of friends on Facebook can provide good fans in the same way that following the Twitter followers of like-sounding artists can. People are often friends because of similarities in interests, pastimes, location and so forth.

TweetReach
atnmusi.ca/ch2h7

"How far did your tweet travel?" — TweetReach

This is a great resource for finding out such information as how far your Tweets travel, who the most influential Tweeters are and who retweets your posts the most. This will give you a good idea of who your Super Fans are and whose followers to follow. If you type in the Twitter handle of an artist who sounds similar to you, you can find out who their most active followers are so as to follow and engage with them. You can also type in a word or topic and identify the most influential people tweeting about it. This again can help you to find potential fans. The more information you can add to your Super Fan profile, the more you can find out about your top fans and what their common interests are.

Link shorteners
Link shorteners, other than doing the obvious, give you stats on your links. These stats include number of clicks and saves. This all helps you learn more about your fans' interests.

Not only can you view the stats of the links that you have posted but you can check out the stats of links posted by others. Knowing the stats on links that similar artists post gives you insight into what their fans engage with the most. All links in this book are using shortened links.

Many companies out there offer link shortening. Here are a few:

Bitly
atnmusi.ca/ch2h8

Readability
atnmusi.ca/ch2h12

Goo.gl
atnmusi.ca/ch2h9

Tinyurl
atnmusi.ca/ch2h13

is.gd
atnmusi.ca/ch2h10

v.gd
atnmusi.ca/ch2h14

Ow.ly
atnmusi.ca/ch2h11

Klout
atnmusi.ca/ch2h15

"The Standard for Influence ... "

Klout is an ingenious tool that puts a number or value on your overall social influence. It measures your online influence on a scale of 1 to 100. Having a number associated with your influence is a real motivator to improve your online presence if you have even the smallest competitive bone in your body! It is a great barometer of how influential your fans and their followers are.

In regards to profiling your Super Fan, the Klout profile descriptions can help you learn more about your fans as well as the community that they influence and those that influence them.

I suggest focusing your attention on the followers who are the most influential in their circles—those with the highest "Klout Score." Influential on Klout does not mean having the most followers; it means having the most engaged followers.

Klout allows you to compare yourself to other Klout users. Comparing your Klout to that of another similar artist will give you insight into who they influence. The people they influence should be people you connect with. I recommend that, once you have used Klout to gain information about people's influence and networks, you connect with them via Twitter. You can also use Klout to input the Twitter handles of those who follow you, to identify the most influential followers.

My favourite way of using Klout is via HootSuite.

HootSuite
atnmusi.ca/ch2h16

HootSuite is a way to have all your social sites controlled from one location or dashboard. Although I will talk about HootSuite later on (see Chapter 5), for now I want to discuss how you can use it to profile your fan(s).

HootSuite has a number of analytical tools. For example, it provides stats from its own link shortener. You are able to see which links get the most action based on number of clicks, as well as what day they are opened. This gives you feedback about your audience's interests.

One of the coolest features in HootSuite is the ability to create streams. Once you choose to "add stream," you are able to set it up as a search or a Twitter list. You can then filter the stream by keyword or by using Klout. This enables you to narrow down what appears in a stream by setting the filter to display only people of a specific Klout Score or by specific keywords.

Additionally, when creating a stream as a search you can choose to use your location to show local results. This automatically displays the results within a 25-kilometre radius. However, if you want you can change the longitude or latitude of your current location to that of anywhere in the world (you can use Google Maps Labs to find longitudes and latitudes). This allows you to create searches for specific geographical areas. For example, while located in Vancouver, Canada, you can find out within a 25-kilometre radius of downtown London, England (this can be set to a greater radius if you wish) who is talking about U2 and filter the stream so that it shows only people of a minimum Klout Score. I am sure you can see the benefits.

Blog, website and Google analytics

Using the analytics or stats provided by blogs, websites and Google can give you key insights into various things, including where your visitors are from geographically, what keywords they have typed to come across your site, how long they spend on your site, which content gets the most action, which days and times of the week get the most traffic and which posts or tracks got the most views or listens on specific days.

Use your blog to find out how people came across you. Seeing the search terms used can give you an idea of what brings people to your site. These search terms can give you an idea of your viewers' interests. It also is a good barometer of what your brand is attracting. In turn it can help you to create content, tags and so on that can help with search engine optimization (SEO).

People who comment are potential Super Fans. They are the ones you want to be sure to engage with. From the perspective of profiling your fan, you can check out each commenter's profile or Gravatar to gain more information on the person. You can even find out what blogs those who comment are subscribed to and learn more about their interests.

Use the blog analytics to discover where your audience is coming from. This again will help you focus your marketing efforts, your distribution strategy and your tour scheduling.

Use TV to profile your fans

If you have had the opportunity to license your music to television, you can tap into the resources of the TV show involved to find out more about the demographic of its audience. You can find out where the show's ratings are highest, so as to have an idea of popularity based on geographical location.

Quite often TV series have music players on their websites with the names and songs of the artists featured on their shows. This can give you an idea of other artists that sound like you. Once again, this can help you when it comes to comparing your fan profile to that of another established artist.

If your music has not been licensed, you can still use these resources as long as you are able to identify shows that play music of a similar style to yours.

TuneFind
atnmusi.ca/ch2h17 can help you identify the music that you hear on movies and TV shows.

Adtunes
atnmusi.ca/ch2h18 can help you identify the music used in commercials.

Pinterest
atnmusi.ca/ch2h19

Once you have found your fans on other sites, you can search for them on Pinterest and you can also search the Pinterest pages of artists who sound similar to you. Pinterest will give you a very visual idea of what your fans' interests are. Because your music is only a part of the engagement with your fans, it is important to know some of the common interests you might share.

Keep in mind that if you were to find out that your fan is a female between the ages of twenty-five and thirty-seven who enjoys yoga and outdoor living, is a vegetarian and has no kids, you might decide to approach your music marketing from the angle of a yoga-equipment company. You might choose to establish brand partnerships with companies unrelated to the music industry that are influential in the lives of your targeted demographic. Finding your way into the hearts of potential fans via lifestyle choices and brand consumption is a great way to set yourself apart from the pack.

iTunes

atnmusi.ca/ch2h20

Use iTunes to see other albums or artists purchased by the people that bought your music. This gives you an idea of who else your fans are a fan of. As mentioned here many times, you can use the fans of others to build the profile of your own fan.

Keep in mind that people who go to the extent of commenting and engaging on blog posts and leaving reviews on sites such as iTunes and Amazon are potential Super Fans.

As a side note, when a comment or review is negative, you can give yourself a pat on the back for generating passion in people! With passionate diehard fans come passionate "haters" too. Great brands create passion. Author and branding expert Marty Neumeier puts it best when he invokes the words of human rights activist Elie Wiesel: "The opposite of love isn't hate, it's indifference." Negative comments can be opportunities to start a conversation and ultimately lead to converting that bad reviewer into a new-found Super Fan.

As for how to get featured on iTunes, mobilizing fans to download your music around a specific day or event really does increase your chances of spiking and arousing attention. The number of downloads it takes depends on the genre. But if you are able to get attention with enough action in one day and everything available online shows that you are the real deal and not just trying to cheat the system, you could get featured on the front page of the genre you are in.

For example, if it takes one hundred downloads of a folk artist in one day to create a spike, how could you organize at least one hundred fans to purchase your latest single on the same day? Get creative. Here are some ideas to get the juices flowing:

- You could include a $10 iTunes gift card as part of the ticket price to your concert, or even with the purchase of a physical album, and then find a way to have everyone use it to purchase your album during the show. Make it some sort of a ritual. They get it for free, you get the majority of the money you spent on the gift cards back via your digital distributor (from the iTunes sales), and you get the chance to be featured on the iTunes page. What happens if you were to give out one hundred cards a night on an extensive tour?

- You could call your mailing list into action to purchase your latest single on a specific day and in return gift them the rest of the album electronically. All you would need is proof they purchased it, such as an iTunes receipt or a screenshot of the download. While you're at it you could ask them to leave a review on iTunes in return for a bonus song.

- You could have a laptop at your merch stand and have people log in to their iTunes account and purchase your single. They could also use their phones and mobile devices to log in and buy it. In return you can give them a link to download the entire album digitally for free. The pitch is "99 cents for the full album."

Being featured is an editorial process. Be sure to communicate with your aggregator (such as CD Baby, TuneCore or Ditto Music) to ensure they include your content on the list that goes to the iTunes editorial teams.

Every little bit counts and the potential exposure is more than worth it!

Facebook
atnmusi.ca/ch2h21

Use Facebook Insights to understand more about your audience members and how they interact with your posts. By knowing what posts pique your audience's interest, where your audience is from geographically, the languages the members of your audience speak and the gender and age group they belong to, you have more information for the profile of your Super Fan.

You can also use Facebook Graph Search to identify your fans, learn about their favourite interests and hobbies, pinpoint the interests of the artists who sound similar to you, find potential co-branding opportunities and refine the types of contests you create. All this adds to a better understanding of your audience and how to target the Super Fan. Here is a link to a great article on using Facebook Graph Search, with Facebook's information link afterwards:

17 Ways Marketers Can Leverage Facebook Graph Search
atnmusi.ca/ch2h22

Introducing Graph Search
atnmusi.ca/ch2h23

YouTube
atnmusi.ca/ch2h24

YouTube provides analytics for its videos, which give you insights into where the most views are from geographically; details about the age demographic, the gender of the listeners, likes and comments; as well as top playback locations, and top traffic sources. YouTube recently added a function that allows you to identify your most engaged and influential subscribers. You can use the information from your own videos and also find the same information for videos from artists you consider to be similar to you. Use their fan profiles to help shape your own! YouTube annotations and keywords are also important tools as they help you learn more about your demographic and target them more efficiently.

Learn more about YouTube Demographics
atnmusi.ca/ch2h25

Google Trends
atnmusi.ca/ch2h26

Use Google Trends to search for similar artists, song titles of similar-sounding tracks, lyrics, brands and so on. You will be able to gauge such factors as the online interest that currently exists, whether the artists and songs are actively being searched for and whether there is more or less interest presently than in the past. You'll also find out such information as what search terms are most popular, how popular the topic is and where most people are searching those keywords from geographically.

For example, by searching for "Kings of Leon" you will find out in which countries people are most actively searching information about them and what search terms people are using, and you will be able to compare dates of when people were most actively searching for the name and particular events and articles that took place at the time. Consequently, you can learn about what in particular sparked people's interest in doing a search. This information helps you learn more about the audience that exists for artists that are similar to you and so gives you more information to add to your own Super Fan profile. It is a good source of marketing ideas and research too. Additionally, Google Trends gives a lot of insight into keywords to use in your online content, as well as topics to blog about to help with your SEO.

Trends are cyclical. In the cycle of a movie, there is talk of the film being made, then you see the trailers, the interviews and pre-release articles, then the movie comes out and there are more reviews, then the DVD, and so on. During that process, people will be actively searching for information online. However, once the cycle is over the searching stops. It is only when a 3-D version is made, or, for example, a movie is remastered, brought back in colour or released on BlueRay and marketing and media come into play again that we see new spikes appear in the trends.

When "new" information is released or "new" events take place around a previous trend, new spikes appear. The interesting thing is that a topic may not have lost people's interest—they may still be fans of Harry Potter books and films, for example—but it may simply be over the novelty phase. To create Google Trend peaks you need to create conversation, media interest, online content and so forth around your brand. If it is a matter of peaking old trends, you need to bring something "new"—something that once again generates media interest, conversation, online content …

Sonicbids

atnmusi.ca/ch2h27

You can use Sonicbids to find out about gigs that other artists who sound like you have landed. This gives you an idea of who might be interested in you and which opportunities might exist. If you start looking into the types of audience that the people, companies or brands supplying the gigs have you will obtain more information to research, more search terms to use and more potential Super Fans to win over.

ASK YOUR FANS WHO THEY ARE!

After all the previous suggestions, I cannot leave out the most direct approach: ask your fans who they are. Use online surveys and have sign-up sheets at your concerts, with pertinent fields for fans to fill in.

Many companies offer surveys that can be sent out in different ways, including via social media or in newsletters or emails.

Always consider the fan and the WIFM (what's in it for me) factor, by giving back something in return for someone's time. Get creative. Get creative with the questions and get creative with what you offer in return.

Here are a few companies that provide surveys:

Constant Contact
atnmusi.ca/ch2h28

Survey Monkey
atnmusi.ca/ch2h30

KwikSurveys
atnmusi.ca/ch2h29

Survey Tool
atnmusi.ca/ch2h31

WHAT NEXT?

All accumulated data plays an immensely important role in how you market your brand. It helps you create Facebook ads to target your fan demographic. It helps you know which platforms to focus on and which to forget about. It can affect your tour routing and the types of venues you approach, as well as the choice of radio stations you send your music to. Even the merchandise you create will be affected once you know who's buying it. You can create marketing strategies that will appeal to your fan base and not miss the mark. Without knowing your fan base it is all just a shot in the dark.

It's obviously preferable to send out newsletters whose content appeals to your fan base. Just think: with all the accumulated data, you can create a newsletter containing information people want to read about as well as details of experiences and products that they not only want to purchase but that fit their personal income. Keep in mind that knowing where your fans are from and what their ages are means you are able to find out what average incomes are in their area. If you know where your fans are and what they do for work, you can use a tool like Salary.com (atnmusi.ca/ch2h32) to know their average income.

ADDITIONAL THOUGHTS

- When creating a sign-up form for a newsletter, request information that will tell you the most about your fans.

- When you give music away for free, be sure to gather as much data in return as possible. The more data, the easier it is to create a profile.

- Gather more info from fans at live performances by handing out free download cards that will entice them to give information you request when redeeming the download online.

- It is said that what we are passionate about when we are younger—in our teens—is what continues to be our deep-rooted passion as we get older. If you know the age of your fans, you can find out what the pop culture of the day was when they were in their teens and that too can spark ideas in your marketing efforts.

Other sites to check out

ArtistX
atnmusi.ca/ch2h33

Beluga
atnmusi.ca/ch2h34

Big Champagne
atnmusi.ca/ch2h35

Buzzdeck
atnmusi.ca/ch2h36

Genre-X
atnmusi.ca/ch2h37

Hottest Artist
atnmusi.ca/ch2h38

Simply Measured
atnmusi.ca/ch2h39

TuneGlue
atnmusi.ca/ch2h43

The Appreciation Engine
atnmusi.ca/ch2h40

Understanding Music
Recommendation
atnmusi.ca/ch2h44

The Echo Nest Labs
atnmusi.ca/ch2h41

Vocus
atnmusi.ca/ch2h45

The Music Maze
atnmusi.ca/ch2h42

The following sites are useful for monitoring media mentions.
You can use them to monitor your own mentions and also those
of similar-sounding artists, brands and so on. That can give you
insight into good places to focus your own media attention.
These sites are especially useful for measuring the success
of your campaigns (and you can directly apply the tools they
offer to the "Music PR" and "Social Media" chapters of this
book—Chapters 4 and 5 respectively).

Conventional and Social Media
Tracker
atnmusi.ca/ch2h46

Social Mention
atnmusi.ca/ch2h51

Google Alerts
atnmusi.ca/ch2h47

Topsy
atnmusi.ca/ch2h52

HowSociable
atnmusi.ca/ch2h48

TweetAlarm
atnmusi.ca/ch2h53

Meltwater IceRocket
atnmusi.ca/ch2h49

Twitter Counter
atnmusi.ca/ch2h54

Reddit
atnmusi.ca/ch2h50

CHAPTER THREE

Branding

Branding

Branding is so far-reaching and penetrates so deeply into the essence of what we do that essentially everything we do becomes our brand.

I asked my friend Josh Nychuk, an award-winning Canadian graphic designer with a focus on brand identity design, to write the following introductory section for this chapter. He has all the qualities to rise above the noise and his is certainly a name to watch out for. Music also happens to play a large part in his life.

BRANDING FUNDAMENTALS, BY JOSH NYCHUK

The strategies and techniques of branding are easiest to understand when we look at the basic ideas they are built on—knowing what you believe in and knowing your purpose—and communicating these in your art. My aim is to provide a general understanding of modern branding practices, using a fundamental framework so that you as a musician can apply the knowledge to your situation.

First, we need to establish a definition of the term *brand*, or *branding*. Branding has given rise to a language or vocabulary of terms that even professionals working in the field sometimes misuse. Various definitions have evolved over time. Until recently, the term *brand* was widely used to describe a company's trademark or logo. A brand is much more than that, but we still sometimes call a trademark or logo a "brand." So why this confusion? The 2006 book *C/ID: Visual Identity and Branding for the Arts*, by Emily King and Angus Hyland, puts it well, describing the reason for the frequent misuse of the term *branding* as "partly because of the ever-changing semantics of marketing jargon and partly because their purposes are sometimes better served by a certain ambiguity." This ambiguity is not meant to be interpreted in a negative sense, as a large number of meanings can ultimately enrich and deepen the subject. What the ambiguity does is allow people's interactions with a brand to form into unique perspectives based on their own experiences. When we talk about a brand we are talking about our perception of it, which includes a lot more than the company logo. For this reason I think that branding expert Marty Neumeier has given us a useful, simple way to express what a brand is:

> *"It's not what you say it is, it's what they say it is."*
> —Marty Neumeier, *The Brand Gap* (2003)

Neumeier goes on to say that a brand is "a person's gut feeling about a product, service or organization" and that brands "are defined by individuals, not companies, markets or the public." This definition says that (1) a brand is about perception, (2) everyone has his or her own perception of a brand, and (3) each perception is formed from an instinctual (gut) feeling. The fundamental aspect that I would like to highlight in this definition is the intuitive nature of how our perception is formed. To use the analogy of music, this intuitive nature can be compared to the visceral emotional reaction we experience when we hear a favourite song. The emotional connection we form with a piece of music or an experience is a fundamental characteristic of branding.

Our scientific understanding of an area of the brain called the limbic system helps explain how emotions affect behaviour, learning and memory. The limbic system is predominantly responsible for our emotional life, memory formation, behaviour and learning. This region of the brain is recognized as having a faculty for developing trust, and when we hold something to be truth, it forms a belief. When a group of people come together under a shared belief we feel a sense of belonging. Branding is able to communicate with us in these ways, forming beliefs and making us feel a sense of belonging.

No discussion on branding would be complete without at least one mention of Apple, simply because it is a modern example of a business with a particularly strong brand. So let's look at one example of how the company has successfully developed a unique level of trust and sense of belonging with its audience group. Apple says it believes in revolution by empowering the individual. The company has developed an emotional bond and sense of community with its audience through consistently revolutionizing technology, just as it promised to do. Apple's advertising focuses on product culture rather than product features, thereby creating an attitude and outlook that people can relate to. Certain Apple fans have been willing to camp overnight outside retail stores to be the first to own a new product. This type of behaviour is associated more with the music industry, as music provides a deeply meaningful element to our lives. For a company that makes consumer products, Apple has reached an unprecedented level of influence in the culture it has created.

To demonstrate how effective branding can be in a less benign example, we could look at its use within the historical context of totalitarian governments. In *Iron Fists: Branding the 20th-Century Totalitarian State* (2008), design historian Steven Heller analyzes the use of branding within four totalitarian regimes—Nazi Germany, Fascist Italy, the Soviet Union and Communist China. Heller gives factual examples of how these regimes used branding aesthetics, icons and mythology in their propaganda to effectively coerce and persuade nations. This is obviously a malicious use of branding, and the atrocities these regimes committed coincide with their strategies in branding. My point here is that branding is a powerful communication tool—it can obviously be used for good or evil, and its effects can be far-reaching.

A brand's ability to embody a set of values and beliefs and to create a sense of belonging is arguably the first and most important fundamental function. The second is identification.

Every brand has an identity, the role of which is to orient us to the brand and provide us with a means to recognize it. The term *brand identity* evolved from the term *visual identity*—the logo or trademark, typography and colour(s) that served as visual markers to distinguish ownership and characteristics of a company.

A musical band, just like a company, has a visual identity—made up of the group's logo or signature name or symbols, album artwork and occasionally the frontman or the members themselves.

A brand identity is broader in nature than a visual identity, though. It consists of the sum of all visual, verbal and conceptual aspects of the brand. The identity becomes an image that exists in our mind as an abstract symbol, enabling us to recall certain feelings and ideas when we think or experience the brand.

To use music as an example, consider a solo artist like Johnny Cash or a band like The Beatles. What images or words come to mind? For Johnny Cash, we might think of "rebellion" or "rock star"; for The Beatles, "love" or "peace." No one could draw you a picture of love or describe to you in words what it is—you have to know what it feels like. An identity is simply an easy way for us as humans to visually evaluate whether we should get involved, buy into, or believe in something. It's about assessing inner characteristics through outer forms.

Acting on values and beliefs gives us a sense of purpose.

Behind every good brand there lies a purpose, and if that brand is a company or product, that purpose goes beyond solely existing to make a profit. A purpose is not simply "to offer unsurpassed customer service" or "to play the loudest rock music"; it's a set of values or core beliefs that you are willing to act on. It's like having something to say with your music, beyond just being able to play music. It's not an easy thing to establish for oneself, and even harder within a group because egos are involved.

In his 2009 book *Start with Why: How Great Leaders Inspire Everyone to Take Action,* Simon Sinek offers excellent insights into how all great leaders operate on the principle of knowing their purpose. Sinek gives many compelling examples, from individuals to organizations, of those who have either changed the course of history or made radical innovations in their fields—all from knowing and acting on their purpose. When a brand embodies its purpose, it is communicating a set of values and core beliefs. It attracts others who share these values and beliefs, and eventually forms fans, followers and an audience. This is how a brand leads. It says: "We believe in something, and if you like you can join us on this journey." This journey becomes a narrative, and as leaders you chart the territory.

So where will you go next? Bands and musicians have access to the same tools as businesses to build a brand—they too can hire artists, designers, consultants, managers, marketers, photographers and writers for their expertise. The largest barrier is often finding access to capital or finance and the time to ensure original quality results. A wealth of technology is available today to empower individuals and to allow those who have the knack for using it to take a more entrepreneurial approach to their art.

My intent has been to make clear the fundamentals of branding so that you can consider how they apply to your endeavours. Beliefs are powerful, so don't be surprised to find that the people who share the beliefs you hold will actually want to help you out, offering their talents or time. History has shown us that to "make it" in music, business or life, you need a lot of help. Find what you believe in, demonstrate it through your actions and communicate your purpose to start finding the people who are going to help make it happen. Those are the fundamentals of branding.

—Josh Nychuk

MAKING BRANDING WORK FOR YOU

When it comes to the nuts and bolts of making the latest branding knowledge work for you as an artist, it makes sense to look at what some of the top experts have to say. The following three international figures come at branding from different perspectives:

- Marty Neumeier (author, *The Brand Gap*), of San Francisco, has a background in design, is now a major business adviser, and his name has already appeared in this chapter.

- Douglas Van Praet (author, *Unconscious Branding*), of Los Angeles, uses neuroscience to plan advertising strategies.

- Daniel Levitin (author, *This Is Your Brain on Music*), is an American-born Montreal university professor who is a cognitive psychologist, musician and renowned music producer.

It makes sense to read their books if you can, and seeing their ideas have helped influence my thoughts on the topic of branding you will read more about them in the pages that follow.

BRAND POWER

The value of music has never changed—it is the format in which we purchase it that has changed. The value of music is the experience it gives us and the emotional connection we have to it. It is the memories it brings back and the moments it embellishes. So the true value of a band is not just the amount of units and downloads the group sells, but the overall value—including the money-generating aspect ("monetization")—of the band's brand experience.

Great brands all do the following:

Create positive experiences to generate positive memories. In order to have a memory that stands out, we need to consciously engage the brain. Nothing commands the attention of the mind better than novelty, the unexpected, the element of surprise, and ultimately the disruption of patterns. Once the mind is engaged, the experience needs to maintain the engagement of the mind to become a positive memory. Connecting with raw, meaningful primary experiences and emotions takes place at a much deeper level than any materialistic, technological experience.

Connect the consumers/audience with each other, not just the product. A brand that represents a community—that builds a "tribe" whose members connect with each other—is immensely stronger than a brand that connects the audience with a product that is here today and gone tomorrow. There will always be better products but the experience, the community, the culture you create should be one-of-a-kind. From a band perspective this means connecting your audience members with each other because of what you represent and not just because of the latest single you released. In fact, the songs should represent the greater meaning you stand for and be only part of the brand experience. Everyone wants acceptance, validation, social status, to be part of something greater than themselves, and successful brands become a way of representing just that.

Undersell and overdeliver, which creates unexpected value and results in positive experiences. It is these types of experiences that enable word of mouth to become a large factor in the promotion of the brand. When something is better than you expected and your repeated experiences are consistent with the first, then you tell your friends and take pride in being the one to introduce them to the brand. The global management consulting firm McKinsey & Company estimates that two-thirds of the US economy is now driven by word of mouth. So as bands, don't spend all your time promoting yourselves as being the greatest thing since sliced bread, or telling the world that your latest single is going to make you bigger than The Beatles; spend all your time creating music and experiences that are better than anyone could ever imagine so that your audiences can tell the world how great you are!

The internet has created a new transparency: now people can write reviews and comments about the brands as they experience them. There is no amount of money that can pay for advertising to say differently. As author Steve Jones points out in his book *Brand Like a Rock Star: Lessons from Rock 'n' Roll to Make Your Business Rich and Famous*, a great example is the Guns N' Roses album *Chinese Democracy*. Thirteen years and millions of dollars later, the album could never have lived up to all the hype that surrounded it. And of course although it was not a "bad" album, it flopped as it was not worthy of the time, money or hype given to it. So create incredible products and experiences and let people discover them and they will spread the word.

Have great stories. Because storytelling is such a huge part of how we remember and how we spread information, having a great brand story is key to having it spread. Stories create deeper emotional meanings and connections to the brand. A compelling story can create trust as well as lead the imagination of the consumer or audience to experience the brand before the real experiencing happens. Because the same neural functions are activated when imagining and when experiencing, storytelling is a large part of creating a strong and valuable brand. We have all experienced a musician recounting a story about the song she or he is about to play and the fact is that, more often than not, by the end of the story we want to hear the song. There is a huge difference between wanting to hear a song and being subjected to a song—for starters, we are much more likely to pay attention and consequently remember the song we wanted to hear.

Lead, not follow. All the successful brands or people I have ever met or read about have actively put themselves out of their comfort zone by not following other successful models and ideas and by creating something new instead. When Apple created the iPad, there was nothing like it and also nobody asking for anything like it. By taking the lead, the company created a need and a niche. By pushing our limits, by thinking outside the box, by believing in our ideas before anyone else does, we enable ourselves to create a niche and to position ourselves as the top contender in our field—the rest are all followers!

MUSIC & BRANDING

What is really interesting is that all the above elements occur naturally in the world of music. Music generates emotion and feelings, which are the very things that drive behaviour. Feelings become walking thoughts, which turn into intentions and finally actions. Music connects people socially; builds emotional ties to memories and experiences; has the ability to make us feel good; can create a sense of purpose; enables us to overcome great challenges; gives a voice to its tribe; and has the ability to unite people no matter what political, social, racial or sexual preferences and prejudices may exist. Songs carry stories; great songs carry deep meaning that everyone can relate to. Music that is authentic and pure finds its way to the right audience because it simply "must" be shared with people. When music is performed on a stage, the true power it carries can be delivered to new levels.

I believe that the future of music lies neither in the format in which tunes are delivered nor in how we pay for them, but 100 percent in the experience that music creates and in how we monetize that experience. The way to create a movement, a tribe, is by making people pay attention through the unexpected, delivering content that makes sense to the conscious mind, connecting audience members with each other and the brand that represents them, and having a story that becomes everyone's. The monetization comes from selling access to the tribe. Access brings social acceptance, a sense of belonging, status, a feeling of being part of something greater than just the membership ... People will sacrifice logical thinking over social acceptance.

If we look at the monetization of music coming from the experience and the access to the tribe that surrounds the experience, then it makes sense to understand who is going to be most affected by the experience and benefit the most from joining the tribe.

I don't believe there is one all-encompassing way and technique to target everybody, because there are too many types of people. We experience different things at different times in life, so our social needs change. For example, in late adolescence we usually experience the physical and emotional separation from our families. This time in our lives gives us more of a desire to be part of a tribe that can give us a new sense of belonging. If you look at the music that becomes popular in these age groups, it is clearly representational of the period of life the people in those age groups are in. The music connects them with other like-minded people experiencing similar things in their own lives. We all tend to experience music differently at different times in our lives. The first time you discovered and shared a band with a friend — and the types of emotions connected to that — will be what you think of when you hear the same music later in life. We certainly have times in our lives in which we are more prone to be influenced. Just think about it: if you started liking rock music at a young age, you probably still tell people that's what you like. You're likely never going to say you "hate" rock music even if you find other genres that appeal as you get older.

The interesting thing is that the times in people's lives in which they are most likely to be influenced by a brand and the time in life in which people have the money to spend on a brand do not necessarily line up.

Branding, music and the subconscious mind

I am fascinated with how branding works on a subconscious level—why we gravitate to the brands we do and ultimately spend our money and time on them. Why do we pick a Fender guitar over a Gibson? Why do we associate with Pearl Jam fans or those of Bob Marley? At the end of the day, bands are brands so it only makes sense to think like one!

BUILDING A TRIBE

> *"Belonging to a brand community only serves to accentuate that feeling of belonging, which is a central element of any social species."*—Gad Saad

Branding today is about building a tribe. Great brands create an experience and following not unlike a religion. Researchers at Tel Aviv University in Israel, the Stern School of Business in New York, and Duke University in North Carolina found that non-religious people in the United States rely on brands to a much greater degree than do religious people. A 2011 article on the study—"Brands: The Opiate of the Nonreligious Masses?" by Ron Shacher et al.—suggests that brands and religion might act as substitutes for one another. Like religion, brands can provide people with a measure of self-worth and ways to create meaning and identity. For this reason it is no surprise that brands represent social groups and can provide social acceptance. When we buy a brand, we are given a sense of belonging to something greater than ourselves.

> *"Apart from economic payoff, social status (social rank) seems to be the most important incentive and motivating force of social behavior."*—John Harsanyi, economist

Brands are a means of displaying our personal traits to others. We are telling potential mates and friends something about our values through the brands we purchase and flaunt. Usually, wearing sports apparel indicates our interest in physical fitness and the car we drive says something about our social status or care for the environment; likewise, the music we listen to and buy says something about the "tribe" we belong to.

In *The Brand Gap*, Neumeier gives an overview of how the value of branding has changed since the early twentieth century. In the early 1900s, he says, brands focused on features, or "what it is"; by 1925 it was about the benefits, or "what it does"; in 1950, the focus was on the experience, or "what you feel"; and since the start of the twenty-first century, brands have been about identification, or "who you are." It is imperative that a brand stand for something greater than just its product.

The artist is the brand and the fans are the tribe. People belong to tribes, not products. So an artist needs to represent something that is greater than just the music alone. Career artists do this and understand it is not just about a hit single. When you represent something people associate with that goes beyond just the music, the fans don't leave when one song bombs.

In his book *Subliminal: How Your Unconscious Mind Rules Your Behavior,* Leonard Mlodinow, a theoretical physicist, states: "Both experimental and field studies have found, in fact, that people will make large financial sacrifices to help establish a feeling of belonging to an in-group they aspire to feel part of." Changing your perspective from selling music to selling access to your tribe should open creative doors to new revenue.

What fascinates me is the fact that music connects with us emotionally, brings us together socially, creates belonging and acceptance and has strong ties to memories—all vital elements of a strong brand.

> *"The objective of branding should not be to connect people to the company that sells stuff. The real role of unconscious branding is to connect people to other people."*—Douglas Van Praet

"The only thing that really matters in life are your relationships to other people." This is the conclusion that psychiatrist George Vaillant came to after a seven-decade-long Harvard Study of Adult Development. Numerous studies have shown that social interaction, identification and acceptance of others have been critical to our survival and happiness. Not only that, but some scientists believe that the need for social interaction was the driving force behind the evolution of superior human intelligence. There are even studies that have proved that people with more social interaction live longer. Because of our social interaction, co-operation and intelligence, we have the superior ability over other primates to band together and co-ordinate complex activities. Brands need to find ways to bring people together, and music is a driving force behind social events and has been a way to bring us together for centuries.

THE EFFECT OF MUSIC

"Music taps into primitive brain structures involved with motivation, reward and emotion." — Daniel Levitin

A study conducted by David J. Diehl and Samuel Gershon, of the department of psychiatry at the University of Pittsburgh School of Medicine, shows that levels of dopamine activity directly relate to mood. Decreased levels of dopamine activity are involved in depression and increased levels are associated with mania. The findings of studies like theirs are why newer antidepressants act on the dopaminergic system.

According to one study in Daniel Levitin's book *This Is Your Brain on Music: The Science of a Human Obsession*, listening to music causes regions of the brain to become activated in a particular order. The starting point is the auditory cortex, which processes the components of the sound; next are the frontal regions that process musical structure and expectations; and finally it's the mesolimbic system, which is involved in arousal, pleasure, the transmission of opioids and the production of dopamine, climaxing in activation in the nucleus accumbens (p. 191). Levitin goes on to suggest:

> The rewarding and reinforcing aspects of listening to music seem ... to be mediated by increasing dopamine levels in the nucleus accumbens [NAc], and by the cerebellum's contribution to regulating emotion through its connections to the frontal lobe and the limbic system. (Ibid.)

As more evidence of the connection between music and dopamine, Levitin references an interesting experiment carried out in 1980 by Avram Goldstein. The experiment showed that the pleasure of listening to music could be blocked by administering the drug naloxone, as it was believed that naloxone interfered with dopamine in the NAc.

Levitin goes on to reference a 1999 study by Anne Blood, a postdoctoral fellow working with Robert Zatorre at the Montreal Neurological Institute. She was able to show that the intense musical emotion her subjects described as "thrills and chills" was associated with brain regions thought to be involved in reward, motivation and arousal. The study proved that one of the regions stimulated was the ventral striatum, a structure that includes the NAc. Levitin describes the NAc as

> the center of the brain's reward system, playing an important role in pleasure and addiction. The NAc is active when gamblers win a bet, or drug users take their favorite drug. It is also closely involved with the transmission of opioids in the brain, through its ability to release the neurotransmitter dopamine. (*This Is Your Brain on Music*, p. 189)

Clearly, music affects dopamine function and consequently affects mood. Levitin explains that music mimics some of the features of language and invokes some of the same neural regions. So as well as making you feel good in general, music conveys the kinds of feelings and emotions that vocal communication can but without the barrier of language.

With this information you can see how music connected to a brand has the ability to intensify the reaction of the brand experience on the consumer's brain and to help associate the brand with specific feelings and emotions.

If the experience of music connected to a brand has the ability to stimulate the nucleus accumbens, could you turn your fans and consumers into brand addicts? Something to think about …

COMMANDING ATTENTION

> "When someone does something different or unexpected they interrupt our anticipated pattern of perception which sets off a neurobiological process that commands our notice."
> —Douglas Van Praet

If you are able to create novelty, engage your audience members in physical action and stimulate them emotionally, you have the ability to have a brand that becomes a rock star.

Novelty or the unexpected demands the brain's attention. Expected patterns do not demand your attention. When you're driving a car, you're usually able to also talk or sing because your unconscious mind is in control; however, when something unexpected happens— when something darts across the road—your conscious mind kicks in, requiring your full attention.

In *Unconscious Branding*, Van Praet notes that Jeff Brown and Mark Fenske, both Harvard-trained brain experts, say we remember better and "encode more strongly" when "(1) We are in a highly emotional state; (2) The message has significant meaning; (3) It's really unusual; and (4) We are paying close attention."

Haydn's *Surprise* symphony (no. 94 in G Major) added an element of novelty in the form of a loud combination of percussion and brass in the Andante. It is said that he did this because he was tired of people falling asleep during performances. This element of surprise would shock the audience and command their full attention.

In another example, John Cage's opus *4:33*—four minutes and thirty-three seconds of silence (complete with page turns)—was intended to get the audience to pay attention to the sounds around them. By doing the unexpected, Cage ensured the audience would pay attention. And by paying attention they opened themselves to hearing the turning of the pages, the shuffling of feet, people coughing and all the other sounds they usually failed to notice.

There have even been studies to show that exposure to new experiences improves memory. One study on the brain's response to novelty, involving Nico Bunzeck and Emrah Düzel and described in *Neuron* in 2006, concluded that when we introduce completely new facts to the mind it has a better chance of remembering the experience.

Consider the fact that only 1 percent of humankind's existence has been spent living the way we do now—the rest of the time we were hunter-gatherers. We have survival instincts ingrained in us, including our fight-or-flight reflex. In certain situations our body prepares us to fight for our life or run for our life. This reaction is connected to our "reptilian brain," the part that developed first way back when. How many times have you jumped when seeing a stick in the woods, thinking it was a snake, and then immediately realized it was just a stick? This is because our subconscious reacts to danger and then our conscious mind takes over to make sense of the situation. We can take advantage of how our minds work by creating novelty, the unexpected or surprise, and then backing that up with something the conscious mind is going to want to stay engaged with. As musicians, if we provide a memorable experience we will have successfully made a lasting mark in the mind of the audience, fan or consumer.

> *"Awareness of our surroundings occurs only when the things we experience violate our expectations."*—Douglas Van Praet

When we lose things like glasses, quite often it is because we were not consciously aware at the time we put them down. It was not a conscious action—it was like driving the car while talking. As a band or brand the same thing happens: if the audience is experiencing a live performance, listening to a piece of music, looking at a piece of art, experiencing a product or service, and nothing interrupts the expected, then chances are they will forget about the experience altogether.

What can you do in your career to command attention? If you are performing live what can you do that is unexpected? Live producer Tom Jackson talks about creating moments. These are moments that engage audiences, moments they will remember, and so moments that will make them purchase your music to relive the moments. You need to create the unexpected and command your audience's full attention. You need to create moments and consequently memories that people in your audience attach to your music.

If you think about it, you will quickly realize that every notable musician and brand has been a leader of change, has broken the existing patterns, has surprised the public with something new— something unexpected. Then after such a success, others have followed, copying the steps that led to the original success. Most never reach the success of the first person to achieve it, as what was once different, a surprise, unexpected, a disruption of patterns now becomes expected and falls into a pattern. The Beatles have never been replicated; nor has Jimi Hendrix. I suspect that Amanda Palmer's Kickstarter success will not be replicated either, certainly not by copying her success. However, the ability to break patterns and do the unexpected is unlimited!

CREATING POSITIVE MEMORIES

As we've discussed, Marty Neumeier says that individuals—not companies, markets or publics—define brands. *"It's a gut feeling because people are emotional, intuitive beings,"* he says in a PowerPoint presentation on *The Brand* Gap (atnmusi.ca/ch3h1). Gut feelings are built on accumulated experience and knowledge. The more positive memories connected to a brand, the more likely people are to trust and ultimately invest in them. It is our remembering self that makes purchase decisions.

> *"When we love a piece of music, it reminds us of other music we have heard, and it activates memory traces of emotional times in our lives."*—Daniel Levitin

Music, like smells, can connect you so vividly to a memory that it can feel like you are transported in time. The smell of certain spices mixed together can remind you of your mother's cooking, even a particularly memorable occasion on which you enjoyed it. Music can bring back memories of significant moments in your life (in the world of advertising, a song can make you think of the dog-food commercial it was used in ...). There are powerful associations between memories that are linked to music and smells. Creating experiences with your art that are deeply connected to music and smells can allow the memories of the experience to be triggered in the future by those same sounds and smells. The Black Crowes always light incense at their live concerts. If you are a fan who attends their shows, chances are you might think of The Black Crowes when you smell the same type of incense at a friend's house.

We are constantly bombarded by so much information that it is virtually impossible to remember everything with exact detail. What we remember is what matters to us and what we feel are the important aspects of the experience. Repetitive positive brand experiences are the key to marketing a brand successfully. Positive memories of a brand experience are more important than the details of the experience itself. The elements that move us physically and emotionally are primarily how we will formulate our judgments of the brand. This is what Daniel Kahneman, the Nobel Prize-winning behavioural economist, refers to in his book *Thinking, Fast and Slow* as the "peak moments" and "concluding impressions." Kahneman's "peak-end rule" suggests creating powerful, positive peak physical and emotional experiences that leave audiences on a high note. This rule enables you to have more control over the way your brand is remembered. Funnily enough, the focus of his study was on pain and how we remember it—not for the sum of the experience but rather its average. Kahneman's peak-end rule is widely used in marketing today. You can apply it directly to your music career and you can especially apply it to your live performances.

Douglas Van Praet writes:

> When we motivate people into physical action, engaging more than just their perception, cognition, and emotion, we involve more of their neurology impressing the brand deeper into long-term memory. Not only do real-life experiences involve our vast motor systems, they vividly engage our multiple sensory

systems. Through sight, sound, touch, smell and taste, they give us more ways to firmly establish and represent the memory in the brain that drives response. (*Unconscious Branding,* p. 228)

Music, especially live music, has the innate ability to do exactly that. In Seoul, South Korea, Dunkin' Donuts had a marketing campaign in which the company put atomizers in public buses that would emit the smell of freshly brewed coffee. These devices were activated by the sound of the Dunkin' Donuts commercial when it came on the radio.

The combination of the smell and an audio prompt that cleverly came on only before stops with a Dunkin' Donuts nearby—suggesting listeners purchase coffee at their stop—was enough to significantly increase their sales during the time of the campaign. Altogether 350,000 people experienced the ad during the campaign, leading to the number of visitors to the Dunkin' Donuts stores increasing by 16 percent and sales going up 29 percent, according to Dunkin' Donuts advertising.

Brand equity equals positive memories. Positive memories build trust in where you spend your money. Applying that concept to live performance as an example, if the experience is worth remembering people will purchase your music as a way to relive the experience over and over. It is not as much about the songs as it is about the emotional connection to the songs and the experience they generated.

A prime example of connecting memorable experiences and physical action with a brand is Red Bull, because that strategy has been key to the energy drink company's success. The brand has come to have fans that are notably loyal, much like those of Apple. Right from the beginning, Red Bull GmbH focused on creating hands-on, fun experiences around the brand. The Austrian company would spend its marketing dollars on organizing, and sponsoring, exceptionally memorable parties for college students. The combination of the right audience with the right experience meant that consequently the memory of the experience remained—and connected to the Red Bull brand.

According to Van Praet, the three key experiential ingredients to the Red Bull's brand success are novelty, physical action and emotional stimulation.

Red Bull is a great example of a company that has been "on brand" (jargon for being in keeping with a brand's values and vision) with the types of affiliations, endorsements and experiences it generates. These affiliations and experiences have been key to gaining exposure and trust with the audience involved. The company has successfully aligned the brand with extreme athletes as well as created its own extreme sports.

Most recently the "Red Bull Stratos Space Jump" had millions of people watching live online as Felix Baumgartner broke the sound barrier and set the record for the highest free-falling jump. The space jump was, again, in line with what the brand stands for. These types of associations and events don't sell the drink's taste, but rather the power it gives the consumers when they drink it.

I was interested to find out that the toughest personal challenge of the jump for Baumgartner was having to deal with feeling claustrophobic inside the space suit. At one point he actually fled to the airport instead of participating in a test run, not able to get himself to spend six hours in the suit. A psychologist had to help him through the phobia. You can be physically prepared for success, but ultimately it is your mind that needs to be conditioned.

It is no surprise that Red Bull has been a pioneer in signing artists to a company brand. It has successfully picked artists that are on brand and connect with Red Bull consumers. This can certainly be a win–win situation for both artist and brand, and is something to watch out for as more and more brands are looking for creative ways to partner with artists.

B(r)anding—a recap of points to keep in mind:

- Be authentically, confidentially yourself. Be different.

- Focus on creating positive experiences that result in positive memories.

- Surprise people in emotionally meaningful ways.

- Make people feel good and their lives easier to live.

- Long-term success is based on trust plus recommendation.

- Be a fan of your fans. Reward brand "ambassadors" (i.e., the Super Fans).

- An effective brand should speak more about the person who chooses it than about the product it represents.

- Be sure to listen to what is being said about you and use the information to strengthen your brand.

- Be a leader, not a follower. Create the unexpected. Use the element of surprise backed by values that people relate to.

- Give value greater than just the "product." Give a valuable and meaningful experience.

- Connect people with people; let the brand represent them.

- Overdeliver and undersell. Let the experience and product be greater than the expectations.

- Build trust through positive experiences.

- Engage with your audience. Be transparent. Recognize mistakes and celebrate successes.

- Develop your brand story. Let your brand experience start in the audience's mind by stimulating the imagination. A brand is a living, breathing thing—it evolves, and your story should be the same way.

- Create community, a sense of belonging, a place of acceptance. Monetize admission to the community.

- A great brand should represent the inner person its fans strive to become.

- Never substitute real experiences with online experiences. Use the internet as an extension of your physical brand. Use it to build awareness and gather data. Activism is always more effective than "clicktivism."

- Don't let "freemium" marketing (i.e., freebies) dictate the value of your brand.

- Build brand affiliations that add value and focus to your brand, that help tell your story. Be creative in choosing your partners and strive to surprise.

- Follow Marty Neumeier's "Five Disciplines of Brand Building": differentiate, collaborate, innovate, validate, cultivate.

- Answer these questions in order to ensure the focus of your brand: Who are you? What do you do? Why does it matter?

- Create a recognizable image. Symbols defy literal definition and require emotional interpretation. As Carl Jung said: "The sign is always less than the concept it represents, while a symbol always stands for something more than its obvious and immediate meaning."

Nashville audio branding expert Steve Keller offers some excellent advice in the following points:

1 **Be congruent.** The brands that are most recognized and familiar are the brands that practise congruency in their communication. Authenticity is one thing. Alignment is another. Research shows that the brands that make the strongest impressions are the brands that align their identity across multiple consumer touch

points: visually, verbally, sonically—even considering how haptic and olfactory touch points might affect brand identity. If your verbal message isn't aligned with your visual image, it can result in a perception of the brand that feels inauthentic, disingenuous, and even dishonest.

2 **Be consistent.** It takes time to establish a brand identity—and to build equity in it. Super brands understand the importance of consistency. They connect with their consumers as often as possible in as many contexts as possible—and they make sure that when they do, the consumer experience of the brand is always the same. As a result, the brand feels familiar. Consistency creates—and then delivers on—consumer expectations.

3 **Keep your promises.** A brand is ultimately the promise of an experience. Make sure you understand what that promise is—and continually take an inventory to make sure you're keeping that promise. That's how you build fans—and loyalty.

For some in-depth discussions on branding, please check out my interviews with the following brand experts:

Steve Jones (author, *Brand Like a Rock Star*)
atnmusi.ca/ch3h2

Karen Kang (author, *BrandingPays: The Five-Step System to Reinvent Your Personal Brand*)
atnmusi.ca/ch3h3

Steve Keller (Nashville audio branding expert and CEO and strategist of iVGroup)
atnmusi.ca/ch3h4

Marty Neumeier (author, *The Brand Gap*)
atnmusi.ca/ch3h5

Josh Nychuk (graphic designer, Nychuk Design)
atnmusi.ca/ch3h6

CHAPTER FOUR

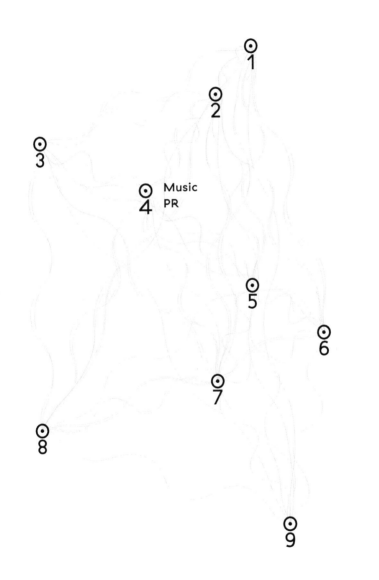

1

2

3

4 Music
   PR

5

6

7

8

9

Music PR

"Without publicity a terrible thing happens ... NOTHING!"
—P.T. Barnum

Public relations (PR) ensures the world knows you exist, learns your story, hears your music, is aware of your tour, finds out about your products ... More specifically, it is the voice that communicates directly with the media and the people who can impact your career.

The results of your PR campaign should build on your existing reputation, be a voice to your brand and support your overall strategy. Taking these factors into account will affect which outlets of exposure you approach as well as how you go about it.

PR VS. ADVERTISING

PR has always stood apart from advertising. Now more than ever, paying for expensive advertising in the hopes of "buying" quality, trust or reputation is less effective than having good PR. Thanks to Google reviews and all the tools of web 2.0 (the new age of web technology and applications), people can share their feelings and experiences of products, services, live shows and almost anything else as they are experiencing them. The internet has added an element of transparency that means the consumer is the voice of quality control. With all the outlets available to express opinions and experiences, word can travel at breakneck speeds. So spending money on advertising to be the "best pizza place in town" or the "Greatest Rock Band Alive" doesn't mean much—ultimately it is going to be what word on the street (and now online) says is the best and the greatest. The good thing is that the word does spread and the internet makes "far and wide" take on a whole new meaning. The power of word of mouth has moved to the next level!

For this reason hiring a good publicist can be more cost-efficient, and ultimately more important, in today's internet-based world than paid advertising.

The online world of PR

The fact that so many print publications have gone out of print because of the internet has inevitably changed PR. This development has affected timelines and opened masses of new outlets for exposure.

Thanks to the tools available, it's easy to find out who the influential people, publications and media are that are connecting with, influencing and affecting your target audience on the deepest levels.

Using social media is a great way to monitor your brand. You can find out who is talking about you positively as well as those who are talking negatively. Using social media as a tool, you can provide assistance and information, start a conversation and ultimately turn bad reviews and negative words into opportunities to establish meaningful relationships.

Your interests, age, location, gender and so on work as guides toward choosing specific media and technology to digest information. There is more information than ever on the demographics that online and offline publications are targeting. This information is priceless as it allows us to know where our PR work is going to create the largest impact on our audience and which platforms will reach our "Super Fan."

With many new ways to interact with your audience, the ability to find out what your audience is talking about, and new data-mining tools to help you learn more about your fans and what influences them, the game is changing! Combining these elements gives you the opportunity to create razor-sharp PR campaigns that connect in a meaningful and organic way to your targeted audience.

The first segment of this book on profiling your Super Fan (see Chapter 2) applies directly to profiling your ideal media outlets when creating PR campaigns. As an example, knowing where bands similar to you are being featured can help you work out which media outlets to approach. Just take a look at "Press" pages on artist websites and see if they include publications that are relevant both geographically and demographically to whatever upcoming event you want to promote.

Get to the point

The ability of social media and the internet to provide information instantly has affected the attention span of a significant segment of the developed world. As an example, Twitter's 140-character Tweets require creative thinking about your wording, but have affected how much people want to read elsewhere. Keep this in mind when you are creating content. More than ever, the first line of your press release, your bio, or any of your other written content has to get the point across immediately. Think of it as a Tweet!

ASKING THE PROs

I asked renowned publicists Eric Alper, Ariel Hyatt and David Weiss a few questions on the topic of PR.

1. Eric Alper

Eric Alper is based in Toronto and is the director of media relations at eOne Music Canada. He has handled PR for clients such as Ray Charles, Ringo Starr, Sir Bob Geldorf, Steve Miller, Sinéad O'Connor, The Smashing Pumpkins, Slash, Cradle of Filth, Chickenfoot, Bush, Kris Kristofferson, Snoop Dogg, Joan Baez and Pete Seeger.

Aaron Bethune:
   What is PR?

Eric Alper:
   PR is essentially that relationship between the record label or band and the media. So it's my job to ensure that the music gets heard and to do follow-up. It's not necessarily to make the media love the band, because that's totally up to them. But just to give them a fighting chance.

For PR from an independent side, your competition is U2, your competition are the Katy Perrys of the world. So, it's just to ensure that press releases get written, that bios get written properly, and that they [the artists] are written about in such a way that is interesting and has a couple of angles for the media to write about.

It is also to ensure that everything goes smoothly, whether it's booking a day's worth of media for a band, contacting MuchMusic and MTV, or ensuring that the videos get played and so forth.

It's utilizing all the tools that the band have and the record label have in order to work with the media. The media need people to write about, and it's my job to come up with as many different angles and pitches as possible to get them interested in what the band have to say or what they sound like.

AB:
What makes for a good press release?

EA:
You have to go on the idea that nobody's going to read your second line, so your first line has to be good enough for people to continue reading.

It has to be well written without obvious grammar and spelling mistakes. If the press release isn't well written, it can give the impression that maybe the band isn't good either.

Your perception of something when you're reading about it can be that if it sounds dull and boring, then chances are you will think that the band, movie or TV show is probably boring as well. So you want to pepper it with excitement and be able to give the information in a quick manner.

A band bio can reveal a lot more information about the band than a press release, such as how they met; where they've come from; what kind of influences musically they have; what they want to say on this album that might be different from the past records; where song titles come from; what their inspirations are;

where the album title comes from, etc. ... For example, when you know more about Adele, her break-up, it makes the media and audience appreciate the album a little more because they know where it's coming from.

When it comes to a press release, it's just giving the media that information about why you're contacting them in the first place. If it's a show, is it just another show in your city? Is it a Battle of the Bands? Is it part of a larger tour? Because sometimes by listing all the dates in your press release, even if you're only hitting that city once, it gives off the impression that the tour is a fairly big deal. Sometimes I don't put all the tour dates on the press release because maybe the band is playing a residency in the city that alone is worthy of a press release.

A press release is to provide all the necessary information in a quick, to-the-point manner, so the reader gets interested and calls you back to say, "You know what, I'm really excited about this."

AB:
At what point does a band need a publicist?

EA:
I tell bands now that unless your songs are for sale somewhere, you have no reason to contact either a publicist or radio. The bottom line is that you have to start to sell something.

A lot of the bands that I knew growing up had somebody in the band contact the media themselves. Sometimes they were upfront about who in the band was calling; other times I've heard of people making up assumed names and business companies just to give off the impression that they were a lot bigger than they actually were. I would say: be realistic. Nobody really cares that an indie band has a show in your city and you don't have a lot of media. But if you really truly are doing something different, or if you happen to be based in Canada and a US publication features you, whether it's *Pitchfork* [a major daily internet publication] or getting on a really cool blog, then that's worthy of a press release. Just to let people know that you exist.

Nobody should really be touring or trying to reach the larger general population without having songs available to sell, because you never get to choose which media are going to write about you. You could be sending out a press release and the next thing you know, it's up on a huge blog like *Pitchfork*, and all these people within minutes are on your website and want to buy something, and you've missed out. That might be, to some bands, the only opportunity to actually reach the media and hit them in that way.

There's the thinking now that sometimes the best publicity is no publicity by not reaching out to the media and letting the media discover the band. Letting the fans do the "PR" for them by getting their music and sharing it, sticking it on their SoundCloud page or on Facebook under "I Like."

There are a slew of bands, like Odd Future, that never really reached out to the media, and let them discover the band themselves. It put them in a position of a bit more of a mystery rather than, "Here's 15 press releases, a bio, all of our recordings, please write about me!" There's a great deal of bands that simply don't care whether the media is writing about them; they're just reaching the fans directly and they're doing a very good job at it.

AB:
How much lead time do you need for a successful PR campaign?

EA:
I usually go at least two months in advance, which is not a lot of time. But, for instance, eOne just signed Bush and their album comes out in four months. So, the first press release for Bush is going out tomorrow. That's just to whet people's appetite. We probably won't have music to give to media, my guess, probably for another couple of weeks. And then there's the plan of, do we want to give away a song? If we don't give away a song, does it benefit or harm them?

Radio can go six weeks in advance, but in some cases you're planting those seeds for the band. At least with radio, sometimes a year in advance, just simply because the competition is too heavy.

If you're a rock band in Canada, not only do you have to concern yourself with CanCon (Canadian content), but you've got to realize that there's probably going to be five singles from the Foo Fighters from this album alone, and then you have to worry about bands like Bush, Cage the Elephant, and whatever Jack White's project is that month. So, when you're talking about radio, there's a lot more seeding, growing and planning.

In terms of the press, it's great to have something two months in advance, but again the problem becomes if you're an indie band and you start sending out press releases ahead of time, you may get on websites, whether it's *NOW Magazine*'s or, if you're in Vancouver, on the *Georgia Straight* and the next thing you know, you've got all these people coming on your website and you've got two months to sell an album before your album even drops. So, I tend to send out a press release with the ability that somewhere out there the fans can actually get the music and that the bands can actually get that music heard, because who knows how often the media are going to warm up to your ideas on it.

2. Ariel Hyatt

Ariel Hyatt is a renowned New York publicist, author, educator and speaker. She is the owner of the online PR company Cyber PR.

Aaron Bethune:
  What is PR?

Ariel Hyatt:
  I asked the same question on the first day of my first internship at a PR firm in London. I'll never forget the answer the guy gave me. I was nineteen years old, it was my first internship, and I said, "Can you tell me what PR is?" He said, "PR? It's PR!" I thought, "Wow. Thank you for that." You can imagine that internship was a disaster from that moment on. Anyway, the process of PR is the communication of a product, a good, a service, or a person, to the media. So when you hire a publicist, you're basically hiring a mouthpiece to communicate to the media world your message or what it is you would like to promote. Until I started working in PR firms, I really didn't understand the depth of how PR touches almost everything

you read in the media. For example, if you're a woman who likes fashion magazines, when you pull open a magazine and you see "Our favourite shampoo of the month," or "Our favourite lip gloss," or "The best pants to wear this season," that is all 100 percent the work of a publicist. The editor did not go walking around to find the best anything. The publicist worked very, very hard with the editor to place the product. Every facet of almost every business has publicity—politicians, products, goods, services—almost everything you can think of. Stores, cities, towns, and of course musicians all have publicists. When you hire a publicist, what you are doing is hiring someone to represent you to the media. When I say the media, I mean newspapers, magazines, television, radio, and now it's been vastly expanded in recent years to blogs, podcasts, internet radio, almost anything. So that is, in a nutshell, what it is.

AB:
How important is a band's pitch?

AH:

I believe a pitch is the most important thing a band or artist can develop. Without a pitch, people will have no context for understanding who you are or what you sound like. Unfortunately, many bands are terrible at creating pitches. It's critical because we have very, very short attention spans in today's world. If you don't have a concise pitch that gives people an instant hit, you're basically robbing yourself of possibilities.

AB:
What makes for a good pitch?

AH:

Something that's extremely descriptive and catchy; descriptive doesn't mean you have to sound like somebody else, though that's a very helpful context. Catchy could be anything from fun, like "hillbilly flamenco," or "polyethnic Cajun slam grass," or it could be really descriptive like "Joan Jett meets Jessica Rabbit." Those are three of my favourite pitches … they are really good. If I was in an elevator with Devil Doll and I asked her "What kind of music do you make?" and she answered "It's Joan Jett meets Jessica Rabbit," that's dead on. She's a rocker who's got a really sexy, curvy look. A pitch like that, a short concise piece, is crucial. Bands are normally terrified, they don't want to say they sound like anybody, they don't want to pigeonhole themselves. It really is a disservice to try to invent a new genre of music to explain what you are—it may feel creative, but people don't understand it.

AB:

What is a realistic time frame for a PR campaign to show results?

AH:

Depends on the type of results you are looking for. If you're talking about a traditional PR campaign in major publications—these are known in the PR world as "long-lead press" (*Spin*, *Rolling Stone* and *Vanity Fair*)—that means you have to begin thinking about your press placement at least three months before the issue comes out. So for Christmas press you must have your Christmas tracks ready to go at the end of August, and your publicist should be lining up your Christmas pitches for long-lead press by September. This takes planning and foresight and I have met a lot of artists who don't think this far in advance. Of course, for daily and weekly newspapers, there is a shorter window. If you're promoting a live event in a local newspaper, the editor needs a minimum of four to six weeks' notice to schedule you in. They have to get interviews and artwork and they are getting inundated by hundreds of other publicists and events that month, no matter what city you are playing in, so again: planning and foresight are key.

With the internet, it's very fast and can be instantaneous. Blogs are looking for information quickly and efficiently. We've released MP3s on a Monday and by Tuesday there are internet radio stations streaming, blogs posting, and people sharing it all over the social networks. So when you talk about an online PR campaign, that's a whole different beast.

3. David Weiss

New York journalist David Weiss co-founded SonicScoop, *an online "news source and community," and writes about audio for magazines such as* Mix *and* Drum! *He co-wrote the book* Music Supervision: The Complete Guide to Selecting and Licensing Music & Sound Design for Media *(with Ramsay Adams and Dave Hnatiuk), and he is an electronic music producer.*

Aaron Bethune:
Does journalism affect the music industry?

David Weiss:
They are there to affect each other. You've heard of *Pitchfork*, which was started as a magazine in the early to mid-'90s and has grown into arguably the most influential tastemaker publication media outlet online now. They've got enormous traffic and it's very important to get your album reviewed in *Pitchfork*. What I've heard is that those who are in the know battle very hard to get their music reviewed on *Pitchfork* to promote their albums. I've heard that bands are actually changing their music and shaping it so they'll get a positive review from them. I guess it is kind of disturbing to hear that.

So there's one example of journalism affecting music. There's probably a myriad of other examples like that. We use media now to learn facts, get analysis, get opinions and get help with the outside world. We're looking for something that we're going to act on, whether it's travel or weather information, or to know about music that's going to fulfill us in some way.

AB:
What is the process for an artist to get a review or article in a publication?

DW:
Today it totally depends. It used to be pretty cut and dried. Several years ago, when an artist came out with an album, they would print up many, many copies of the album and send it to the journalist three months before it came out. It would be the publicist or the

band that would get the music to the journalist and then try and get some type of ink.

Now, you still get a little bit of that. I still get several CDs a week in the mail. For the most part, I'm bombarded with email from publicists, and it's welcome. The internet makes it a lot easier to spread a ton of information about artists. But there's millions and millions of people competing for other people's attention. So that's the rub.

Today, someone might send me a link to their album online, and if I get a chance I'll download it and give it a listen. That's just one of many ways that things get to me, but there are lots of others. There's pure osmosis — we're in NYC, and I'm going to be out and seeing a band, or someone's going to tell me about it, or I'll find out about it via my own site, on *sonicscoop.com*. I find out about a lot of great music by writing about a producer who's produced ten bands, and I listen to all those bands when I get a chance. That's a terrific channel for finding out about music. Every editor and writer has their processes and filters for what music they actually listen to and cover.

AB:
What makes for a good press release?

DW:
They need to be succinct. Keep them to a page; if you present someone with too much information these days, they're going to decide they don't want to read any of it. "Please forgive me for writing such a long letter; I didn't have time to write a shorter one." I hear this quote all the time. Keeping things succinct requires a lot more thought and effort than just throwing a whole bunch of information out there.

Always ask yourself: Are you providing the Who, What, Where, When and Why?

Always make sure your contact information is there. One piece of advice I give to bands is to avoid naming yourself as the press contact. For example, if this press release is about John Winters, jazz guitarist, and John writes it and puts it out, consider making an alternative email address such as *press@johnwinters.com* and make the media contact your boyfriend or your girlfriend. From an image perspective, if you're making yourself look completely like a one-man shop, it just doesn't have the same impact. I deal with some one-man companies and I tell them to find a way to make it look like this is from a press representative.

One of the things I learned from Steve Karas, who gave me the internship at IRS Records and is still a top publicist in the music field, is to never compare a band to another band—he would never say "They sound like Faith Hill and Queens of the Stone Age" ... You've got to find a way to describe the music without invoking other bands or artists, unless you think that's really essential.

Make the artist appear to be an interviewable entity—someone that would be interesting to talk to.

I actually don't call them press releases very often anymore. I refer to these public communications as news releases, because I think there's a big difference—there is a lot less press now. Your news release, if you're an artist, it's going up on your website, it's going out on your email list, you're linking to it on Twitter and Facebook, etc. ... It's news that you're putting out and it's going to a great deal of people who aren't with the press.

AB:
How have blogs affected the business?

DW:
It depends what you actually define as a blog. I can't say for sure what a blog is now—I don't think of a blog as being different from any other kind of media resource. A blog, to the general public, simply means a website that is updated frequently with some type of opinionated slant of reporting on a particular topic. Due to the ease that blogs can be created, just like the extreme ease that music can now be recorded, anyone who wishes to be a taste-maker, have an opinion, and be instantly internationally published

can be. If you're a person using all that stuff, hopefully blogs are going to be a way to point you to some of the stuff you really like, but we all have to apply our filters at some point.

AB:
Are there any in particular that you pay more attention to?

DW:
One of my favourites is written right here in New York City. It's called *Create Digital Music*, and that's written by a guy called Peter Kirn. It's a very geeky blog about producing music with digital tools—and it's funny. *Mashable* is regarded as a blog and also *Tech Crunch*, but they're not necessarily music-related. I find those three very important to check every day.

What I'm about to recommend next isn't a blog, but everyone should subscribe to the "ASCAP Daily Brief" [available through the online home of the American Society of Composers, Authors and Publishers]. It's an excellent, daily email aggregation of breaking news about the music business.

AB:
What defines a good story?

DW:
What we're most interested in at *SonicScoop* are stories that [co-founder] Janice [Brown] or I haven't thought of—when someone proposes it we realize it's interesting and relevant to our target audience. It comes down to what we think our readers are going to sink their teeth into. We're not always right about what that is, but that's the thing.

A good article pitch is based on the potential journalist's demonstrated knowledge of your site or outlet. You're going to have to be persistent. In my *Music Supervision* book, one of my favourite quotes is from Adam Schlesinger of the band Fountains of Wayne, who talks about the fine line between persistence and annoyance. It's a tough line to walk. The squeaky wheel gets the grease. If I don't know you at all and you keep coming to me because you believe in yourself and you're doing it in a way that's not crowding me, eventually I'm going to write you back. Eventually, I'm going to be able to read this thing you submitted and see where you really fit in.

AB:
Has the internet affected printed publications?

DW:
It has devastated the economic model. These types of transitions go hand in hand with human development. One of the key aspects of our evolution is how we communicate. ... Humans are extremely well organized — it's our advantage and our downfall; it's what made us incredibly awesome at what we do, and may bring disastrous consequences in the end. But we organize astonishingly well and communication is definitely at the heart of that.

Print ruled for a long time and probably put some people out of business at first ... people who pounded stuff into stone tablets or something. Now the internet is putting print out of business, making it irrelevant in almost every way, shape and form that is used. There will always be printed communication, but the internet has made it incredibly hard — not impossible — to make money with printed communications. Someday something will come along and do that to the internet.

YOU HAVE TO SOUND GOOD IN WRITING!

With a wealth of tools available to us to promote our music and our brands, how we use them is key to our online and offline success. The most used technique to promote ourselves is writing. For this reason, it is important to know how to sound equally outstanding in writing and music.

> *"No matter how brilliant a website's design, no matter how elegant its navigation, sooner or later visitors will decide whether to take action because of something they read." —* Brad Shorr

Keep in mind that when you submit your music to people, they read what you write before they listen to the music. So the music has absolutely no weight in creating interest and impact with your first impression. Think about that. Unless someone heard you playing live, or on radio or TV, perhaps, your music is not going to be the first impression!

I can't begin to estimate the number of press releases, bios, even emails and voicemails that I get from bands, and the majority all have the same spiel. They've been playing since childhood, when they play as a band it's magical, they are charting on ReverbNation and can I check out their music and somehow help them out …

When you get a ton of submissions you would be surprised at how few have great stories that engage you and consequently both create intrigue to check out the music and make it obvious how to promote that music.

When a band's pitch has the engaging qualities of a story, by the time you get to the music the songs have added emotional value. No matter who you are pitching to, in order to stand out and give a reason for people to pay attention you need to have a story that sets you apart.

STORYTELLING

"All stories are built around human truths, no matter what channel they live on. The best songs, the best movies, the best ads let you see yourself in them somehow." —Deutch Inc.

Storytelling is a primal form of communication. It has traditionally been a way of passing on knowledge, lessons, events and experiences from generation to generation. Stories are the threads that tie us to ancient traditions, legends, myths, even symbols, and they connect us to a larger self and universal truths. Through stories we can experience extreme situations and intense emotions with a safety net.

Think of how easily we can remember stories from our childhood, yet how difficult it is to remember a statistic or piece of data we read about this week. If you want to sell something—whether music, merch or yourself—you have to do it within the context of storytelling. Achieving true engagement happens when you wrap your products in a story, helping consumers to accept them organically into their lives and to share the story as if it were their own. If you approach your career, band, brand, content and so on from a storyteller's perspective you have the ability to spread it far and wide.

Much like your songs and live show, you need to develop your artist story. It takes practice. Learn to tell it in a way that is engaging and easily spread by others. Your story will make it clear to newspapers why they should feature you, give radio a reason to play you, and so on. Your story will set you apart, add another dimension to your brand and give greater emotional connection to your music.

Your story should be unique. It should set you apart. We are all different, so your story should be too! Once you have developed it, your story should be incorporated into everything you do, especially your PR. In interviews, always bring the answers back around to help tell it. By clearly communicating your story, you will help spread it further than you can ever imagine.

Your favourite bands and brands have a story. Whether it is the classic "hero's journey," or a tale about the underdog's victory or the simple overnight success, it is how we remember and tell others about our favourite performers and brands.

Here are a few reasons why stories are so important:

- They are how we share human experience.
- Unlike facts and data, they are easily remembered.
- They make us, our products, songs, brands, etc. ... unique.
- By wrapping brands, bands, songs, products and so forth into stories, we can spread them virally in the real world.
- In a world inundated by information, a good story can cut through the noise like nothing else.

The Power of Storytelling

"Stories are easier to remember because in many ways stories are how we remember." —Daniel Pink

Stories take place in the imagination and, to the human brain, imagined experiences are processed in the same way that real experiences are (see Chapter 3, "Branding"). Because of a story's ability to create genuine emotions and behavioural responses, the brands, products, songs, bands and people that we connect with stories will inevitably be more memorable and stand out.

The Introduction to this book is a story. It recounts a life-changing experience I had while mountaineering in the Andes when I was younger. I wanted to draw on the similarities between climbing a mountain and finding success in music, but I also wanted you to know more about the person typing these words—the real me. By sharing my story, I have in turn told you a lot about myself. It gave me the opportunity to start building trust with you right from the start. It meant acknowledging a bittersweet truth upfront, that I didn't reach the summit, but the overall authenticity of the book depended on that.

Sharing personal experiences in stories engages your audience through emotions and allows the audience to feel connected to you. Stories allow us to overcome our differences, understand ourselves better and find our commonalities. They are the highway to our right brain and a way of triggering the imagination. And through imagination we tap into creativity, which in turn is the foundation of innovation and change. If you want people to take action, put the message in a story!

The key to a great story is a compelling beginning, an absorbing middle and a satisfying end. A great story doesn't "tell" the audience something—it makes them "feel" it, because feeling allows the audience to become involved with the story. By feeling we step out of our own shoes and are able to see things from another person's perspective and feel empathy. We can use stories to persuade others as well as to explain how we justify our own decisions.

With the ever-growing number of platforms available online, there have never been as many places and opportunities to share stories.

Creating Our Own Story

We all have a personal story. In fact, we share our individual stories with the world through the way we live our lives and the way we communicate with the people around us.

The fact is that we create our own stories, we live them, we tell them to others and we become known by them. We each have to create the story we want to live, share it with the world and have others spread it. That is how we will live the reality we want to live.

I'm sure you know people who have the "gift" of good luck, are happy, never short of work or money, live their dreams and reach the goals they set ... How about people who are hard done by, whose lives are tough, who struggle to find work, for whom money doesn't come easily, and so on? People tell us the stories they choose to live by and those become the stories we know and associate with them. Moreover, it is how we describe them to others.

How often has a friend or family member changed their story? It's not easy! Those who do change do it by making a conscious decision and then taking action. They start telling a new story and living by it. It starts with waking up and saying: Today is going to be great! This is who I am and this is my story!

Writing the story of success can include visualization, believing that your thoughts create your future, being open to endless possibility, and making the present the past you want to remember as well as a stepping stone to the future you want to have.

Even though we are discussing personal stories right now, note that the same tactics apply to our careers, businesses, brands and so on. We each need to write and live the story we want to be known by.

The Piano Man

The small Isle of Sheppey, off the coast of Kent, England, made international headlines after a drenched and disturbed man was found walking on a windswept seaside road there. He was taken to hospital, where he failed to answer any questions. Then one of the staff gave him a piece of paper and pencil, and he drew a detailed grand piano. When the staff took him to a piano, he proceeded to play sections from *Swan Lake* by Tchaikovsky. As time passed and the "Piano Man" remained unidentified, a photo was taken and sent to the media in the hope that somebody would recognize him.

The man would play the piano for hours and would have to be physically removed from it. He mostly played his own compositions, which were compared to the work of Italian composer Ludovico Einaudi. When he wasn't playing, he would carry a plastic folder around that contained sheet music.

There was much discussion about how he had landed where he had. Theories included the suggestions that he had swum ashore after falling off a boat; that he was a professional musician who had been performing not long before he was found (which would account for his smart clothing); that he was a French street musician; that he was a Czech concert pianist; and even that he was a Canadian eccentric. But the truth was that nobody could identify who he was and how he had got there.

There was a lot of speculation until one day he was identified and the true story came out.

The story of the Piano Man spread because it had all the right ingredients to engage an audience. I still find it remarkable, and consequently have included it here. I have posted a couple of links below so you can learn more, because the story does have a conclusion. I am sure somehow you'll want to check it out now that I have got you interested!

The Story of the Piano Man
atnmusi.ca/ch4h1

The Piano Man Follow-up
atnmusi.ca/ch4h2

Here a couple more interesting links to check out:

Better User Experience with Storytelling
atnmusi.ca/ch4h3

Jay O'Callahan : The Power of Storytelling
atnmusi.ca/ch4h4

BE CREATIVE

Find ways to creatively get your story told in the media without going the route of advertising. Reviews, articles, interviews and the like are always more organic ways of introducing your music and career to an audience than paid ads.

Local media are always looking for good stories and relevant local content to publish. You would be surprised at how many bands will never approach the media because they don't think the media would be interested. There are also just as many bands that do approach the media but expect the media to be the ones to come up with the story. The fact is that if you can present an engaging story and you reach out to the right people, you will be pleasantly surprised with the result.

IDEAS, REMINDERS & CONSIDERATIONS

I started this book by suggesting that the best thing you can do with the information within these pages is turn it on its head, get creative … The following points include the obvious people to contact and ways to reach out to them, as well as some more creative approaches. See what outside-the-box ideas you can come up with!

- **Be sure to submit your live dates and press release to all relevant local media.** This should include local papers and radio stations as well as magazines and e-zines. Often the person who books the venue you are playing can provide local media contacts.

- **Be sure to look into college papers and radio stations too.**
  Get in touch with student unions so you can get connected with
  people who are influential with the student body. There are bands
  whose careers have been made on college radio and campus
  tours—think Dave Matthews and the Tragically Hip.

- **Look into local charities, local businesses and so on that are
  potential fits for your show and brand.** Consider co-branding
  for a show and give yourself more angles to approach the
  media with.

- **Present different angles for interviews.** Contact the entertainment editor of a relevant publication with an interesting story
  on how the artwork for your new album came about and why
  it is newsworthy. An image of the album as well as a story that
  creates intrigue around the music is always more effective than
  paying for an ad that features the album art. Check out the story
  behind the artwork for John Mayer's album *Born and Raised:*
  atnmusi.ca/ch4h5

- **Think outside the box.** I worked with a band that had inspired an
  artist friend to create a cartoon based on the band. The cartoon
  became part of the album artwork, the website, the merch, the
  stage set-up … Because of the concept, we approached the
  local paper with a comic strip. This was fitting for the band's
  brand and was able to generate intrigue and consequently traffic
  to the band's website. The artistic twist opened up promotion of
  the band in the art world too!

- **Look for new and unexpected ways to be interviewed.** Identify
  influential people in the markets you are touring in by using the
  online tools we have discussed previously. Ask if they would
  interview you before you tour through their towns. You can do
  many things with the interview, including featuring it on your
  blog, submitting it to the local paper and putting it up on your
  website. You will create a connection with an influential local
  person who will have actively become involved in your career.
  This adds another important influencer to help spread your story.
  It can even make for an interesting interview to submit to e-zines

and print media, especially if the person interviewing you has an interesting story too.

- **Write your story as a min-saga.** No more and no fewer than fifty words. Learning to condense your story in a way that can be transmitted in a short email or phone call is extremely important. No one wants to wade through an essay to understand why they should interview or feature you.

- **Reverse the roles.** Interview a local (to your tour route) entertainment editor at a paper, publication or blog, or even a radio music director, and feature it on your blog or website. Everyone likes their turn in the spotlight and often the people who are used to doing the interviewing don't get interviewed themselves. This can be the start of building a relationship and ultimately result in features, mentions, interviews, spins and so on in the future when you tour through town. Plant the seed and watch it grow!

- **You need to build relationships early on.** The more relationships you make in the industry, the more likely you are to "make it." To be a good publicist you need to know a lot of people and have the gift of the gab. As in the preceding point, you have to find ways to connect with influential people without making it about your music. Shine the light on them; give more than you ask for!

- **Don't just think music media!** Just because you are promoting your music career doesn't mean you need to promote yourself like every other musician, in all the same places musicians promote themselves. At the end of the day, do you want to promote yourself to other musicians or to your Super Fans? If members of your fan base all share the common love of yoga, then research how companies whose primary clients are yoga lovers handle their PR. How are they promoting themselves? What media are they appearing in? How are they connecting with their audience? Is there an opportunity to approach them for co-branding or cross-promotion?

- **Make your news release search-engine-friendly using Google keywords and Google Trends.** Here is a great case study that can help you to apply SEO techniques to your PR: atnmusi.ca/ch4h6

- **Follow up. Follow up. Follow up.** People don't do this enough. That said, there is a fine line between being professional and being a pain in the ass. Whenever you contact somebody for the first time, ask when and how would be the best way to follow up. As an example, I get so many emails a day that older emails can get lost at the bottom of the list as new ones come in. When somebody follows up I appreciate it because that person goes back to the top of the list. Also, musicians seem to be notoriously bad at following up and consequently miss many opportunities!

OUTLETS FOR OPPORTUNITY

There are endless outlets and opportunities for promoting yourself and creating a presence both on- and offline. A large part of going from "invisible" to "incredible" is tied in with whether or not you are making use of all the tools and outlets for your music and story. Our ability to be creative and find unique places to establish our presence is huge. Here are a few of the more obvious:

- Albums
- Blogs
- Electronic press kits (EPKs)
- Flyers
- Magazines and e-zines
- News releases
- Newsletters
- Newspapers
- Posters

Here are more outlets for exposure, including some of the less obvious:

Applications to festivals. I don't expect people to get on a festival's bill the first time they apply, but I do believe that if your name comes up enough and your music and show are appropriate, it will eventually happen! The point is that you're getting yourself out there.

Emails. Send emails. Look up the contact info of publishers, labels, music supervisors, producers, editors, radio personalities, music directors, radio promoters, managers, agents, entertainment lawyers, venues, brands … Don't expect things and don't ask for help, but ask for feedback. You will have made them aware of you and if you're lucky you will gain important feedback. I remember being in a band and sending out eighty-five personalized emails one weekend—it literally took the whole weekend, because I also took the time to research the people who would receive the emails. It was a lot of work but it was worth it. So send emails! Put yourself out there!

Radio. Terrestrial and online. Submit your music to all eligible stations. Most will have indie nights or feature indie bands. Whether you get one spin or get put in rotation, it's all part of getting exposure. (See also Chapter 9, "Radio Promotion.")

Social sites (Facebook, Twitter, MySpace, ReverbNation, SoundCloud, YouTube, Pinterest, Vimeo, etc.).

Submitting to competitions. I don't believe in competitions. However, I do believe that if your music is going to be reviewed by influencers it is worth putting yourself in front of them. The more people who hear you and the more your name comes up the better! There are many examples of performing artists and songwriters who entered competitions and didn't place first but catapulted their careers into stardom as a result.

Websites (your home page, your venue's home page, your sponsor's home page, links on other artists' home pages, etc., etc., etc. You would be surprised how much follow-up you have to do to ensure you appear in all the places mentioned).

Wikipedia. Having a page created on *Wikipedia* (be sure to read the guidelines) not only gets you more visibility but affects your Klout Score.

And let's not forget:

Parties. Be social—get out there and mingle. Even if it is not the whole band, somebody's got to do it! The internet is great, but it is no substitute for getting face time. There are always music schmoozes, so just look up your local music association and see when the next one is. Creating moments with people when everyone is relaxing is a perfect opportunity for networking and getting yourself out there. It's the perfect way to be remembered with a real-life "story." At a lot of music conferences, including the annual Midem (Marché international du disque et de l'édition musicale) in Cannes, you can find the best networking opportunities happening in the hotel lobby bars after the day is done. On your local scene, get out there and party. Play at parties. Next time you play in town, let your new-found friends know that the party's at the venue!

Do what they do. Even if this sounds distasteful, the fact is that surrounding yourself with the type of people you want to know for your music can be part of getting to the top. This applies to local music schmoozes and music conferences, but it also applies to golf clubs, gyms and yoga classes. The truth is that you have a love of music in common, so you can turn this into an authentic part of your life. But you have to put yourself in the best position to create the opportunities with the people you need to know to get where you want to be.

As a side note but in reference to this last thought, let me give you an example of why you might want to surround yourself or "hang out" with people who live the life you want. We all have an internal thermometer that lets us know when we feel comfortable. It is our success thermometer. If we feel comfortable at 30 degrees Celsius, then when the temperature drops to 10 degrees we do whatever we can to get back to 30 degrees, but when the temperature rises to 50 degrees we do whatever it takes to get back down to 30 degrees.

If you want a higher standard of living, if you want greater success in the conventional sense, if you want to make more money, you need to raise your comfort temperature. Surrounding yourself with people who are living the way you want to live makes raising your own thermometer a lot easier. Surrounding yourself with people living at lower levels of success is always going to make it harder for you to change.

It is amazing how many people ruin opportunities because they are out of their comfort zone. Whether it is ruining a relationship with your dream girl or guy or losing a dream job, if you want your thermometer for success to rise, one way to move the process along is to surround yourself with people who feel and live comfortably at "high temper-atures." We all hear comments such as "I'll never be able to live there," "I'll never get to play there," "I'll never be that good," and the truth is that they become the reality. But if you surround and involve yourself with people who do "live there," "play there" and are "that good," you will see that what seemed like a dream is the reality being lived around you. Your perception of dream and reality will change. This applies directly to believing in yourself, because surrounding yourself with people who believe in themselves and are experiencing success is a way to help you feel that you can achieve it to. It's like Henry Ford said: "Whether you think you can, or you think you can't—you're right."

Interestingly enough, when I was speaking with Steve Rennie, manager of Incubus, he told me that the band members came from middle- to upper-class families and so *they knew what it felt like*." Their internal thermometer was already set at a level of success because of their backgrounds.

WRITING YOUR NEWS RELEASE

Instead of telling you how to write a traditional press release, I am posting some links that tell you how to do it. I encourage you do your own research as there are a ton of resources online and one may resonate more with you than another.

10 Ways to Make Press Releases More SEO Friendly
atnmusi.ca/ch4h7

How to Create a Modern Press Release
atnmusi.ca/ch4h8

Press Release
atnmusi.ca/ch4h9

Write Your Press Release Online
atnmusi.ca/ch4h10

Save your press clippings to build your résumé. Next time around you'll have more to show!

A GOOD PUBLICIST

Good publicists have established connections and relationships in the industry that they can tap into when needed. They are able to connect the right artist with the right publication so that it is a good fit and all parties benefit. They understand the artist's vision and know who can connect the artist with the right people to see it through. A good publicist can be your evangelist and ambassador, as we all know it can be very difficult to talk about our own art and career.

A publicist can get you exposure in publications and in other places that start a conversation, generate reactions, and get people writing reviews, creating blog posts, and so on. A good publicist understands your story, knows how to tell it and knows who is going to want to hear it! A good publicist will put you in the right place at the right time, whether it's a party or a TV show, or an interview on radio or at a local paper. What is for sure is that if you want to rise above the noise you need to be heard and that is the job of a publicist and a PR campaign. A publicist won't give you talent or turn a bad product into a great one, but if you've got the talent and have a great product, then a publicist and a good PR campaign can get you the exposure you need to rise above the noise.

A FEW FINAL LINKS OF NOTE

First, here is a link that offers many ways to stay on top of your online PR:

Twitter apps to manage your online presence and reputation
atnmusi.ca/ch4h11

Here are links to some more interviews I have conducted with prominent publicists in the music industry:

Eric Alper
atnmusi.ca/ch4h12

David Weiss
atnmusi.ca/ch4h14

Kevin Fetterplace
atnmusi.ca/ch4h13

Some free online press–release distributors

These are links to sites that will distribute your news release for free:

24-7PressRelease
atnmusi.ca/ch4h15

Mynewsdesk
atnmusi.ca/ch4h20

Express-Press-Release Inc.
atnmusi.ca/ch4h16

PressReleasePoint
atnmusi.ca/ch4h21

Free Press Index
atnmusi.ca/ch4h17

PR-inside
atnmusi.ca/ch4h22

Free Press Release
atnmusi.ca/ch4h18

Release-News
atnmusi.ca/ch4h23

Live-PR
atnmusi.ca/ch4h19

Your Story
atnmusi.ca/ch4h24

CHAPTER FIVE

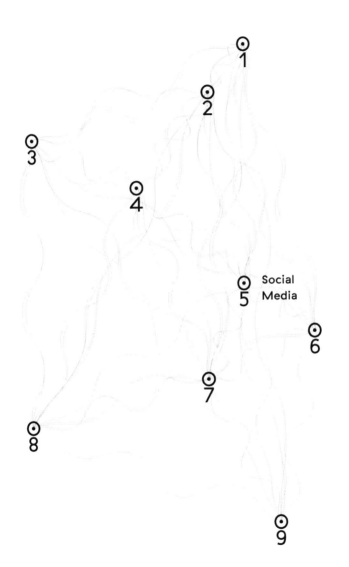

1

2

3

4

5 Social
Media

6

7

8

9

Social Media

Social media is the most powerful networking and marketing tool available to musicians today. It allows you to share information with large virtual communities. It is made up of platforms that have the capacity for two-way interaction, and you can use it to connect with industry movers and shakers, build and retain a fan base, establish your brand, increase sales on- and offline, promote concerts, even get gigs and endorsements. Social media directly applies to all areas of your career.

There are so many resources available online and great books to read on the topic that it would be crazy for me to not post links to the ones I like the most. So I have, and you'll find them along the way. What I want to focus on is the approach, the mindset behind how you go about using the platforms available and analytical tools they provide. The strategy you apply and the approach you take are far more valuable for reaching your goals than the platforms you use. Once you have a strategy, you find the platforms to execute it and you learn how they work to fit your needs.

WHY BE SOCIABLE?

In music communities, certain people's names always seem to come up as the go-to bass player or the must-have drummer, and so on. If you're looking for somebody to fill a gig, these are the people whose names crop up. Is it because they are the best? No. It is because they are the ones who are putting themselves out there, playing at every opportunity they get and socializing with the right people; they're the ones you "know," so you recommend them. There are a ton of people making music in their bedrooms and basements (some even make it to their garage to play with others), and many of them are technically unbelievable and amazingly talented, but unfortunately we will never know about them because they don't put themselves out there.

Be sociable. Social media is just an extension of who we are and how we meet people, connect with old friends and market ourselves. Interact with people just like you would if you were at a party: find interesting topics to talk about and, if people find you interesting, they are naturally going to want to know more about you and what you do.

The internet has become a new venue for hanging out and socializing. So consider social media to be that new hangout, treat your online friends like you would your offline friends (hopefully they'll all become one and the same), and when you're hanging out online don't be the person others would avoid in real life—be a good conversationalist and a good listener. Be the person that people talk about and recommend!

Social media makes connecting, networking and communicating directly with both fans and industry folk a piece of cake. You can log onto Twitter right now and reach out directly to a musician, a fan, a potential sponsor or an industry mover and shaker, and chances are they will tweet back! How cool is that? This business is built on relationships, and social media is a great place to start them. It allows us to develop and maintain those relationships every day, "one Tweet at a time."

When you interact via social media, it's about starting and joining conversations, it's about being sociable. It's not about bombarding people with your latest single or upcoming gigs before you've even given them a reason to be interested, but rather about creating friendships with people who consequently will want to learn more about what you do.

The key, however, is not to substitute real encounters with online ones. Take every opportunity you can get to solidify the online relationship by meeting in person. It really is not surprising that people who are sociable offline are more likely to find social success online.

GET WITH THE TIMES

Gone are the days of static websites that read like magazines or catalogues. Web 1.0, as it was called, was a passive experience with only a one-way conversation from the site creator to you.

With the arrival of web 2.0, we had a two-way conversation on our hands: it immediately required participation. It is web 2.0 that gave birth to social media. In fact, the main features of web 2.0 are the social networking sites (e.g., Facebook, Twitter, MySpace, YouTube, Flickr and Instagram), as well as applications and sites that users contribute to (e.g., wikis and *Wikipedia*), not to mention ways to self-publish (e.g., blogs, podcasts and vlogs—video blogs) and of course social bookmarking and tagging web services and sites (e.g., the bookmarking service Delicious, the news aggregator Digg and the discovery engine StumbleUpon).

With web 2.0 you cannot rely solely on advertising and having a website as a way of establishing yourself and your brand. Anyone can add their opinion to a blog, leave a review on iTunes or start a group about your brand. And what the world has to say about you is ultimately more important than what you have to say about yourself. Making use of all the tools available on web 2.0 allows you to gain insights into what people are saying about you, your music, your brand ... and also to join the conversation and have a voice.

For this reason, don't be a broadcaster—harness the power of social media and web 2.0 and join the conversation.

BE AUTHENTIC

It is so important to be authentic when it comes to social media. If you want to create authentic relationships and have an authentic and dedicated fan base, you need to be yourself and share the real you! Worrying about what others think or want to know when it comes time to write a blog entry or post a Tweet results in staring at a blank page or, even worse, writing something that doesn't represent the real you.

People connect with like minds. That's why talking about things like your hobbies, social views, favourite teams, favourite foods and other bands results in better fan engagement. Also, it sure is easy to develop content when you're not just trying to make it about your own music and career!

Thanks to the different tools available, some of which we have already discussed, you can track your stats and gain insight into which posts receive the most views and interactions. This information will help you focus your content.

Strategy is important. This book can help with that, but it will be up to you to make sure that the interactions, conversations and relationships you develop are real!

STRATEGY

Have a strategy. Just having one puts you ahead of the game, because most people don't get that far.

Be sure to:

- have a clear brand message.
- know the profile of your "Super Fan."
- build an audience.
- engage and interact.
- be consistent.
- give more than you ask for.
- create calls to action.

This is a relationships business and who you know is a major factor in your career development and overall success. Social media is by no means the be-all and end-all; however, it is a great place to start the conversation. The strongest relationships will be those that go beyond the cyber world. Whether it's on tour, at conferences and festivals, at coffee shops or in boardrooms, meeting people in person takes the relationship to the next level.

When it comes to building relationships you really have to start by finding the people you want to connect with. Once you know who you need to meet, you need to get creative about how you can start a conversation. Sales pitches are *not* good conversation starters!

Keep in mind that it is unlikely that someone at the top level is going to acknowledge you if you try cold-calling them. You have to strategically work your way up by developing relationships with people who can introduce you to the next person who can help you on your way to the top. Getting an introduction by somebody is a great way to start a relationship. My father once gave me a great piece of advice: "You don't need to know everybody. You need to know the person who knows everybody."

Recently *Billboard* put out its "Power 100," which covers the top 100 most influential people in the music business. My thought process would be to research who some of their connections are and then who those people are connected to and so on until I found somebody I was connected to. Then I would work my way back to the top by finding a way of getting introductions to the next person, starting with the person I was already connected to. Make sense?

When it comes to building an audience online, you can use a lot of the tools we talked about under "Fan Profiling" (Chapter 2). Knowing the profile of your Super Fan, you can go about using the same tools to locate and follow other potential Super Fans.

There is a technique for building a large following in a short period of time on Twitter. It involves following large numbers of people, then giving them a set amount of time to "follow back"; if they don't follow back after a given time, you "unfollow" them. The idea is that you keep the number of followers high and the number of people you are following low, which makes it look as though you are influential. Everyone worth their salt will tell you that this is *not* the way to build a true following. Just because you have 100,000 followers doesn't mean they are engaged Super Fans. In fact, Twitter has put in place ways to prevent this type of mass following and unfollowing. Usually the people who do this have no consideration for who they are following—they haven't profiled their Super Fans and followed them, which just adds to how ineffective a following they have. I completely agree that this is not the way to build a following. You really do have to build a fan base one person at a time.

However, I think there is a happy medium as long as you abide by the rules of social media conduct. It makes total sense to follow as many potential Super Fans as you can, and if they don't show interest remove them from your list. You need to start by locating potential fans and then engaging them. However, you do *not* need to be following three times as many people as are following you. This tells me that you are not engaging enough, or that you are engaging with the wrong type of people and hence the lack of people following you back. The process would be: (1) establish brand positioning, (2) profile fan, (3) target fan, (4) engage fan, (5) develop brand, and (6) create calls to action.

Although mostly for Twitter, this approach can be used for social media fan-building in general:

- Clearly define your brand and what sets it apart (ideally your niche). This affects everything from your Twitter description to the type of content you create and curate. You need to know your brand to know its target audience.

- As discussed under "Fan Profiling" (Chapter 2), learn more about your Super Fan.

- Follow and befriend potential fans based on your research.

- After following potential fans, allow three to four days for them to show some sort of interest (following back, accepting the friendship, etc.) before deciding whether to choose to continue following them.

- Look for opportunities to connect, interact and converse with potential Super Fans.

- Create lists so as to organize the new connections into relevant groups. These can be by location, level of engagement, expertise, interests, artists they are fans of, online reputation/Klout … (I especially like to have lists of people I am particularly keen to establish a connection with; I keep an eye on these lists and when the opportunity arises, I interact.)

- Use lists to strategically organize and interact with the right people, in the right places, at the right times surrounding new releases, tours, media, crowdfunding and crowdsourcing projects, and so on.

- As you build an audience, simultaneously create, curate and publish content that represents your brand. Give a reason for people to want to be connected, especially why they should stay connected.

- Create calls to action with a clear message as to what is in it for the fan.

- Create stats and build data to learn more about your audience, the level of engagement, what's working and what's not. This information is also a valuable resource for potential sponsors, co-branding partnerships, endorsements, advertising and the like.

CHOOSING THE SOCIAL MEDIA PLATFORM THAT IS RIGHT FOR YOU

Many social media platforms are available and although there is something to be said for having a presence on them all, what is most important is to be a part of those that best fit your brand and fan demographic.

There is a school of thought that advocates claiming your stake on all social media platforms and securing your brand's name. However, that has real value only if you are also able to update the sites on a regular basis as well as engage with the different audiences.

My experience has shown me that once you have profiled your Super Fan, it will become clear which social media platform is best suited to engaging with them. I have worked with legendary bands whose millions of fans were mostly active on Facebook and YouTube. I have worked with clients who have built their online success on Twitter alone. The fact is that the best results came from focusing on sites that were the best fit for their particular audience. The more you know about your fans, the easier it is to know how to connect with them.

From a marketing perspective, finding out that your fan base shares a love of football would give you insight into how and where to market to them. You could then research which social sites the teams use, how they market their brands online, even how other companies are marketing their products successfully to football fans. Now you're not thinking as much about how to market your music in places where music is marketed but how to market your music where football is marketed. This is bound to affect your approach and with it the social media platforms you use.

APPROACH

Your approach and strategy should be personalized—to you. There is no set template to social media success, just as there is no set template to musical success. You ultimately want to connect with your audience in a way that is meaningful and effective, and that fits your personal brand.

The platforms you choose to use should be directly associated with who you are trying to reach. Everyone has a preferred platform. For example, I love Twitter and have made some great connections that way, which have gone beyond the cyber world. I use LinkedIn strictly for business, and am very wary of the people I add. I am not a huge fan of Facebook (in my personal life) or MySpace, although I have a presence on both and certainly use them for researching people. Just because a social media site exists doesn't mean you need to be on it. You need to know where your fans are and be there.

Every artist is unique, and for that reason the approach should be too. It might seem easier to look at what everyone else is doing and do the same, but what works for one person doesn't necessarily work for another. And as mentioned earlier, being different is the key to commanding attention. So get creative, remove the box!

When I used to have guitar students, I would give a lesson in which I would challenge my students to find ways to make sounds with the instrument that didn't include the traditional use. I wanted to see what they could come up with by using their creativity. There were no rules and anything went—the crazier the better! The reason I encouraged them to do this was to emphasize the fact that there is life beyond traditional rules; you can develop your own way to make your own music. I wanted to take away the box and let them be creative.

I see social media the same way. How creative can you get with your approach? How can you use the platforms available in unique ways to generate the greatest results? One of the reasons why I feel this is such an exciting time in the music industry is that you can write your own rules, and if you are able to use the tools available in creative and new ways you will stand out from the crowd.

This is the checklist for my social media approach:

- Be authentic and show the real you from day one.

- Share enough of your personal life to give people insights into who you really are and establish a closer relationship.

- Interact with your audience; don't just broadcast.

- Create added value and intrigue to your songs, life and career by being a storyteller. A good story will spread far and wide!

- Be talented, be a star, work hard, but don't sacrifice being yourself. Authenticity allows people to champion someone who is real and consequently to feel part of their success.

- Balance your content 80:20, with 80 percent fun, personal and interesting, and 20 percent sales or calls to actions.

- Find unexpected and meaningful ways to reward your audience.

- Know your fan demographic and target them. Develop a fan base of people who feel like friends, and treat them that way. You don't need to appeal to everyone; just cater to those who allow you to be yourself.

- Be sure to show your appreciation of others, give back to those who give to you, share the love and get involved in championing others.

- Make sure that everything you do is consistent and supports your brand. All parts need to work together. Your content should fit your sound, personality and image.

- Let yourself be discovered where your demographic or Super Fans will value you the most. Don't worry about being every-where—be where you know they will find you.

- Stay humble.

- It's okay to have a presence on some platforms as a broadcaster, but be sure to establish the platforms that allow you to connect directly with your fans.

- Don't have all your information available everywhere. Keep the home page as your "Grand Central Station" and the other plat-forms as a way to get there, while still giving those other plat-forms a reason to be visited in their own right.

- Always check back in with your brand. Are you creating content that builds its value or are you diluting it? Make sure aesthetic touches like colours and fonts are all supporting your brand and its target demographic.

TOOLS AND TIPS

A. SOCIAL MEDIA—THE PLATFORMS

An online presence is essential in today's music industry. If I hear your song on the radio, or if your name catches my attention on a piece of printed press, can I google you, find your music and get to know more about you? It is surprising how many bands have spent money on recording songs but not put any effort into creating somewhere for people to learn more about them.

I worked with a band that wrote and recorded some great songs with commercial radio in mind. They spent money on tracking their first single to radio and got fantastic results, including a national hit. However, if you heard them on the radio and wanted to learn more about them, hear more music and, most importantly, purchase what you heard, there was nowhere to do it! I lie—there was a MySpace page with quotes. Same thing. When you get a hit on the radio, or you get mentioned in *Pitchfork*, you need to have a place that people can be directed to, a place where they can become fans of the band and not just fans of the song. To go even further, there is no point in promoting your music if you don't have a site that offers creative ways for people to spend money, share your music and join a newsletter!

The most important social media sites in my opinion, and in alphabetical order only, are Facebook, Flickr, Google +, Instagram, LinkedIn, MySpace, Pinterest, Reddit, StumbleUpon, Tumblr and Twitter. If nothing else you need to at least be acquainted with these. I suggest starting with Facebook and Twitter as a foundation to build on.

When thinking about a user name, be sure to pick one that you can use across all platforms. So check what is available on all the sites you are considering. Be sure to maintain your brand imagery, colours and description across all sites.

Every time I check out new artists I check out their social media. If I can't find your music, videos and other content online, you can tell me all you want but you are not benefiting from the biggest net-working and marketing tools available to you. And that is not going to look good!

Here are the sites and apps I believe you should be connecting to your project. I have included lots of links.

1. Twitter atnmusi.ca/ch5h1

Be sure to register an account with your personal names as well as band name. Have your personal account connect to your band's Twitter account—for example, on your personal Twitter account's bio, you could write "guitar player for @thegreatestbandalive." That way, no matter how people search for you they will always find a way back to your band account.

Also, make sure that your Twitter and Facebook accounts are connected. You could go a step further and have your Twitter account feed to your other social sites, blogs and websites.

When I have somebody add me on Twitter I look at their description, how many people they are following in comparison to people following them, and what some of their last Tweets are. Ultimately all these things have to add up to being somebody I want to follow and not just spam. Twitter accounts that follow a large number of people with few following back and that have a lousy description and spam-like posts are not likely to get people interested in following them.

Keep in mind that social media is replacing face-to-face meet-ups and also phone calls. Facial expressions and tone of voice are lacking, which means everything from photos and descriptions to content and conversations are what we are basing the relationship on and how we build trust.

When going about finding quality followers, a good place to start—beyond friends and family—is by finding similar artists as we discussed in the "Fan Profiling" segment (Chapter 2). Then start adding their followers. Give them a few days to follow back. If the other artists' fans are compatible, you will find a lot will follow you back. After a few days you can use Tweeter Karma or Tweepi (links below) to unfollow those who don't follow back. These two tools will list the people you are following who are not following you back in order of how recently they tweeted. If somebody has not been active on Twitter for a month, the cold truth is that you probably don't want to be connected with them for business reasons anyway.

Keep the number of people you are following fairly close to the number following you back, and never too many over those following you. Ideally, you want to have more people following you than you are following. However, having 100,000 followers and following 80 people clearly indicates that the social triangle is not complete. You are obviously not truly connecting with your audience.

Numbers aside, the most important aspect of all is engagement and building real relationships.

Tools and analytics

Commun.it
atnmusi.ca/ch5h2

TweetReach
atnmusi.ca/ch5h8

Fake Follower Check
atnmusi.ca/ch5h3

TwitBlock
atnmusi.ca/ch5h9

Listly
atnmusi.ca/ch5h4

Twitilist
atnmusi.ca/ch5h10

Socialbakers
atnmusi.ca/ch5h5

Twitter Counter
atnmusi.ca/ch5h11

Tweepi
atnmusi.ca/ch5h6

Who.Unfollowed.Me
atnmusi.ca/ch5h12

Tweeter Karma
atnmusi.ca/ch5h7

Twitter lingo

As with any new language, the best way to learn is by throwing yourself in the deep end and giving yourself no other option than to learn to swim! However, here are a couple of things you should definitely know about for your first week on Twitter:

- **#, @, RT and DM:** Use # (hashtags) to be more searchable; @ to direct your conversation or Tweet at somebody; **RT** to retweet other people's great Tweets; and **DM** to direct-message people when you don't want others to see your conversation.

- **#followfriday (#FF):** On Friday, tell everybody about the people you think they should follow! Share your friends with others. Here is how somebody would tweet to follow my company and a few others on FF: **#FF** @playitloudmusic @futurehitdna @shadesof-solveig @wesdavenport

- **#musicmonday (#MM):** On Monday, tweet about music! What you're listening to, bands people should check out, music news, and so on. Put **#MM** before your Tweet to get the most exposure and to make it search-friendly.

Hashtags are used for events, conversations, and so on. A great tool that allows you to view specific hashtag conversations in one place is TweetChat (atnmusi.ca/ch5h13).

Online articles such as the following can deepen your Twitter knowledge:

14 Twitter Tips and Tricks for Power Users
atnmusi.ca/ch5h14

2. Facebook atnmusi.ca/ch5h15

Set up a band page on Facebook.

You can add a number of apps to enhance the fan experience and also to sell and feature your music, newsletter sign-up form, merchandise, to pull stats as well as use creatively, for marketing purposes, for example.

Here are some apps I can recommend:

Bandcamp
atnmusi.ca/ch5h16

Publishing to Twitter
from Facebook
atnmusi.ca/ch5h20

BandPage
atnmusi.ca/ch5h17

YouTube for Pages
atnmusi.ca/ch5h21

Band Profile by ReverbNation
atnmusi.ca/ch5h18

Vevo
atnmusi.ca/ch5h22

FanBridge
atnmusi.ca/ch5h19

One way to build up your "likes" on Facebook is by creating an additional Facebook profile and then going to pages of similar bands and adding their fans. You can of course add too many people, which will trigger Facebook's spam controls and get your account suspended. The way things work as this book goes to press, if you ever get a warning, stop adding people immediately and wait thirty-six hours before adding any more. It is hard to come up with an exact formula as to how many people you can add before you are considered a spammer. This link explains a little more about how Facebook used to clamp down on spammers:

Explaining Facebook's Spam Prevention System
atnmusi.ca/ch5h23

Here is a link to what Facebook considers to be spam:

Facebook Help Center
atnmusi.ca/ch5h24

When adding people, pay special attention to the fans who comment and "like" posts, because an engaged fan is the kind of fan you want. Interacting and commenting on the same posts is a good way to build up to recommending they "like" your band "page." Facebook Graph is a great way to discover the fans of other pages of similar artists.

However, the best way to build your Facebook page likes is by creating ads and, most importantly, content that people want to share. At the end of the day you can find many ways to get people to your page, but if the content you are posting is not engaging then there is no reason for people to like it in the first place. So start with great content!

One quick search online and you will find a ton of information on what the going trends and techniques are for generating likes.

Common Facebook questions

What are Facebook impressions?
atnmusi.ca/ch5h25

How do I use Facebook page insights?
atnmusi.ca/ch5h26

How do I create a great Facebook ad?
atnmusi.ca/ch5h27

Facebook ads and sponsored stories

How do I create a Facebook ad or sponsored story?
atnmusi.ca/ch5h28

How Facebook ads work
atnmusi.ca/ch5h29

Facebook ad secrets
atnmusi.ca/ch5h30

Using Facebook and Twitter trends to write PPC (pay per click) ads
atnmusi.ca/ch5h31

When creating any kind of Facebook ad, keep in mind that Chapter 2 of this book ("Fan Profiling") can help you establish the demographic to target.

When creating Facebook ads for which you pay per click or per impression (i.e., each time the ad is seen), you can keep in mind whether the aim of the ad is ultimately to create exposure or if it only has value when clicked on. For example, if your ad says "10pm April 2nd at the Roxy LA" with your band name and image, perhaps it is worth paying per click because the ad is less likely to attract clicks or need them, especially if you're in the Los Angeles area. Seeing the ad is enough info to get you to the show. In other words, the ad is simply for the relevant demographic to "view" but not click. Consequently, the intention is that you get a large number of impressions but a low number of clicks and you pay per click. This type of ad could be worth it from a perspective of building brand visibility.

When creating click-on ads, consider having the ad drive traffic away from your Facebook page. This could obviously be to many places, from your website to a YouTube video. However, something else worth considering is to have it take you to your newsletter. Most third-party newsletter companies (such as MailChimp, Constant Contact and Mad Mimi) provide links for you to share particular newsletters. You can use those links to drive traffic from Facebook ads to your newsletters.

Whoever clicks on your Facebook ad will be sent to your latest newsletter, so the newsletter concerned should include a mailing list sign-up form. That way, if visitors like what they read they can sign up through the official process. In the body of the newsletter you can include content as well as apps so the viewer can learn about the band, download a free track, stream music, view videos, like your Facebook page, follow you on Twitter and so on.

Generally a newsletter with a lot of embedded apps will have a higher bounce rate when it's sent to email addresses, but if you are simply sending people to a link then the more apps the merrier!

The difference between linking an ad to your newsletter and linking an ad to your website is that you are able to customize the newsletter to the demographic you are targeting. It allows you to give those people a sneak preview of why they should join your mailing list and it gives you a chance to reward them with something that is not necessarily available for the general public on the website. And, of course, you can add a "like" button so that you can build your Facebook likes while you're at it!

Another alternative is to have your ad link to a secret page on your website. You can add all the same apps and information and have the added benefit that those who get to the secret page may well continue browsing your site.

Facebook "lookalike audiences"

Although reading this book equips you with ways to know who your target audience is, Facebook has added a feature that can make it even easier. If you provide email addresses, user IDs or phone numbers of your current audience, Facebook cross-references that information with its database of one billion-plus user accounts and looks for an audience that matches the demographic patterns of your current audience. That "lookalike audience" is of course the target of your ads. If you organize your audience in lists by (1) people who have already purchased, say, an album, merchandise or tickets, and (2) just the casual fans, then you would want to use the information of the fans who are already spending money as the audience to "clone" with Facebook's lookalike audiences.

There are a few things to keep in mind. First, for cross-referencing and finding patterns, Facebook requires a minimum number of email addresses (one hundred-plus at the time of writing). Second, you need to be accessing Facebook with Google Chrome to use this feature. Last, even though Facebook cannot legally use your audience's information in any way at this point, I suggest that you read the privacy policies as these do have a tendency to change.

This video by music marketer John Oszajca does a great job of explaining how to use the "lookalike audience" feature:

How to Create Facebook's Lookalike Audiences
atnmusi.ca/ch5h32

Facebook's news feed algorithm

Ads are a good way to reach new audiences and strengthen your brand exposure, but once you have built your audience and gained new friends, how do you ensure your content appears in their news feeds? This question is not easily understood and Facebook does not disclose all the details as to how the news feed algorithm works. However, here are a few links that shed enough light to at least give you the best chance for your posts to appear in the news feeds of others (keep in mind that technology is changing at the speed of light so I highly recommend doing your own research whenever possible to stay up-to-date):

EdgeRank: A Guide to Facebook's Newsfeed Algorithm
atnmusi.ca/ch5h33

EdgeRank Is Dead: Facebook's News Feed Algorithm Now Has Close to 100K Weight Factors
atnmusi.ca/ch5h34

What is EdgeRank?
atnmusi.ca/ch5h35

f8
atnmusi.ca/ch5h36

3. MySpace atnmusi.ca/ch5h37

MySpace is certainly not as important as it once was. However, it helps you to be more searchable and, with its millions of visitors (twenty-five million a month in 2012, according to MySpace), having a presence there isn't a bad thing. The pages are highly customizable and easy to set up, which gives you no reason to avoid having one.

Make sure your overall brand, content and top song are consistent on all social media platforms. When you are promoting a single you want to make sure it is the first track people hear. As mentioned already, you can have your Twitter or Facebook account feed into your MySpace one, reducing the need to update it separately.

Here are some tips from MySpace:

MySpace Artist HQ
atnmusi.ca/ch5h38

Additionally, make sure you:

- add a certain amount of new friends a week, and if you're in a band get other band members to do the same.

- comment and interact on your own page as well as other people's.

4. LinkedIn atnmusi.ca/ch5h39

LinkedIn is one of my personal favourites, along with Twitter. I use it as a way to develop business connections and for networking, as opposed to promoting artists. I have made more lasting business relationships resulting in monitory benefit on LinkedIn than on any other site. Twitter comes very close.

Once you have made a connection you gain access to a person's personal email address, which in turn opens the door to a more personal way to connect. I also love some of the features, including recommending and endorsing somebody as well as the ability to see who has been checking out your profile and how often your name comes up in a search.

A few simple yet effective tips on expanding your network follow:

- Always include a personal message when adding a new connection. Do *not* use the generic greeting!

- Join relevant groups, because you need to be part of the same groups as the people you add if you are not their friends or somehow already connected. Another way to approach this is find who you want to connect with, see what groups that person is a member of, join the groups and then add the person as a connection.

- Post and interact in discussions. Be consistent so that you are visible and group members become familiar with your name, brand or band.

5. Blogs

For starters, get a Gravatar (atnmusi.ca/ch5h40), so that people can see your image or branding when you leave comments. Readers are more likely to click on your Gravatar and consequently discover more about you if you use your photo or brand image than if you don't have any visual representation other than the preset standard image.

You need to find blogs that are already featuring bands similar to yours. Here are a few sites that will help you find what you are looking for:

Google Blog Search
atnmusi.ca/ch5h41

Technorati
atnmusi.ca/ch5h42

The Hype Machine
atnmusi.ca/ch5h43

Next build a relationship, starting with comments and working up to asking if the blogger will check out your music. If you are commenting, the chances are good that the blogger has already checked you and your music out.

Don't bother trying to have music featured on a blog or in the traditional press if you don't have it available for sale or at least a free download or streaming option. You need to be ready for the new visitors and potential fans to be able to leave your site with both a reason to come back and something to "share" with their friends!

By the way, Google loves blogs. So, if you don't already have one you can sign up for one here:

Blogger
atnmusi.ca/ch5h44

Tumblr
atnmusi.ca/ch5h45

WordPress
atnmusi.ca/ch5h46

6. More Social Sites You Need to Know About!

I have mentioned some of these before, but they definitely deserve to be singled out at this point:

Bandcamp
atnmusi.ca/ch5h47

ReverbNation
atnmusi.ca/ch5h53

Google +
atnmusi.ca/ch5h48

SoundCloud
atnmusi.ca/ch5h54

Instagram
atnmusi.ca/ch5h49

StumbleUpon
atnmusi.ca/ch5h55

NoiseTrade
atnmusi.ca/ch5h50

Twitter Music
atnmusi.ca/ch5h56

Pinterest
atnmusi.ca/ch5h51

YouTube
atnmusi.ca/ch5h57

Reddit
atnmusi.ca/ch5h52

TIP: Create Lists

Lists help you stay organized. They also help you to connect with people who are in a position to help your career. Here are a few specific ideas:

- On Facebook, list your friends based on location so as to never inadvertently send a concert invite to someone who is in another country and obviously won't make it to the show tomorrow night! In fact, generally only invite people who can drive to the event in thirty to sixty minutes max. More importantly, make lists so that you can strategically create calls to action in support of tours, new releases, radio campaigns and so on.

- On Twitter, create lists of people you want to connect with so as to see their conversations and be able to jump in. Use the lists to search for content to retweet. Use lists to categorize people by location, jobs, interests, "fans of" and so on.

- Use lists in the real world to stay on track. Never give yourself more than ten things to do a day. Write down five successes a day on a list to celebrate your achievements.

- Build a list with your Dunbar 150 number (see Chapter 1). Add people whose group you want to be a part of and be sure to interact on and offline with them.

TIP: Create Content

Creating content is the key to generating traffic, building your brand, building engaged fans and generating comments, likes, follows, and so on. Creating content means everything from blogging to posting photos, from tweeting to posting songs. Having content allows others to retweet and post links that lead back to you. Posting other people's content, retweeting it and so on can create followers, based on your ability to curate appealing information that caters to their tastes and interests, and at the same time supports your brand. However, unless you provide a small segment of the third party's content on your own blog or website (usually with a link to the original post), it will not drive traffic to your website. Keep in mind that you want everything to ultimately come back to your website, where you can sell products, have sign-ups for your newsletter and ultimately capture and retain fans.

You can talk about certain topics—such as your new music, your next show and the competition you need people's votes for—up to a point before you start to sound like spam. It's like that 1-800 number that calls selling something you don't want and didn't ask to be called about. If all you do is "sell" to your audience, chances are you will be treated like that 1-800 number. People will want to "hang up" and never pick up the phone when that number calls again. You will be seen as spam. So how do you avoid that? You need to find content that is relevant to your brand's qualities, your interests, your hobbies and so on, and post it. By sharing more personal information you allow people to find authenticity in your brand and discover things in common. If you post about such topics as a hobby, other bands, life on the road, experiences in the studio and culture in general, not only can people find common grounds of interest but it leads to naturally "wanting" to hear what you do!

Remember that you are not going to appeal to everyone, and in fact you shouldn't! You want fans who are passionate. Some will love you and consequently some will hate you. That's the essence of passionate fans. You don't need to worry about appealing to the masses, but rather whether you are being authentic to yourself and your brand. This makes picking content easy as you don't need to think about the opinion of others.

Don't know where to get content? Want to know what is trending and actively being searched for? Check out Google Alerts and Google Trends—not only can you have content sent to your email inbox, but it is all "breaking news."

Google Alerts
atnmusi.ca/ch5h58

How to Use
Google Trends Like a Pro
atnmusi.ca/ch5h60

Google Trends
atnmusi.ca/ch5h59

B. SOCIAL MEDIA-RELATED TOOLS & EMAIL MARKETING

1. HootSuite atnmusi.ca/ch5h61

Like many of you, I find myself not wanting to spend all my time updating the many social media platforms available individually.

HootSuite provides the perfect solution. With a web-based dashboard and a mobile app, you can update all your social media sites from one place. Not only that but it offers the ability to geo-target your searches as well as filter out the most influential people by using Klout (as I mentioned in Chapter 2, "Fan Profiling").

I thought that this was a great opportunity to ask the experts at HootSuite if they could answer some questions on their product and how to put it to best use for musicians:

Aaron Bethune:
Briefly tell me what HootSuite does and which social networks you integrate with?

HootSuite:

HootSuite is a social media management system for businesses and organizations to collaboratively execute campaigns across multiple social networks from one secure, web-based dashboard. Users can launch marketing campaigns, identify and grow audiences, and distribute targeted messages using the dashboard's unique layout. HootSuite streamlines team workflow with scheduling and assignment tools and reaches audiences with geo-targeting functionality. Users can invite multiple collaborators to manage social profiles securely, plus provide custom reports using the comprehensive social analytics tools for measurement.

AB:
How can I use HootSuite to help me find influencers of specific topics in specific markets and geographical locations?

HS:

You can set up a tab labelled "Influencers" (or whatever works best for you), then create up to ten geo-located searches or keyword streams that focus on specific topics (or keywords) that are in line with your industry of interest. This search stream provides you with results within a specific radius in a location of your choosing. Once you've created these streams, filter each of them by Klout Score to find the influencers of these specific topics and start tweeting, retweeting and creating strong relationships.

Adding Geo-Located Search Streams
atnmusi.ca/ch5h62

Filtering Tweets by Klout Score
atnmusi.ca/ch5h63

AB:

What does an influencer look like? What are the key ingredients to deciding if they are influential? How do you decide who is actually "influential" versus who just appears to be?

HS:

Klout helps you determine who the quality influencers across different social media networks are. By simply looking at their Klout Score, you are given a good idea of someone's influence in a specific industry or subject area. The evaluation of an individual's influence is dependent on what they share and what level of engagement they have with others. An influencer will push out timely and relevant content using credible sources, and provide his or her opinion on that topic. The higher the Klout Score, the more influential they are considered to be in their field.

AB:

If I wanted to find out who the most influential people are in London, England on the topics of music innovation and branding, how would I go about it?

HS:

You can follow the steps on creating a geo-located search stream for London, England, and use search queries that include relevant terms such as *music innovation* and *branding*. Then, use the filter feature to filter that geo-located search by Klout Score.

AB:

Can I pick a specific geographical radius for my search? Where can I find the information to customize it?

HS:

Yes, you can pick a specific geographical radius for your searches. The geo-targeting feature allows you to monitor status updates in a stream within a targeted location. All you need are the co-ordinates of the location and specified radius (kilometres or miles) of the area you would like to track. This search stream can provide you with results within a specific radius in a location of your choosing.

AB:

How can I filter the search so that it contains only the most influential people?

HS:

Tweets can be filtered by Klout Score for your Home Feed, Mentions and Direct Messages (Inbox) streams. Filtering Tweets by Klout Score is a great way to monitor and engage with the most influential people you follow, and can be done from the Streams section of your HootSuite dashboard.

Filtering Tweets by Klout Score
atnmusi.ca/ch5h63

AB:

How can I see what others are saying about the influencers?

HS:

You can create one or more keyword search streams with the influencers' Twitter handles.

AB:

Is there a way of seeing their conversations so as to know how engaged their audience are with them, i.e., what people write to them or mention? Is there a feature that allows me to factor this into searches?

HS:

As above, you can create one or more keyword search streams with the influencers' Twitter handles and then monitor those conversations.

AB:

Can I add the people I decide to be influential to lists that I can filter and how would I do that?

HS:

If you have these users in a keyword search stream already, you can filter the most influential ones by filtering by Klout Score. You can then create a list stream for the specific group of users you want to keep track of. From there, simply drag and drop user photo thumbnails from your keyword search stream into your list to add them in.

Creating and Adding Twitter Lists in Streams
atnmusi.ca/ch5h64

AB:

If I wanted to "trend," how would I use HootSuite to help?

HS:

It's up to the rest of the Twitter population to make topics trend by tweeting about them, but there are ways you can push them in the right direction. Make use of hashtag keywords, and track the use of the hashtag by creating a stream to follow the activity. Don't be afraid to be part of the conversation. Share relevant material with your followers, and engage with other Tweets that you find interesting.

AB:

How do you recommend setting up my dashboard to make the most of my searches?

HS:

You can personalize your dashboard by creating lists and streams of people and/or keywords that are relevant to your interests. To further organize your dashboard, you can create tabs to keep track of several streams within a particular social network or topic of your choice.

AB:

What is your recommendation regarding building relationships with influencers?

HS:

Engage with your favourite influencers via Twitter and other social networks on what they've posted or other topics they might be interested in. You can also retweet—RT—messages you find interesting to share with your followers (it shows you're reading their material and support their causes!) and Direct Message—DM— other users privately.

AB:

What are some of the features people should be taking advantage of with HootSuite and why?

HS:

HootSuite contains a wide variety of features that streamline social media usage. The features are dependent on what level of account you have (Free, Pro, or Enterprise), but even the most basic Free account includes up to five social profiles, unlimited app integrations, basic analytics reports, message scheduling, and 2 RSS/ Atom feeds. At the Pro and Enterprise levels, you can add teammates and use HootSuite Conversations for easy collaboration, and make use of Google Analytics and Facebook Insights integrations for more detailed analytics reports.

HootSuite also offers HootSuite University, a social media certification program that trains its users on the features and functionalities of the dashboard via video-based courseware. The program features webinars that reveal best practices and tips from industry-leading brands, platforms and educators. It is included for HootSuite Enterprise clients, but is available to Pro and Free users at a nominal cost.

atnmusi.ca/ch5h65   atnmusi.ca/ch5h66

AB:

What are the most important features to your integration with YouTube and also the Statigram app?

HS:

They would have to be the following:

YouTube

- View YouTube videos in large format.

- Monitor thirteen available feeds and custom-label stream names for easy management.

- Stream your account and channel activity, including viewing history.

- Access your favourites, subscriptions, playlists and videos marked to watch later.

- Search for videos and filter for most viewed, top rated, most popular, and more.

- Upload videos from the HootSuite dash, add title, description, tags, category, privacy level and licence setting.

- Share videos to all your social networks in HootSuite.

Statigram

- View your Home feed and feeds for Your Photos, Your Likes, and the Popular feed from Instagram.

- Stream and monitor your Instagram community, including your followers and those you follow.

- Analyze your Instagram photos and community growth with summary statistics, rolling thirty-day trends and monthly history.

- Gain insights into and manage relationships you have with your Instagram community.

- Search for photos by hashtag or username.

- Share photos to all your social networks in HootSuite.

HootSuite App Directory
atnmusi.ca/ch5h67

2. QR Codes

QR (short for Quick Response) codes have been popular in Asia for years. QR Code is the trademark of a type of two-dimensional bar-code. It was invented by Denso Wave, a subsidiary of Toyota, and developed for the Japanese automotive industry so as to keep track of vehicles during manufacturing. Now they are everywhere! You see them being used in magazines, TV ads, posters, products, business cards and so on. I love them because they make it possible to connect physical marketing with digital marketing. There is no end to creative ways you can incorporate QR codes into your marketing and branding.

Generate QR Codes
atnmusi.ca/ch5h68

Places and ways to use the codes:

- On posters
- On CDs
- On flyers
- On products in general
- Projected onto walls
- On business cards
- In treasure hunts (each QR code has a hint that leads to the next QR code and ultimately treasure!)
- As the "secret code" that leads an audience to a "secret show"
- In street language.

The link below explains it best:

Modern Hobo Code
atnmusi.ca/ch5h69

QR codes can lead people to websites, social media platforms, newsletters, downloads, secret pages … your imagination is the limit.

3. Mailing Lists and Newsletters

Newsletters aren't necessarily the first thing artists think of, but they can be extremely useful.

By way of example, recently, while I was doing consulting work for the publicist of a Juno-nominated singer-songwriter, we were talking about the different performance outlets and revenue streams available to the artist and the importance of building and retaining fans. The artist was performing at venues ranging from clubs and theatres to people's living rooms; his performances were always personal and connected with the audience. Unfortunately he was not building a mailing list that would allow him to maintain that connection with his fans throughout the year.

The type of concerts combined with the type of music and the delivery of his performances allowed an ideal environment for creating positive memories and developing meaningful relationships with his fans. A newsletter was the missing link that could generate greater revenue and a stronger following.

Newsletters allow you to maintain relationships and continue the conversation after a tour. If you make ten new friends at an out-of-town show, you need to maintain and reward the relationships. Next time you play in their town you put them on the guest list and ensure they bring more friends with them by adding a "+1" to each of their invitations. Having that type of relationship and giving the fans special treatment will ultimately result in their wanting to share that experience with their friends. They'll spread your music and bring their friends to your shows. I'm sure you've heard it before; in fact, maybe you've even said these words yourself: "You need to come check out this band … they were in town last night and after the show we hung out, we exchanged info and they told me next time I'd be on the guest list … you have to check them out!"

I use third-party newsletter providers in a ton of different ways. I love the ability to track the stats and analytics.

I use them to present songs to music supervisors. It creates a visually pleasing way of presenting the music, with images and even info on the bands. I use embedded SoundCloud (atnmusi.ca/ch5h70) tracks to stream the music, and links to Hightail (atnmusi.ca/ch5h71) to download the files they want.

Because I am able to monitor when the relevant email is opened, when a track is streamed and which tracks get downloaded, I can follow up accordingly. If a track has been downloaded, I don't follow up quite as quickly, but if I see an email hasn't been opened and tracks have not even been streamed, I might follow up a little sooner to prompt the music supervisor to review the material. This would be the same if sending to anyone in the industry, as with an EPK (electronic press kit).

The newsletter format is also useful for tracking radio singles (see Chapter 9, "Radio Promotion"), which is something I do in a way that's very similar to what I've just described in regards to sending music to music supervisors.

I use a newsletter format to follow up with new connections whether it be someone I just met in person or a new connection on LinkedIn. Again, this allows me to include imagery as well as know if they opened the newsletter or clicked on any links. This gives me an idea as to what they found interesting and ways to continue the conversation.

I create personalized greeting cards each year with my newsletter format. It allows me to add images and also music. If I include a link to some kind of free download, I am able to see who clicked on it.

You can see that there are many creative ways to use newsletters and make use of the important back-end stats.

Newsletters are a vital part of your ability to build relationships, connect and retain fans, generate calls to actions, as well as sell experiences and merchandise. They should be a part of your online strategy and used correctly they are a big part of how you generate income.

Here are a few companies you can use to get started creating your own newsletter:

Band Letter
atnmusi.ca/ch5h72

MailChimp
atnmusi.ca/ch5h75

Constant Contact
atnmusi.ca/ch5h73

Mad Mimi
atnmusi.ca/ch5h76

FanBridge
atnmusi.ca/ch5h74

Nimbit
atnmusi.ca/ch5h77

A few things to keep in mind:

- **Subject lines.** The subject line is often the deciding factor as to why I open an email from a stranger. You want to be personal— mention the recipient's name!

- **Content.** Follow the 80:20 rule and be sure that 80 percent of your content is fun, interesting and informative and that 20 percent is marketing/selling/calling to action.

- **WIFM ("What's in it for me?" factor).** Give more than you ask for. Don't expect people to do something for you before you do something for them. If you are going to ask your fan to do something, make sure it is clear what is in it for them.

- **Call to action.** Create calls to action that will impact the attendance at your shows, spread your brand virally, sell your experiences and so on. What is for sure is that if you don't ask, you don't get!

- **Sign-up sheets.** Create a sign-up sheet so that you can collect data to build your mailing list wherever you play, speak or appear in general.

- **Get creative with how you build your mailing list.** You can build a mailing list by getting business cards dropped into a hat for an onstage draw, or by giving music away in exchange for an email address, but there are much more inventive and creative ways to do this and you have all the resources you need to come up with your own! (I have included a few in Chapter 6, "Live & on Tour.")

Something you might find of interest is the average "open rate" of a newsletter (i.e., what percentage of the newsletters you send out are actually opened). It varies by industry. Based on an *Email Marketing Benchmarks* report put out by MailChimp, if you are in the business of selling vitamin supplements, an average open rate of a newsletter is 26.5 percent; however, for artists the rate can be a lot higher— 43.1%. So the good news is that it is a lot easier to have a fan open a newsletter than to try to get someone to open a newsletter that promises cheap vitamins. Nonetheless, 43.1 percent is still a far cry from 100 percent. If you want people to open your newsletter, they need to have signed up to receive it in the first place. The next part is making sure the subject line is enticing. Here is a great tool for creating subject lines (and it works well for blog titles and blog ideas too!):

Portent's Content Idea Generator
atnmusi.ca/ch5h78

4. Crowdfunding

You would be surprised to know how many people are willing to help finance your projects. You just have to ask. The most success comes when you already have an engaged audience and large fan base. Starting your career with a crowdfunding campaign might not be the way to go; start by building a fan base first!

Amanda Palmer's Kickstarter success in 2012 came from many years of building a loyal fan base. Altogether $1,192,793 was pledged by 24,883 people in thirty days. It helped that her previous band, The Dresden Dolls, had been signed to a major label. They played to large audiences, which added to the exposure and building of her independent fan base, but most importantly the way that she developed her relationship with her own fans resulted in the loyalty that they show her. Like anything that gets a lot of media attention, there are mixed opinions about Palmer's success through Kickstarter and what she's done with it. A lot of people complain that other music on the radio sucks and that radio should be playing theirs. There is always a reason why some people are successful and others are not. I will say one thing in that regard: only in the dictionary does success come before work! The fact is that Amanda Palmer's success has set a new bar for finding funding in the current independent music industry. A lot can be learned from her success. I recommend checking out the following video on the art of asking:

Amanda Palmer: The art of asking
atnmusi.ca/ch5h79

Find creative and out-of-the-box things to give away to your fans in return for their money. Mail yourself to them so you can spend a day together; sell the publishing rights to a song; join their band for a gig; play a private show at their house or place of work; write a bio for them; give a recommendation; write an introduction to their book; work for them for a day; write them a customized song ... the opportunities are endless!

These are a few of the principal crowdfunding platforms:

Indiegogo
atnmusi.ca/ch5h80

RocketHub
atnmusi.ca/ch5h83

Kickstarter
atnmusi.ca/ch5h81

SellaBand
atnmusi.ca/ch5h84

Pledge Music
atnmusi.ca/ch5h82

Ulule
atnmusi.ca/ch5h85

Remember: *If you don't ask, you don't get!*

Also, don't keep all your creative ideas and ways for people to spend money on you for crowdfunding campaigns. Use the same concepts on your website store and your merch tables! .

Dutch music futurist Bas Grasmayer talks about two types of consumers: the time-rich money-poor and the time-poor money-rich. In other words, there are the people who have all the time in the world to find something for free (like an illegal download of your music) and there are those who don't have the time to spend hours finding a way to get something for free and would rather just pay and get it immediately. Get creative about ways to cater to both types, whether it is online or offline. You should offer freebies as well as expensive items. Spending money and acquiring your products should be easy. Freebies and sales should be presented in a clear, "one-click" format.

LEARNING FROM OTHERS

Whether I like a style of music or not, I want to know why a song has become a hit or an artist a star. I am fascinated by understanding what makes somebody rise above the noise and what elements play a role in success. Do fans become fans of a song or do they become fans of an artist?

Think back to the discussion on fan profiling in the early part of this book (Chapter 2). Understanding the fan demographic of artists similar to you makes part of the fan-profile process easier. I recommend keeping an eye on the online efforts of those artists. Make notes on what you think works and what doesn't and apply what you discover to your own efforts—with your own twist. However, don't just look at what they do online; look at it in the context of their overall marketing and branding.

1. Learning from ... Adele

I recently viewed English singer-songwriter Adele's *Live at the Royal Albert Hall* video and was interested to see how her live performance related to her online presence. As you probably know by now, I believe that it's a smart move for all artists to take the time to see what works for others who have a similar sound to them and to apply what they discover creatively to their own career! Here are a few things that stood out when I watched the video and that fit into my own social media approach, as discussed under the "Approach" section earlier in this chapter:

Waste no time in connecting with your audience. Be authentic and show the real you from day one.

Adele wasted absolutely no time in establishing a connection with the audience. After the first song she introduced herself, then told the audience how special it was to be performing at a venue she had seen her idols perform at and thanked the audience for giving her the opportunity to do so. To make it even more personal, she told the audience how nervous she was. By being herself she set the atmosphere for a close interaction between artist and audience.

Share enough of your personal life to show people who you are and build a closer relationship.

Adele acknowledged a friend in the crowd and then told the story of their falling out and making up years later. She had written a song for her friend when she was sixteen and dedicated it to her at the concert. Sharing a personal story allowed the audience a glimpse into the type of friend and person she is.

Interact with your audience, don't just broadcast.

She frequently asked for the lights to be turned on the audience so that she could see them and interact with them. This involved the crowd and gave a more intimate "living room" atmosphere. Making the audience a part of the show meant the experience was more personal to the audience. It made them closer by taking down the barrier between artist and fan.

Create added value and intrigue for your songs, life and career by being a storyteller.

Adele was giving her songs intrigue, personality and deeper meaning by sharing the stories behind them. By introducing every song, she gave the audience an opportunity to digest her songs and have something to remember them by. When songs are played one after another, unless there is a recognizable moment to connect to a specific song it is all too easy to forget what you just heard. Another band might find Adele's style of introducing songs disruptive to the energy and flow of a concert, but this worked perfectly for Adele and her audience.

Be talented, be a star, work hard, but don't sacrifice being yourself. Authenticity allows people to champion one of their own and feel part of the artist's success.

When Adele talked to the audience, she was at ease and relaxed. It was as if she was hanging out with her friends—as if she could have easily decended from the stage and blended right in. When she sang, she was focused and delivered passionate performances. She truly came across as an average person with an above-average talent. The people in her audience were visibly proud of her achievements and were obviously a part of the journey that led her to perform at the Royal Albert Hall.

Have balance in what you share.

Her down-to-earth, light-hearted and funny interactions with the audience were a nice contrast to her emotionally charged, heavier songs.

Find unexpected and meaningful ways to reward your audience.

Adele had written a note after doing an interview earlier in the day and left it on a seat for an audience member to find later. Along with the heartfelt performances, a night of storytelling and getting to know the artist, an unexpected note would be a very special keepsake. The fan would have walked away an ambassador ready to spread the Adele love!

Know your fan demographic and target them. Develop a fan base that could easily be your friends and treat them that way. You don't need to appeal to everyone, just cater to those who allow you to be yourself.

The people in the audience looked as though they would likely enjoy each other's company and could all go for drinks together after the show. Adele has a very specific demographic and she catered to them perfectly.

Be sure to show your appreciation of others, give back to those who give to you, share the love, get involved in championing others.

Adele played a number of cover songs and explained why. She dedicated one to her mom. She gave the songs a personal meaning and in doing so made them her own. Because her version of each cover had a story that went with it, those who heard it are likely to think of her version of the song even when they are listening to the original.

Make sure that everything you do is consistent and supports your brand. All parts need to work together. Your imagery should fit your sound and personality.

Her look, performance and interactions with the audience were a perfect fit. It was comfortable and relaxed and delivered satisfaction; nothing was uncomfortable, conflicting or overdone.

Let yourself be discovered where your demographic or Super Fan will value you the most. Don't worry about being everywhere ... be where you need to be.

I remember hearing Adele for the first time on CBC Radio. And for any reader who is unfamiliar with the CBC (Canadian Broadcasting Corporation), this serves as Canada's national public station and is not where you would expect to hear top-40 hits—it is where you go to listen to indie, roots and so on. I would go a step further to say that the average person listening to music on the CBC is doing so because she or he is interested in discovering new bands and is opposed to hearing "commercial top 40s." In my mind this was a perfect fit for discovering Adele's music. It was via a station that is associated with discovering "real music" in a grassroots way.

Stay humble.

Adele was appreciative at all times, never once presenting herself as being a cut above the audience. She was confident, yet humble.

The performance encouraged me to take a deeper look at her online presence as well as overall marketing. Sure enough, every aspect of Adele's music and career fit together perfectly. Everything supports her brand, who she is and how she portrays herself, from the colours to the wording to the emphasis on page placement and the choice of social platforms.

Her approach to social media (in late 2013 anyway!) was like that of an average friend online—direct from her to her fans with what seemed to be no filters. She didn't give a ton of updates, but when she did they were personal, not sales pitches.

She was using her Twitter account as a way of communicating directly with her fans.

Her Facebook page was a different matter, because her team was using it to give musical and career updates to the fans. Her Twitter fed to her MySpace. Her MySpace showcased her music, but essentially was just there making a presence.

So essentially there is a clear distinction between the channels that Adele uses to communicate with her fans and the channels that her team uses to release news. This distinction allows Adele's "brand" to stay true to her.

Adele's YouTube channel was less personal in regards to her interaction when I studied it, because there were no personal comments from her, but of course there were plenty of videos that showcased her personality and transmitted her authenticity.

Obviously Adele is just one artist with a specific demographic. If you look into what Lil Wayne, Justin Bieber, Keith Urban, Diana Krall or OK

Go are doing, it is going to be unique to them. I highly recommend doing similar research into a band that is local to you and making a name for themselves. Don't limit your research to A-level artists!

As a side note in regards to storytelling, I am sure that with all this attention to Adele's Royal Albert Hall performance you are likely to want to check it out, even if you've seen it already. This applies to how talking about your own music is a way to make people take an interest in checking it out.

Adele: Live at the Royal Albert Hall
atnmusi.ca/ch5h86

2. Learning from ... Jack Conte & Pomplamoose

Social media may have given artists the power to broadcast their music to the wider world, but it hasn't really made getting heard any easier. If you want to rise above the noisy clamour for attention on the web, your creativity needs to be working overtime so you not only write great songs but market them brilliantly as well.

A few years back I interviewed Jack Conte—half of the US indie band Pomplamoose—on the band's tremendous online success through the use of social media. Since the time of the interview much has happened in the world of Pomplamoose. Nataly Dawn's album was at Starbucks last time I picked up a latte and Jack has even started his own crowdfunding website called *Patreon* to help content creators live their passion. I encourage you to check the site out here:

Patreon
atnmusi.ca/ch5h87

Patreon Fan Profiling Tip:

You can use Patreon to identify the top contributing Patreons of similar-sounding artists to you that are using the Patreon platform. These are truly Super Fans of those artists. You can view the profiles of the Patreons, which often include their full names, cities and countries of residence as well as how many "creators" they support. You can do

*a quick online search for these Patreons and see if you can find them
on social media platforms so as to connect with them and introduce
them to your music and projects. Of course, start by signing up to
Patreon to get your own Patreons, especially if you already have an
engaged fan base viewing and interacting with your online content.*

With their innovative brand of YouTube-friendly "video songs,"
the Pomplamoose duo have shown the incredible effect that
imaginatively "packaged" music can have in getting your music
heard by large numbers of people. They may have yet to hit it big on
the *Billboard* charts, but they have clocked up hundreds of thousands
of online music sales and millions of YouTube views, and attracted a
long line of licensing suitors—including major brands like Toyota and
Hyundai—and they have managed to carve out that most coveted of
niches: a genuine self-sustaining music career without label interfer-
ence. How have they done it?

Aaron Bethune:
How did Pomplamoose first begin, and then how did you
manage to attract such an enthusiastic online response?

Jack Conte:
Nataly [Dawn] and I started making music together when she was
in her senior year of college. I'd tried producing one of her records,
but it didn't work out so well and so we left it. As we were in a
relationship together and didn't want to mess that up, we decided
to keep the music and personal stuff separate. But two years down
the road, when we were working on our own YouTube channels,
she started complaining that her stuff didn't sound very well produced. So I said, "Let's take one more crack at this!" I produced
one of the songs she had written and it came out so different to
what she'd had in mind originally that we decided to make it a
band and gave it the name Pomplamoose.

When I put it up on my channel it got a way better response than
anything Nataly or I had put up on our own and so we decided to
do a little bit more. We wrote another song, made a new YouTube
channel, and things took off from there.

AB:

As you are both songwriters, why did you decide to cover other people's songs?

JC:

We realized that covering really popular pop songs was the way to go—YouTube's great algorithm for recommendations meant that we could mooch off of other people's traffic. For example, if you've just watched Beyoncé's *Single Ladies*, it will recommend other videos that have "Single Ladies" in the title, and that's how *our video* got out there.

It started to get recommended a lot, and got on the front page of YouTube. That was the big moment for us, and the rest really started snowballing from that point.

AB:

How did your unique brand of "video song" first come about?

JC:

We already knew at the beginning of Pomplamoose that the video song medium was engaging, as I'd been releasing video songs before Pomplamoose started. These multi-layered, multi-angled clips came about around four years ago with a song I wrote called "Push." Nataly is a fantastic editor and her editing gave it an extra layer and an extra spark. It got a really good response when it was released and made me realize that it was a pretty good idea and that I should release more.

AB:

Was there a particular point when your success made you decide to focus on making music full-time?

JC:

That was a pretty clear moment. We were both busy with our own things. I was working for Google as a video producer and in-house composer and Nataly was finishing school—but I was starting to make more and more money through my MP3 sales, and through Pomplamoose's own MP3 sales. And then when we released our covers record *Tribute to Famous People*, we sold thirty thousand songs in the first month. That was the defining moment when we said, "We're not working on other things now, we're focusing on this."

AB:

To achieve that success, were you doing anything to help promote your video songs or were you just relying on the viral effect they attracted by themselves?

JC:

It's just been YouTube. It's only been recently that we've worked with a PR agent or manager or anything and that was because we wanted to go on tour.

We did get a lot of calls from people in the industry, but we didn't want to do that as we felt we were outside the record business—and we liked that. I'd read a lot of horror stories about what goes on behind the scenes in the music industry and so I wasn't waiting for a record deal at all.

And we've managed to avoid it until now—we're talking with this label called Nonesuch [Records]. If we are ever going to work with a label, it will be these guys—they really understand music and have a lot of great artists on their roster.

AB:

What in particular is it about the label that makes you want to work with them?

JC:

They do things in an old-school way, like a 1960s label—they let the artist create and don't just pump out radio hits. They just want really good music, and whether it sells five thousand copies or a million copies, they are happy to put it out. That's the kind of label we want to work with. Sometimes our music can be very poppy, but sometimes it can be a bit weird, and we like that, and don't want a label telling us what to do, trying to mould us into a radio sound.

Plus the other artists they have are people I respect tremendously, people like Brad Mehldau, Joshua Redman, Philip Glass, Björk and The Black Keys.

AB:
Where are your main sources of revenue at the moment?

JC:
Right now it's MP3 sales and licensing deals, not necessarily publishing deals though. We did a holiday ad with Hyundai that was on three national channels and that pays really well. There was also a Samsung product placement for our *Angry Birds* video, and that was another huge income boost.

Those are occasional income streams. The more constant income streams come from when we release a record and get MP3 sales for a year or two based on that record. Unlike the typical record label model, where you release a record and make most of your money in the first week, the way people find us on YouTube means there's a trickling effect from iTunes. We're getting a few thousand subscribers a month, and they keep checking us out, and we keep on getting more and more sales from that kind of fan.

AB:
Do you find that, because of your YouTube exposure, music supervisors and licensors come to you?

JC:
We've always had people come to us—we've been really lucky with that. For the Toyota commercial they got hold of us and said, "We really like your 'Mister Sandman' song. Can you give us a fee?" So we talked to some lawyer friends of ours and sent them a fee. Same with the Hyundai ad—they sent us an email saying, "Do you want to be on TV?"

AB:

Why do you think your music has proved so popular for licensing?

JC:

I think Pomplamoose has a very "sync-able" sound. People who hear it want to put pictures to it.

AB:

Despite now enjoying success with licensing your music free of video accompaniment, do you think Pomplamoose would have found the same level of success if you had not made the video an integral part of the music?

JC:

About 99 percent of our success has come from the YouTube videos, without question.

Before the YouTube thing with Pomplamoose, I tried so hard with my own stuff to get out there. I went on tour three times. People had told me that's what you need to do to build your fan base. I did it and it didn't work [laughs]. I tried playing every two weeks in San Fran, but my friends all got sick of coming to my shows. I tried MySpace and Facebook. I tried releasing music videos, but the truth is nothing really caught on until we started working together and made these video songs.

AB:

Why do you think the combination of video and song has worked so well for you?

JC:

It comes together with the music being pretty good, and the videos being really good packaging. If you ask anyone trying to sell a product, whether they're a musician or a retail store owner, they will tell you that you need kick-ass packaging to sell even the very best products.

Imagine if Apple didn't spend millions on packaging and branding. Their whole approach is the sexy white earphones; ease-of-use gadgets; streamlined, modern computers—that whole package has nothing to do with the function or quality of their goods, it's all external. But would their computers sell as well if they didn't do all that and spend all that money? They have become a worldwide brand because of it. I feel that the Pomplamoose stuff has really good packaging for a really good product.

I don't know how well it would have sold if we had just put the songs up on their own. I don't think they would have gone viral if we had just posted the MP3s on MySpace.

AB:
Is there a definable formula and concept to your videos?

JC:
To some extent, yes. We want to make really engaging videos and in order to do that, we need to make something that we like to watch.

We try to put in a bit of "us" in the videos. One thing we've really learned from being in touch with out fan base and reading lots of comments is that people who watch our videos really like how "present" Nataly and I are in the videos, both as people and as a couple. But there's a fine line between playing that up and it being natural, so we try to just have fun in the studio, and keep it as normal as possible.

Nataly's sense of timing and comedy really come into play with the videos. When we are goofing around in the studio and recording, she is making notes in her head so that when she goes to edit she knows where to put in little funny parts and stuff.

We try to have a variety of things featured in the videos, like close-up shots, faraway shots, and try to show just about every part of how the video was made, so people and viewers can feel a bit closer to us as artists when they watch us. We try not to repeat sections, unless it's a thematic idea.

AB:

You mentioned being in regular contact with your fan base. How do you do that mainly?

JC:

We don't have an email list. We keep in touch with our fan base through Twitter, YouTube, and Facebook. When we have an announcement, we post it on Facebook and Twitter, and if it's a big one, we just put a video out about it. We read a ton of comments as well.

AB:

What was the response like when you went out on tour for the first time, with people having only seen you through your videos?

JC:

It was better than I ever could have expected. We played four shows and they all sold out. Everyone was really excited to be there, and afterwards we met and talked with everyone. It was really cool for us to meet these people who liked our videos so much, and it personalized the "other" side of the YouTube videos. You only get 320 characters and a thumbnail to talk with people in comments and so you just can't get to know someone. So having the people there and talking to you and sharing their lives is so rewarding and nice! To put faces to the viewers was great, and it really increased our appetite for playing more live shows.

AB:

Given the success you've found in helping pioneer the video song format, do you pursue a similar approach for your own music outside of Pomplamoose or do you try to do certain things totally differently?

JC:

We try to use the same format because we both want our own music to be just as successful, but both Nataly's and my music is so different to the Pomplamoose stuff that things are always gonna be a little different.

This might sound a little pretentious, but I think the videos for my own channel are a little more emotional and a little less fun. When we both write for our own stuff, the lyrics and music is a lot more personal as well, so when I'm in the studio singing it's going to be way different than the Pomplamoose stuff, more solemn and less bubbly and poppy. That is the biggest difference and also why the Pomplamoose stuff has done way better.

Nataly's videos are less multi-layered, just her and a guitar, and she can do that because her voice is just so beautiful. I have to compensate a bit for my crappy voice and instrumentation.

AB:
What's next?

JC:
Nataly is releasing a solo record that she is really putting a lot of force into and I'm also doing a solo record, and another Pomplamoose record hopefully by the end of the year. More of the same—no major steps, just more baby steps.

ADDITIONAL RESOURCES

Websites

HootSuite University
atnmusi.ca/ch5h88

Social Media Examiner
atnmusi.ca/ch5h89

Music Success in 9 Weeks
atnmusi.ca/ch5h90

Apps

OneKontest
atnmusi.ca/ch5h91

Mobile Roadie
atnmusi.ca/ch5h92

Vine
atnmusi.ca/ch5h93

CHAPTER SIX

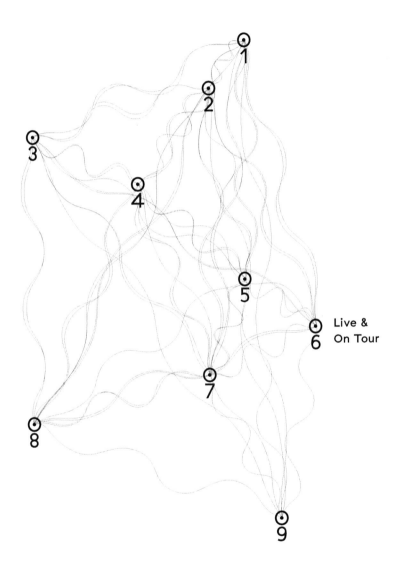

Live &
On Tour

Live & on Tour

Performing music is the main reason most people take up music in the first place! If you can't get out there and share your music with others then you are missing out, not only on the most enjoyable and satisfying part of being a musician but also a principal means to building a fan base and creating revenue. It's like live music producer Tom Jackson says: "All roads lead to the stage."

> "You can't download a T-shirt and you can't download a live experience." — Jonathan Simkin, 604 Records

To be a career artist you need to get in front of people and move them with your music. People buy soundtracks and memorabilia of a night they want to remember.

PLANNING AHEAD

- A reason to go on tour
- Public relations (PR)
- Contracts and letters of intent
- Taxes, visas, work permits
- Anchor date
- Festivals

When are you planning to go on tour? This is an obvious question, but the fact is that you need to give it thought. Too often bands don't give themselves enough time to book a tour that allows them to set up interviews, on-air performances and talks; to give master classes and workshops; and to have the overall ability to efficiently promote their shows.

It is not unusual for musicians to record albums without any thought and certainly without a budget for marketing, resulting in a gift mostly for friends and family. The same happens when people jump into vans without any thought and end up playing to empty rooms and without any PR.

Make sure the tour is supporting your radio efforts, new music releases and so on. Touring should be part of your overall strategy.

A tour should be booked at least four to six months in advance so that you can work all your PR angles to the local papers, radio stations and magazines, as well as fill gaps with events such as house concerts and workshops at local universities, music stores and schools.

If you are booking dates out of the country, you need to allow time for contracting, permits, visas, letters of intent, funding, travel plans, health insurance, gear insurance, international drivers' licences, immunizations, taxes (including finding out what they are and who pays them—e.g., you cannot overlook state or municipal entertainer taxes!), as well as any tax waiver or reduction applications. If you are dealing with a booking agency, the chances are that it will be taking care of this for you.

International performers coming to Canada may be eligible to apply for tax waiver forms. Without them the festivals will withhold a portion of your performance fee (15 percent) to pay taxes. A tax waiver form allows you to be paid and have all income tax obligations waived. For international artists looking to play dates in Canada, it is a fairly easy process and at the bottom of this segment I have included some links to help you go through the steps.

Most countries have withholding taxes for foreign performers. Ireland is one of the few European Union countries that do not withhold taxes from performers. However, in England 20 percent will be withheld unless you apply for a Reduced Tax Payment Application (RTPA). In the United States, 30 percent will be withheld unless you provide Form 8233 or request a Central Withholding Agreement (CWA)—a contract between the Internal Revenue Service and the foreign artist that can reduce the withholding taxes. I encourage you to talk to the promoter from the country you are performing in to find out more.

International festivals and venues require different paperwork. Once again, if you are working with promoters or agents, talk with them to

168   MUSICPRENEUR

ensure they are taking the right steps and know what is required of you. In Canada, for example, you won't need a work permit unless you will be performing in a bar or restaurant (a business in which the primary income does not come from music). If you are going to be playing in a bar or restaurant, you will need to talk to the promoter, booking agent or venue about acquiring the necessary permits.

At the end of 2013, the applications for temporary work permits in Canada had a set fee of $150 per person (including crew members), or $450 for the whole band. Also, since July 31, 2013, a fee of $275 per band member (and crew) has been required when the band applies for a Labour Market Opinion (LMO) document. That cost is usually factored in and split equally across all the venues. So, if the upfront fees for work permits total $450 for a band of four members, and there is an additional $275 per member for LMO and you play ten bar/restaurant gigs, then each venue will need to pay $155 on top of your performance fee.

When it comes to permits every country's rules are different and the fees involved are too. In Europe most countries excluding England and France will allow you to play for up to thirty days without a work permit.

In England, the promoter or booking agent will have to apply for the work permit on your behalf. The cost of the permit and the permit specialist fee will be roughly $880 in total. The good thing is that there aren't any restrictions on picking up gigs once you're there and it's valid for six months. In the United States, you'll need a P2 work permit—which can take up to 125 days to process. The P2 is valid for up to a year and, unlike the scenario in England, is engagement-specific. You will need to submit your performance contracts when applying and any dates booked after acquiring your P2 will need to be submitted and will lead to an additional fee.

So again, allow lots of time to organize all the moving parts before you jump into a van, or onto a plane or boat!

Once you are ready the first thing you need to do is book an anchor date. This date is going to set the pace for all the rest. When you have your anchor date, it's easy to give venues and promoters specific dates that need filling. Without set dates to give the venues, you are reliant on them to dictate their availability and that can really complicate routing and scheduling.

Festivals generally have radius clauses, which impede you from playing within a certain distance during a period of months before and afterwards. This is an important factor to keep in mind. If you are booking during festival season, get your festival dates booked first and then fill in the gaps with clubs.

Quite often festivals will work together to bring certain artists into the country. By working together they are able to offer an artist more dates and consequently pay a lower performance fee as there is then not an exclusive "one-off" date (which are always the most expensive). There are also grants available to festivals that encourage multiple dates. With this I want to point out that festivals communicate; that can be beneficial to you for securing multiple festival performances, but it can also mean that they likely know how much another festival paid you … so keep this in mind when negotiating.

Where?

- Start local.
- Build a loop.
- Swap gigs.

I like to say that you need to tour an area at least three times to start to see a real following develop. And that number is greatly affected by how well you do in all other areas of your career, from marketing, branding and social media to licensing, radio and building relationships!

You need to stay behind at every show and build friendships, create moments and exchange enough information to follow up. That follow-up should include newsletters, opportunities to meet up when back in the city, holiday cards and greetings, shout-outs and so on. The fans really do make your career, so you need to work hard for them and show your appreciation. In order to build true fans, you need to build them one at a time.

Start local. You need to really own your live show before you take it on the road. Playing locally gives you the chance to not only test your show but also your songs and build a following. It allows you to gather important feedback and learn a lot about your fans. Unfortunately artists frequently don't ask for enough feedback and rely on themselves to decide if their show is good. This is a mistake! It doesn't matter what you think of your show; it matters what the audience thinks and the experience they remember.

If you can build and develop your local following, chances are that a local promoter will ask you to open for a bigger act coming through town. Visiting bands will approach you directly to share the bill with them when they tour in your market. Your fan base is valuable to promoters and touring bands alike, as they can help with the ticket sales. Promoters can offer you great opportunities with opening spots that help build your performance résumé and those out-of-town bands can return the favour when you want to tour in their market.

Build a loop. Once you have a local following you can start to expand and get on the road. Keep in mind that touring in a new area is unlikely going to be about the money. You'll be lucky to get a guarantee. For this reason I suggest playing somewhere that is reachable within a day's drive. This allows you to keep the travel expenses down and also to easily follow up.

Once you've built a following in the new town then you expand again. This means that you are always a day away from a "paying gig" and you're only taking a "risk" with the new venue.

Take a map and draw a circle with your hometown as the epicentre, then book gigs within the circle; expand the circle's radius each time you've solidified a fan base in the new area. Consistency is key.

Swap gigs. This is hugely important when you are starting out. Unfortunately some artists' egos will get in the way of "sharing" a bill—they don't want to share their hard-earned paying fans with "out-of-towners." If bands are smart, they put aside the ego element and learn to build friendships with other bands that can help them expand their touring market.

When looking for artists to share a bill with or for touring, do your research before making your approach. Do they have a good local following? Do their fans fit your "Super Fan" profile? Are they playing venues that are a good fit for your show and audience? Do they have a good relationship with local promoters? Do they do a good job of promoting themselves? Are they active with their social media? And so on. This might seem like over-thinking, but if you want to build relationships that are going to take you to the next level you need to think about these things.

When you are booking tour dates you might be interested to know that gigs outside of big cities quite often pay more and are easier to book. So don't just focus on the vanity gigs! Playing in Los Angeles is vanity (and industry exposure if done right) and you'll be lucky to break even on your expenses.

Think outside the box. For example, find out when a major artist with fans that fit your Super Fan's profile are next touring. Follow them on tour and play to their fans in parking lots, on street corners, in campgrounds, and in close vicinity to the venue. Film yourself, blog about it, tell the media, find a way to connect with the band that you are following, make up tour posters, and so on. You might not get paid but you are bound to play to an audience (although it might end up being the police). You will likely make more of a lasting impression than the opening band on the big stage. It would make a great story for the press, a ton of content for the web, and you never know what might come out of it. By picking a band whose following fits your Super Fan's profile, you stand a great chance of picking up fans and building your mailing list. You'll play post-concert house parties, sell merch and build an audience for the next time you come through town. You never know, the major artist band managers might come out and watch you once they catch wind of what you're doing. Get creative and think outside the box!

Booking: Promoters, Agents, Bookers

When you are looking at booking a tour you need to know the players and connect with them.

Interview with Jeff Dorenfield
atnmusi.ca/ch6h1

Above is a link to a great video interview with Jeff Dorenfeld, who is now a professor at Berklee College of Music, on who the major players are in the touring world, who makes money off a live date and how merchandise works.

A promoter's job is to put on a great show. This includes booking the venue, contacting the local press, marketing the show (this can include postering, running ads and a whole lot more), taking care of all moving parts for the night of, including tickets, sound/tech requirements, booking the opening bands, buying the rider ... and generally making sure the show runs smoothly.

When you make a deal with a promoter, you should take into consideration the expenses associated with the show (posters, rider, sound, etc.) so that you know how much you stand to make. These types of deals can range from flat fees to door splits—meaning that after the show's expenses are covered, you agree on a percentage split between promoter and band.

When you are looking into promoters be sure to look for a good match based on the types of shows they promote. Keep in mind that to get a promoter interested, much like everything else we have discussed, you need to have all your ducks lined up—for example, you need to have a great product, a great website, videos of live performances, press, a great online strategy, and a great track record of shared bills and venues you've performed at.

Agents book the shows for you. They're the ones who call the promoters and work out the deal. They know what you need and negotiate on your behalf. The agents are also the ones who generally take care of the tax waiver forms, work permits and so on.

One thing to keep in mind is that a booking agent is going to take between 10 and 20 percent of the fees you receive. This is absolutely worth it if it means you don't have to worry about the booking of your tours. However, if you sign with a large agency you want to be sure you don't end up at the bottom of the ladder, getting fewer gigs than when you were booking them yourself. Typically booking agencies will request that you give them all of your contacts for the places you are already playing. Additionally, if you book your own gigs when you are under contract with a booking agency they will likely request that you still pay them their fee or at least a portion of their regular fee.

A good reason to be signed to an agency, as prominent Canadian booking agent Bill Girdwood told me, is that "a guy phoning on behalf of his band will not get the consideration that perhaps the music deserves just because there is no perceived backup and support. ... One reason venues and also especially corporate clients use agents is so that if a band bails out at the last minute, the agent can pull someone else in from his roster."

Girdwood points out that if you are looking for an agency to sign with, you should look for one that has similar stature acts on the roster as it is more likely to take an interest.

Just like the situation with promoters, you will need to have a reason for an agent to want to work with you. A main factor is income. Are you already booking yourself and generating consistent ticket sales? What size rooms are you playing on average? An agent needs to see money in the deal. For this reason I don't suggest you approach agents until you have a few tours under your belt and have an established circuit. That way you are asking them to expand your touring, not building it from the ground up.

When starting out I suggest a hybrid version: be your own booking agent but work with regional agents and promoters to take care of their areas so as to reap the biggest benefits. It's good to have a trial period when working with someone new to see if the relationship is a fit. Most people don't get married to the person they just met, and it's a good idea to allow time to pass before making a more lasting commitment. Court the agents before you commit.

Bookers are the people at the venues in charge of booking the room. It is important to understand that if you contact a venue directly and the person who books the venue says she will "pencil you in on my calendar," it doesn't mean she is going to be promoting your show! You need to find out exactly what it is that the booker will do and how you are going to be paid. Some clubs have their own in-house promoters who take care of posters and general promotion, but you need to make sure you are clear on what they are going to do. Getting the gig is only half the work!

Contacting the venues, promoters and agents

If you are unsure where to start, you can begin by researching similar bands to find out where they are touring and the venues they are playing. This gives you a good idea as to which venues, promoters and booking agents to contact. Search the web for contact information or even reach out to other bands that are willing to share information with you.

Do the research necessary to find out who you need to reach and how they like to be contacted. Make sure you get hold of people in the way that works for them as individuals—don't use the same approach to everyone. Some people like emails and some people like phone calls; some will want to come to a show and some will want to meet for a coffee.

You are going to need to have a DPK (digital press kit) or EPK (electronic press kit) that you can submit. Below are a few industry standard sites.

EPK examples:

Onesheet
atnmusi.ca/ch6h2

ReverbNation
atnmusi.ca/ch6h3

Sonicbids
atnmusi.ca/ch6h4

Your website should contain all the relevant information. However, you'll want to include information and downloads that are specific to the booking or media process and not necessarily something you want available for fans. For this reason you can create a secret page on your website to be the EPK and simply give out the link.

Mailing a package should not be dismissed, but before using any option find out how the person you are sending it to would like to receive it!

Find out which shows promoters are currently working on and see if you might be a good opening act, especially if it is a band you have already played with.

An effective online strategy will help to get your name out there and help promoters and agents find you easily. It shows you are active and it demonstrates you know how to promote yourself. These are all the hallmarks of somebody I would want to work with.

Moves to consider in courting promoters and agents:

- Cross-promote. What can you do for them?
- Invite them to gigs to preview the band for future occasions.
- Establish relationships with promoters in the areas you plan to tour in. Build and maintain the relationships.
- Have promotional material available.
- Show enthusiasm and willingness to self-promote on- and offline.

When approaching anyone in the industry from whom you want something, it needs to be obvious what it is that you can do in return. You have to build value to your part of the deal so as to make it clear why somebody should want to work with you. If you can present great value to your end of the deal, you'll always get what you want.

When it comes to working with a promoter you need to show them you are going to do your part of marketing the show, that you already have an active fan base that will buy tickets, that you work hard and that you are easy to deal with.

You should be building and maintaining relationships all year round with promoters. But that goes for anyone who helps your career: keep the relationship alive!

Riders

Riders are the extras that you request from a promoter for the dressing room and backstage area. They generally concern food and beverages, but can extend to quantity of dressing rooms, decor, cash for meal buyouts of per-diem meal expenses and so on. If band members are vegetarian or vegan, you might include in the rider that the promoter has to supply a specified number of hot vegetarian meals. If anyone has allergies, a rider is where you would state them.

It is important to be comfortable and give yourself the best chances of delivering outstanding performances. Riders can ensure you the food, beverages and environment you need to put on great shows.

A technical rider covers the technical requirements to put on your show, from the backline (musical equipment) to the lights, inputs and power requirements. If you are an endorsed artist you will want to be sure that the venue is supplying backline that doesn't compromise your endorsement. The technical rider will make for a smooth gig and also prepare the venue and promoter for your show in advance.

If you are interested in viewing the riders of many well-known musicians and get a feel for what they look like, you can visit this website:

Paradise Artists
atnmusi.ca/ch6h5

Seldom does a rider receive the kind of coverage that Van Halen's 1980s "No Brown M&M's" one has. The band inserted a clause specifying that if brown M&M's were found backstage, the promoter would forfeit the show at full price. This sounds outrageous; however, the reason for it wasn't because they were rock gods with strange habits but rather because they had an extensive technical rider with very specific requirements. If they didn't make sure that all the technical requirements were filled, there was the very real possibility that a disaster could happen and somebody could get hurt. For this reason they included somewhere hidden in the middle of their extensive, multi-page rider the "No Brown M&M's" clause. If there were brown M&M's backstage, then obviously the promoter had not gone through the rider and chances were that other things would have been missed and playing the show could be a hazard ...

David Lee Roth telling the story of the brown M&M's
atnmusi.ca/ch6h6

Stage Plots

A stage plot is a visual representation of your onstage set-up. Your stage plot should be included with your contract and riders. The promoter and venue should receive it prior to your arrival so the stage can be readied for your particular set-up. This is especially important for festivals with quick stage turnovers. Below are a couple of websites that offer help for building a stage plot:

How to Make a Stage Plot
atnmusi.ca/ch6h7

StagePlot
atnmusi.ca/ch6h8

Guest Lists and Comps

- Press
- Industry
- Friends/family
- Giveaways, promotions and contests

Make sure you are putting people on a guest list who need to be there. You should be inviting local press, promoters, radio, writers, bloggers, highly engaged local online trendsetters and so on. Maybe even have some tickets set aside for people who are going to post Tweets and Instagrams about you! On the guest list you should also always put your closest supporting friends, fans, street team members and so on. Everyone likes to get special treatment, so be sure to give it to the right people. Also, keep in mind that if you want someone to come from the industry or local media you should make it easy and certainly not something they have to pay for.

As part of your PR, when approaching the media for interviews you should give tickets for sweepstakes and giveaways.

BEFORE THE TOUR AND ON GIG DAY

Once you get in the van and start the tour you want to have fun and enjoy each performance. You don't want to still be securing dates or finding out whether accommodation is included and if you're going to have to find a place to sleep!

The day of the gig should be stress-free and allow you to focus on the music. In order for that to happen you need make sure you are well prepared, have taken care of all the details and follow through with the plan. Here are a few things I would want to make sure of before hitting the road:

- When booking the tour, aim for twelve gigs a week. These should include feature shows as well as clinics, busking, spontaneous concerts, house concerts, private concerts for fans and street teams, radio performances, in-store performances, schools, hospitals and farmers' markets. You need to constantly be promoting yourself and building your fan base.

- Follow up closer to the performance dates to make sure everything is still confirmed and going as planned.

- Ensure your riders were signed and that you'll have all the technical needs to support your show. If you don't have your own sound person, you need to know if the venue supplies one. You'd be surprised how many bands on their first tour show up to a gig that has no "sound guy" and doesn't even have a public address (PA) system.

- Know if you have to go through a union and the union fees involved.

- Discuss and negotiate upfront whether a venue is going to be taking any percentages of merch sales.

- Create a tour plan or booklet and be sure everyone on the road has a copy or at least access to it. If you don't have a tour manager, you'll need to be sure to plan ahead and stick to schedules, departure times, arrival times and so on.

- Know the times of load-in and soundcheck and be early. You have to be professional if you want to be asked back!

- Have your set-up down to an art so that no time is wasted and you can focus on the most important aspects that allow you to be comfortable onstage.

- Allow time for a stunning merch set-up.

- Know your set time and be sure to stick to it. There are laws as to how late music can be played and when clubs close, so don't go over your time slot! An important part of this is in the planning of your set when rehearsing. Rehearse a short thirty-minute set, a forty-five-minute set and a ninety-minute set—that way you are always playing the songs you want to include and you have a great live show worked out. There is nothing worse than having your set cut short and not getting to play your single! Additionally, having not only different-length sets rehearsed but also acoustic versions of songs that are usually electric can make for greater flexibility of the types of shows you can play.

- Be respectful to other bands on the bill and help to make any stage changes run smoothly and efficiently. It should be a family affair, not a battle of egos!

- Know and respect the equipment storage policies. When you've done the gig, know what the policies are for where to put your gear while you interact with your fans.

- Be remembered by the staff. Spend time with them. Be polite and easy to work with. It's hard to get by as a diva or rock star these days …

This is a great tip when it comes to touring internationally and avoiding paying duty on gear you've owned for years (but look into your country of departure's options):

> Before you leave, go to a Canada Border Services Agency (CBSA) office and have an officer verify you have everything on the list and then stamp the list to validate it. And make sure you hang on to the list to show the Canadian customs agents on the way home. (SOCAN—Society of Composers, Authors and Music Publishers of Canada, accessed at atnmusi.ca/ch6h9 on Sept. 25, 2013)

WHAT HAPPENS IF A VENUE DOESN'T HONOUR AN AGREEMENT?

It can happen that you arrive at a gig to find that you are not on the bill, the gig has been cancelled or that at the time of collecting the money the agreement isn't honoured. This is more likely to happen during the earlier stages of your career and less likely once you've worked your way up the ladder and are playing bigger venues, using promoters and have an agent involved!

Although you can pursue legal action (if you have substantial proof), you might factor in your legal expenses versus how much you are losing on the gig. The problem usually exists when a band has not ensured that agreements are signed when a gig is first booked and that copies of these agreements are brought to the venue. There is really nothing you can do at the venue or in court if you don't have the paperwork in order and copies with you to show what was previously agreed.

To avoid problems, deal with money issues when you first make agreements and then bring them up when you get to the venue. Get a deposit. Know who's paying you and have that worked out before playing—don't leave it until the end of the night. At festivals you should be sure to receive 50 percent of your fees at least three months prior to the performance date. Especially for festivals, you should be including a clause in your contract that states you are to be paid on arrival or after soundcheck, come rain or shine.

You can also join a federation, such as the American Federation of Musicians (AFM). Apart from offering health plans, liability insurance, pensions and affordable insurance for your instruments, such a federation can provide legally binding contracts for any type of engagement. As long as you file your contract correctly with the local union, AFM allows the local officer to help collect payments in the case of a default.

Joining the AFM is an option for musicians in Canada and the United States. I recommend looking into your local options. Here is a link for more information on the AFM :

American Federation of Musicians
atnmusi.ca/ch6h10

SHOWCASES

When you are planning to invite industry folk out to a gig, find out what time of day they want to see you play. Playing at midnight is not always going to fly if they have morning commitments the next day, so you might want to do an early show. Also, consider shortening your set to thirty minutes of killer songs, with no fillers. Playing for an hour and a half and leaving your best songs for last is not going to work for busy industry folk. Ensure the venue is a fit for your show and be sure you pack it with fans. Whenever I go to watch musicians I am just as interested to see how the fans interact to the music and personality of the performers as I am to experience the music and performance itself.

STAGE PRESENCE

You can directly apply all the key elements of branding (see Chapter 3) to your show—and you certainly should! Remember that by breaking patterns and using elements of surprise and novelty you command attention; when you have the audience's attention, you can focus on creating a positive experience that results in positive memories connected to your name or band.

Here is a quick checklist for any performance:

- It's a show! I can buy the music if I just want to hear it, so make it a night to remember, make moments I want to buy a soundtrack to.

- Play like you mean it. Be confident.

- Every night is a first night for someone in the audience. Make it one to remember!

- People will buy music and merch when the live experience is worth being remembered.

- Be sure to create space around the songs that you want to make an impact with. Give them a special reason to be remembered.

- Break the patterns in your live show; make sure songs don't just sound different but look different. Sit down for a song, play an acoustic number, get a member of the audience onstage for a song, switch instruments with a band member, have a song sung by someone other than the lead singer, create breakdowns and jams that don't exist on the album version of a song …

- Consider that the volume can sometimes be so loud at a venue that audience members are not actually noticing the musical nuances (especially if they are not wearing protective ear-plugs). This emphasizes the fact that the show and how people remember it is a lot more than just the music. For this reason I suggest giving some thought to what you want people to remember you by. Knowing this can help you to draw up an appropriate set list and deliver your music to its best advan-tage, and it can also help with the interactions between you and the audience.

- The size of your audience should not dictate whether or not it is a good show. You need to put on a performance that is worthy of filling a stadium even if you are in a small club. Your thoughts and actions will become your future.

STREET TEAMS

A street team can build your fan base through street credibility and the kind of awareness generated by fans willing to "hit the streets" to promote you. This model first came about when urban labels like Loud Records, Roc-A-Fella, Ruthless Records and Bad Boy discovered that it was an affordable and "cool" way to reach their target audience. For some independent and smaller labels it was a way of getting around the larger monopolistic record distributors and expensive traditional media (print, TV, radio, etc.) and for others it was a way of building street cred and hype in order to have a stronger negotiating hand when approaching larger record label distributors.

Whichever way you look at it, especially in today's music industry, it is a fantastic way to spread your music and brand by word of mouth. It also helps ensure that proper promotion is done in the areas you are touring in. This can mean anything from proper postering to making sure people are calling in to the radio station to request your latest single.

From the street teams of the urban labels in the early '90s to today's new music industry, a lot has changed. For one thing, we now have social media and the added ability to have street teams that reside entirely online.

I asked Brian Thompson, the Vancouver-based label owner and established new music industry expert (atnmusi.ca/ch6h11), his opinion on building a street team:

Aaron Bethune:
   When do you build a street team and what is usually in it for the team members?

Brian Thompson:

First you have to have had some success with social media. You need to have a number of followers in different cities. That's where the street teams originate. So if you haven't created a fan base outside of your hometown, then street teams just won't happen. Also, street teams won't happen until you have hardcore fans. A casual fan won't want to be a street teamer. There are different levels of fans, and they always start off being a casual fan. So your job using social media is to convert a casual fan into a hardcore evangelist for what you're doing. Once you can recognize that you have a handful of hardcore evangelists for your music in different cities, then that's when you can start approaching them to promote you in their area. Street teams usually are used for when you're passing though their towns. So you can use them to put up posters in their city, hand out handbills, try to use any connections that they might have in their local area to get you some local press; college station coverage; talking to radio stations, music blogs that they may know; or anything like that. Aside from that, if you're not on tour, then really a street teamer can be used to preach to their network of friends and followers and just try to convert their friends to fans, but it's most useful when you're on tour.

PRESS RELEASES

Look again at Chapter 4, "Music PR," and remember:

- You want to grab the reader's attention in the first sentence!

- You want to present a story worthy of publishing! The media are looking for stories, so make it easy for them.

MERCH SALES & MAILING LIST SIGN-UPS

There are a few simple things you can do to make merch tables and mailing lists work for you at gigs:

- Have your merch table in a high-traffic area of the venue. The table should be eye-catching and have good light to feature the items.

- Be sure to have items that fit everyone's budget. The prices should range from $0 to at least $100, if not more.

- Freebies could range from stickers and download cards to hugs and—if you like vintage—signed Polaroids of the artist or band with fans. If you're not into Polaroids, you could take a digital photo and ask for the fan's email address and send it that way (and of course add the fan to the mailing list).

- Other paid items might range from T-shirts, hoodies, CDs, DVDs, hats, panties, cup holders, bags, baby outfits, water bottles, bracelets, posters and photos to more creative merch such as music boxes, hand-painted shoes, iPod/iPad/iPhone cases, handwritten and signed lyric sheets, and custom preloaded flash drives (there are so many cool flash drives out there, from wrist-bands to ones with custom artwork). Keep in mind that the more you know about your fan base the more likely you are to carry merch they will want to buy!

- Your merch table needs to have a mailing sign-up sheet. This sheet has to include names, emails, city and postal/zip codes. This way you can build a mailing list that includes all the neces-sary information to organize your fans geographically.

- Do you take merch with you or do you pick it up? Depending on the extent of your touring, you might want to consider having the merchandise manufactured in the country/province/state you are touring in instead of trying to take it with you. You can save money and Customs hassles. You do not need to be a major artist for this to be worthwhile; I suggest asking the local show promoters if they can help you with the right connections.

- Announce from the stage that you have merch. *Don't overdo it.* Don't be the band that constantly tells everyone to buy its latest album between songs, but also don't be the band that never let you know it was selling merch. Tell the audience you want to meet them and to come see you at the merch table after the show. Once people are at the table and have met you, they are more likely to spend the money (you would be surprised at what a powerful selling aid an authentic hug or handshake can be).

- Give out merch from the stage to winning names pulled from a hat. As a digital variation of that, announce near the beginning of the show that people can add you on Facebook or Twitter and send their names with a hashtag you create for that show. At the end of the show pick a winner that way (this also allows you to create Twitter lists for each show based on the hashtag). Ultimately you want to gather as many emails and as much information as you can! Give the beautiful people working at the venue your merch and ask them to wear it. It just takes a few people to buy, win or be given the merch for everyone to come check out your merch table!

- Reduce the supply and increase the demand. I recently saw a band perform at a theatre and they had a great sales line that went like this: *"We just played a show last night and more people bought our album than we had anticipated, so tonight we don't have enough for all of you as we only have about fifty left."* This came right before the intermission. Were there only fifty CDs left? Not likely, but it sure sounded like a good reason for people to rush and buy a copy while supplies lasted!

15 ways for Musicians to Increase Sales, Fans and Efficiency
atnmusi.ca/ch6h12

How to Sell More Merch at Your Shows
atnmusi.ca/ch6h13

The following device allows you to use your iOS (Apple mobile platform) device or Android phone to read and accept credit cards. Great for selling your merch at gigs!

Square, Inc.
atnmusi.ca/ch6h14

Getting people to sign up for your mailing list
Methods include:

- Give out download cards that require fans' email addresses if they want the download. Apart from handing out the cards from the merch table and at the door, a great way to give the audience download cards is by having the waitresses give them out right after you've played your single and told the crowd you're giving them the song they just heard.

- Instead of using download cards, request people to sign up for the mailing list in exchange for a digital download sent to them on the spot.

- Hand out cards at the door for people to fill out with their info and then put the cards into a hat for an onstage prize draw. Get creative with what the prize is—think outside the box and be remembered for creating a moment.

- Take photos with fans and ask them to sign up for the mailing list with their email so you can send them the photos.

- Record each show live (you can use high-quality hand-held recording devices or your computer with recording software, or you can plug a recording device directly into the soundboard, etc.) and send the recording to your fans in exchange for an email (or a fee). Send a link to a secret page on your website (you could even add photos there from the show, providing ways for people to tag themselves) or to a private SoundCloud track to download.. These tracks should be available only for a limited amount of time.

- Have a rubber stamp made up of your band's logo, including the website. Have the venue stamp everyone's hand as they come to the show. You could even have a link shortener that leads you to the free download page that requires an email address …

- Use QR codes (see Chapter 5) on posters, concert tickets and flyers—even project them onto a screen at your live show or stamp them on people's hands with a rubber stamp. The QR code can direct fans to your free download in exchange for an email address.

These are just a few ideas, but the general idea is that all you have to do is get creative and always make sure there is something in it for the fan!

OVERVIEW

When on tour or playing live you must ...
- bring copies of email exchanges so as to have all your conversations in writing.
- have all contact info in case you are running late, get lost, or simply need to be in touch with the venue.
- have copies of contracts.
- be on time.
- create good relationships.
- have good stage etiquette.
- be respectful and know your own set-up and have it down to an art.
- leave your ego at the door.
- keep healthy and fit.
- be sure that your riders are confirmed and that all elements for a great show are in place.
- consider the ramifications if you are a minor, and always ask if the stage is licensed.

Tips for Surviving and Thriving on Tour
atnmusi.ca/ch6h15

Festivals
- **How do you find out?** Research online, find out where similar bands are performing. (Look at other bands' websites as well as Sonicbids and similar sites.)

- **Who do you contact?** Generally the music director or festival producer. Nonetheless, call and find out who to speak to and how to submit.

- **Submissions and due dates.** Festivals will establish budgets and then want to secure headliners first to ensure ticket sales before they move down the lineup. Festival organizers often start booking the following year's festival shortly after the last one finishes. However, consider end of October to end of March (very latest if at all) to be confirming summer festivals. Find out how to submit and when and follow through.

- **Radius clause.** Don't forget to keep these in mind when booking gigs surrounding the festivals. Be aware that they will often be in place for three to six months before and after the festival date. That said, if you are not a headliner and if you discuss the clause with the festival upfront, they might make an exception and allow you to play certain clubs.

- **Offers and deposits.** The festivals will usually send you a negotiable offer. Once you accept an offer, you need to be sent a deposit, which you can then use for travel expenses and so on (unless they pay for travel).

- **Who is contracting?** Festivals and venues will often give you their contract to sign, but it is important that you have your own standard contract too in case you want to use your own. Sometimes it is easier to send yours than try to amend theirs to suit you. Legal advice is always recommended.

- **Festival meetings.** Keep in mind that many festivals hold joint meetings throughout the year. Among other things this allows them to agree on which artists they want to bring in so as to split the costs between festivals and provide the artist with more dates across a country. You can use this information to your benefit by encouraging a festival that already wants you to perform to encourage other festivals to book you too!

ENDORSEMENTS

Instead of my telling you about artist endorsements I asked John
Wittman to discuss the topic in his capacity as manager of artist
relations at Yamaha Corp. He is in a perfect position to talk about
getting an endorsement because he is the guy you would talk to if
you wanted to be endorsed by Yamaha.

Aaron Bethune:
When should a musician be starting to look for endorsements?

John Wittman:
You must establish yourself as an asset and not an expense before
anyone would want to support you. Every day businesses try to cut
expenses; they try to leverage and capitalize on their assets. Young
players need to get a lot of work done under their belt—they need
to be thrown to the mat many times.

I do artist relations for Yamaha Corporation—the Band and Orchestral Division, which is woodwinds, strings, brass and percussion,
and also drum set, for the United States. If anybody comes to me
and they haven't established themselves as a successful musician—someone who is actually making a living as a musician, be it
a full-time player, performer, or teacher at a conservatory or music
school—how can they expect to be endorsed? They have to have
already proven themselves as a viable commodity before we'd
consider taking them on. That's not to say we don't try to recognize
young talent because we really do—it would be foolish not to.

AB:
**How do you assess whether a drummer is suitable for a Yamaha
endorsement?**

JW:
A lot of drummers just contact us and say, "Hey, we have a lot of
record label interest, and we're going to be the next best thing."
Well, that doesn't mean you've already established yourself. The

band might be getting some good notoriety and may be influential in pockets, but that wouldn't necessarily necessitate a full endorsement, support on the road …

We weigh out, "Is the person a sideman, or is he a soloist? Is he in a band that is ultra-successful?" Carter Beauford—he's the drummer in the Dave Matthews Band—is the dream endorser because he loves the product shamelessly, plays it like crazy, wouldn't play anything else, because he loves the sound. That's the key.

The core of a successful endorsement is when the artist finds the "it," the manufacturer that produces the instrument that makes them completely expressive and free. If that's not there, all the rest will fail. It's like a marriage, if the love's not there then it's not going to work. It's not like, "I kinda like you, so let's get married. But I'm going to date other people." We don't want people to endorse Yamaha for a couple of months, we want it to be an entire lifetime.

Most drummers are pretty cut and dried; they either love the Yamaha sound, the Ludwig sound, the Pearl sound … and want that sound, so they should go to that company once they are established.

AB:
How did your drumming career lead you to getting endorsed by Yamaha, and how did that then lead to you endorsing other musicians?

JW:
My relationship with music started quite similarly to many people who grew up in the '60s; I saw Ringo Starr on *The Ed Sullivan Show* and it literally changed my life. My earliest memories were of just banging on things, and getting a cardboard drum set when I was very young.

Since I was a little boy, watching TV was always, "How did that hi-hat open and close?" … "Why does he have the snare drum that way?" … "What is he doing with that foot?" I went to a small school in upstate New York where they had a very small band program, but I was also playing rock 'n' roll in clubs. It wasn't until senior year that I really got serious about thinking if this is what I'm to be then I'd better be able to speak about it intelligently. I worked like crazy, got into a band, got my butt kicked, auditioned for college, went into undergrad as a music education major. It was a small undergraduate school and because there were not a lot of us, we all had to play everything—marimba, vibes, chimes, drum set, timpani. So it was baptism by fire and I reacted very positively to the pressure.

Upon graduation, I went on the road for three years and played rock 'n' roll six nights a week all over the country. It was 1982, some of the coolest music and some of the worst music at the same time, and it was there that I really honed the relationship with the drum set. And also with music because now you're really doing it for a living; whether you were sick as hell or feeling great, you had to show up every night and give 100 percent.

And that led to me trying to get out of that scene alive, knowing it was time to go if I wanted to continue living. I went back to grad school, got my master's in conducting, and was a band director in upstate NY for six years. I loved it a lot but decided to go back out on the road again and started a band with some friends.

The band disbanded abruptly. It was a very cathartic experience to see your dreams shattered because we were really going for that record deal in the sky. I had to recreate myself and realized I had been going through stages leading me up to the point where I could go back to the woodshed and really work out my weaknesses as a player. I worked endless hours on my drum-set skills, wanting to be a really good clinician. I started to do many clinics, a lot of writing, a lot of teaching … I never went after any endorsements. I developed myself as a commodity and then was asked to endorse Yamaha Drums.

From then I was asked to be full-time, after I was an established artist–clinician, as a studio guy, performer, writer, with these other companies. After that I was asked to come on full-time as the artist relations manager for the Yamaha Corporation. I have been in this position going on fifteen years, and still am very active as a drummer. I play drums for a singer-songwriter named Jenny DeVoe. Also, I still speak a lot at universities and do as much drum clinics and instruction as I can.

AB:
How long is a musician endorsed for?

JW:
We really do want them to stay in the family forever, if Yamaha is the sound that they want. It is really a yes or no thing: you either love the sound or you don't. All the different manufactures make good instruments, but if you really do love the sound and you're a good person, and you're a good business person, and you communicate respectfully and your expectations are realistic, then we want you on the roster forever.

Endorsements don't propel artists' careers—that's a huge misconception. Endorsements are designed to expose the credibility of an instrument through artist endorsement and then to support that artist to continue to be as creative as possible.

AB:
What is expected from a musician in return for an endorsement?

JW:
Good communication. If they're going to be on *Late Night with David Letterman*, if they're going over to Japan, or a new record release is coming out, we want to know about it so we can support and promote them. If you don't communicate well then the relationship's going to be lopsided. There are a lot more artists than there are staff for artist relations. And we don't want to have to not hear from somebody and then they call up and say "You guys never call."

We expect them to play our instruments consistently. In other words, they can't say "I endorse Yamaha" but then when they go down to play a jazz club in the Village, play a competitor's horn or a competitor's electric violin, because that's the sound they really like.

We also expect them to be vocal when appropriate as to why. We do chip in pretty extensively and consistently for support for clinics to help students get good material and information from the Yamaha artist–clinician. When a kid raises his hand and says, "What do you play?" the dude says, "I play a Yamaha trombone, and let me tell you why ... " And the students then go, "I want to sound like him," and hopefully buy Yamaha stuff.

AB:
Do you feel that there's any unique opportunity that exists from being with Yamaha? Is there something other than the instruments and the music?

JW:
Yes. Number one, we are very dedicated to education. If the artist is also dedicated to education, we're going to be consistent with our support of their educational endeavours.

We're very dedicated to the pursuit of sound. The designers in Japan are relentless in the search for really great sound and great quality. Our artists benefit from the consistency of Yamaha's design, which is one thing that makes Yamaha very unique. If you're a trumpet player in Japan and tried a Yamaha trumpet and then were transported to Los Angeles and got the same model of trumpet off the shelf at a music store and played both, the playability and the consistency will be off the hook.

We are a family and we have a worldwide network of support. When our artists travel internationally, the phone rings, and it's like, "John, my saxophone just got run over by a train, I'm in Tokyo, what the hell do I do?" that's not a problem. That's when the endorsement artist says, "Oh my gosh, I'll never leave Yamaha." There's a very high level of expectations working with Yamaha, we expect the best of our people, and when our artists travel to different countries, they're treated with a lot of respect by our staff, and that goes a long way when you're in another country, and your instrument breaks down or is lost.

Another benefit would be there are ateliers, pro-shops, in Tokyo, Los Angeles, New York and Frankfurt where wind people, as well as percussionists and strings, can come in and get work on their instruments by real artisans. This is where science meets art. They trust these people to take their baby apart and make it sound more blue—or more grey. That is an expensive commitment, and it's a huge statement to our artist community.

AB:
Does it make a difference if it's a representative of that artist, or would you prefer to hear from an artist directly?

JW:
Even if management contacts us, I won't sign anyone until I talk to them. It's a relationship. Some major rock stars have great representation—we deal with their techs, personal managers, or business managers—but I prefer to have an artist call me because I really gotta know what makes them tick.

An artist who has a manager call because they're trying to impress does not impress. If they're on such on a high level and it's part of management's job to represent said artist, to talk about an endorsement relationship, I totally get that. But if they are not of the highest echelon of the music business, then pick up the damn phone! Let's be real folks, we're all trying to make it, right? I don't expect anything but honesty and good communication.

We've had some major artists in major orchestras or rock bands that just pick up the phone and say, "Hi, I'm ____ and I just love Yamaha and I love to play your stuff. Are you into that?" That's the kind of call that makes you happy you do what you do because they're really shooting straight.

AB:
Is there a better time of the year to approach you?

JW:

A really rough time to call is December/January because there are many conventions, the Midwest Band and Orchestra Convention, the NAMM Show, Jazz Education Network, Percussive Arts Society ... during December and January I don't field one call from a prospective artist because we're wrapped around major shows. February, March, April is when I catch up and actually listen and call people back.

AB:

What are other mistakes musicians make when approaching for an endorsement?

JW:

The worst thing to do is cold-call, say "Hey I'm Johnny Rotten and I'm really good." The best thing to do is to be an expert on our philosophy and our procedures and go to our website. Most of the people who are really good players and really good people know they've got a few hoops to jump through and will happily fill out an application and send in a press pack.

I'm just asking you to tell me what label you're on, send me a recording, and talk to me about what gear you use. If you can't do that then what's it going to be like two months down the line? There's no relationship if you can't just be normal and stop star-tripping for a minute. We're really interested in good people, good players who are self-propelled, who love our instruments, want to keep playing doing their own thing. If major rock stars can do it, then people who are aspiring certainly can.

It's not a good idea to walk up at NAMM, or another trade show, with a big package and just bombard you. But it's totally cool to come up and say, "Hey I'm ____ and I'd like to send you a package, I'd like you to hear my music. I love Yamaha drums." Approach is everything, and if they take time to look at the website and really just know where we're coming from and know about our instruments and approach us in a good way, then I'm all ears, and really open to opportunities.

AB:
From the other end of the spectrum, can artists be dropped from an endorsement, and what would be the basis?

JW:
It's very rare that we drop people. People stay with us because we make really good instruments, but we also work really hard at having great programs and great support.

Most of the time when people leave Yamaha, it goes something like, "John, I've been playing these other horns and it's just my sound, I love them, and I'm sorry. You guys have been great." To which I answer, "I totally get it." That's life, things change.

As far as really having to drop somebody, it would have to be a real blatant, "No, I'm not going to do any type of support," like I won't put the logo on my drums anymore, or some type of fraud like saying they did these clinics and we paid them and they never occurred.

We just ask people to play our instruments consistently. If they're not really being consistent performing on our instruments then there's no reason for the endorsement. Sometimes you'd watch YouTube things and they're not playing your instruments any more, and then I'd certainly call them to say "Hey what's going on?" If that's the case, if they're not playing and endorsing, then the relationship shouldn't continue.

If you're a young player and you're considering an endorsement, you have to focus on the music first and the endorsements will come. Consistently practise, be a consistent good person, be a relentless good-finder; the mechanics of being a good musician are 25 percent of success, the other components are who you surround yourself with, and how positive a person you are, and how you deal with pressure, and those are the things that propel a career.

AB:

Is there a success story that really defines a successful endorsement relationship with Yamaha?

JW:

Jeff Coffin, saxophone player with the Dave Matthews Band, played a competitor's saxophone when he was with Béla Fleck and the Flecktones. We met him and said, "Hey we're working on some designs of some different saxophones and would love to have you try them out." He was very open and he tried the saxophones, but didn't really like them. We then asked, "What kind of saxophone would make the most sense to you? Where are we missing the target on this instrument?" We involved him in the process of how different saxophones were being developed.

Now he plays all of our saxophones consistently and Yamaha has become his sound. He is über-successful and still always a phone call away. He's one of our most active clinicians. Always just, "What do you need me to do? Let me help." He's always part of the solution, and a good example of somebody who really understands the correct expectations and a healthy relationship as an endorser.

Resources

Here are a few links, mostly directed to Canadian musicians. However, be sure to research online, connect with your local music association, and ask promoters, agents, clubs, festivals and so on for the most relevant and up-to-date information. They will have numbers and email addresses to specific contacts they are used to dealing with that they can facilitate meetings or phone chats with. These contacts can range from government tax people to local media. So look further than just the resources below.

Taxes, waiver forms, work permits and visas

An HM Revenue & Customs guide to how foreign entertainers are paid in England
atnmusi.ca/ch6h16

Central Withholding Agreements for foreign artists playing in the US
atnmusi.ca/ch6h17

Crossing Borders
atnmusi.ca/ch6h18

Form 8233
atnmusi.ca/ch6h19

Immigration advice for performing in the US and Canada
atnmusi.ca/ch6h20

Need a work permit to play in Canada? Find out:
atnmusi.ca/ch6h21

On the Road: Touring Handbook, Presenters Handbook and
Touring Handbook International
atnmusi.ca/ch6h22

Tax waiver form
atnmusi.ca/ch6h23

Temporary Foreign Worker Program (Required for hiring foreign
workers in entertainment and film-related occupations in Canada)
atnmusi.ca/ch6h24

US work permits for Canadian artists
atnmusi.ca/ch6h25

Visa Requirements for US Musicians Working in Canada
atnmusi.ca/ch6h26

Want to play outside of Canada?
atnmusi.ca/ch6h27

Funding and support
There is help out there! Don't be the person who doesn't apply
because you think "I'll never get it … "

There are many little things you can do to capitalize on your live performances. One is to be sure to register your live performances with your performing rights organization (PRO), so you can collect royalties on them. A lot of bands don't know this and are missing out! The following are Canadian resources, but it's usually easy to find local and national equivalents elsewhere:

Canada Council for the Arts: Grants and prizes
atnmusi.ca/ch6h28

Canadian Music Funding Organizations
atnmusi.ca/ch6h29

FACTOR (The Foundation Assisting Canadian Talent on Recordings)
atnmusi.ca/ch6h30

SOCAN (Society of Composers, Authors and Music Publishers of Canada)
atnmusi.ca/ch6h31

Don't miss out!

Booking resources

Association for the Promotion of Campus Activities (APCA)
atnmusi.ca/ch6h32

Book Your Own Fuckin' Life
atnmusi.ca/ch6h33

Concerts in Your Home
atnmusi.ca/ch6h34

Indie on the Move
atnmusi.ca/ch6h35

Indie Venue Bible
atnmusi.ca/ch6h36

Musician's Atlas
atnmusi.ca/ch6h37

MusicNomad
atnmusi.ca/ch6h38

National Association for Campus Activities (NACA)
atnmusi.ca/ch6h39

Onlinegigs
atnmusi.ca/ch6h40

Stageit
atnmusi.ca/ch6h41

VIP Booking
atnmusi.ca/ch6h42

Merch resources

These are just a few of many companies out there. As always, look into your local options and be sure to ask other bands.

Big Cartel
atnmusi.ca/ch6h43

Kill the 8
atnmusi.ca/ch6h44

My Custom Band Merch (MCBM)
atnmusi.ca/ch6h45

Topspin
atnmusi.ca/ch6h46

Toto Merch
atnmusi.ca/ch6h47

Learn to excel in your live performance

Singing Success
atnmusi.ca/ch6h48

Tom Jackson Productions
atnmusi.ca/ch6h49

Additional links

Bandposters
atnmusi.ca/ch6h50

Eventful
atnmusi.ca/ch6h54

Bandsintown
atnmusi.ca/ch6h51

HitQuarters
atnmusi.ca/ch6h55

CrowdSync
atnmusi.ca/ch6h52

How to market and promote music in Italy
atnmusi.ca/ch6h56

Eventbrite
atnmusi.ca/ch6h53

How to market and promote music in Sweden
atnmusi.ca/ch6h57

Ovature
atnmusi.ca/ch6h58

Pollstar
atnmusi.ca/ch6h59

smartURL for showsnear.by
atnmusi.ca/ch6h60

Songkick
atnmusi.ca/ch6h61

Soundhalo: Watch, download and share artist-endorsed live music as
it happens
atnmusi.ca/ch6h62

Ticketfly
atnmusi.ca/ch6h63

TicketZone
atnmusi.ca/ch6h64

Tour Smart: And Break the Band, by Martin Atkins
atnmusi.ca/ch6h65

Welcome to the Music Business You're Fucked, by Martin Atkins
atnmusi.ca/ch6h66

CHAPTER SEVEN

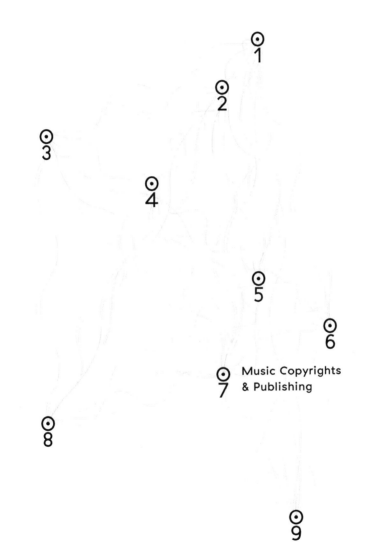

1

2

3

4

5

6

7 Music Copyrights
& Publishing

8

9

Music Copyrights & Publishing

This is a complex issue, but an extremely important one for musicians. The aim here is to give you a basic understanding of copyrights and how publishing works, and I encourage you to continue exploring the subject, as there are many valuable resources available—some of which I mention in this chapter. Note that the laws vary from country to country, so some readers may need to take a good look at their local resources too.

MUSIC COPYRIGHTS

You may be aware that you own "copyrights" to your musical works, but do you actually know what they are? The first thing musicians need to understand is that the moment you create a song and it becomes tangible by "fixation," you automatically receive a bundle of specific rights. This means that as soon as a song is recorded in any format, whether it is jotted down on a scrap of paper, sung into a phone or self-recorded on YouTube, you instantly receive these copyrights. This is the law and it is there to protect your rights.

A career in today's music industry is global whether you like it or not. If your music is digitally distributed through any of the readily available distributors—such as Ditto Music, DistroKid, MusicJustMusic, Indie Pool, CD Baby or TuneCore—it is being distributed worldwide.

Copyright laws, however, are not global. They differ from country to country, some significantly and others in minor ways. This said, because of recent revisions due to international treaties and trade agreements, a certain amount of harmonization is under review in several countries.

Your music is governed by the laws of the country in which your music is being "exploited" (e.g., played on radio, sold, distributed or streamed) regardless of where it was originally created. So if you are Canadian and your music is available in France, Canada and the United States, then the French copyright laws govern your music in France, the *Canadian Copyright Act* governs in Canada and the *US Copyright Act* governs in the United States. This is due to what is commonly known as the Berne Convention.

The *Berne Convention for the Protection of Literary and Artistic Works* is an international agreement governing copyright that was first adopted in 1886. It requires that signatory countries recognize the copyrighted works of authors of other signatory countries as they would their own nationals. It also requires that there be a high minimum standard for copyright law. This means that although the copyright laws are not the same for every country, when it comes to the members of the Berne Union, there is some amount of standardization.

I recommend taking a moment to learn which countries are signatories of the Berne Convention:

World Intellectual Property Organization (WIPO)
atnmusi.ca/ch7h1

Throughout this chapter I reference the Canadian and American copyright acts. Be sure to research those relevant to you.

As applied to music, copyright is best viewed as a bundle of rights. Each country defines the rights in this bundle in its own terminology. In the United States, six clearly defined copyrights make up the bundle of rights that are granted. They are essentially the same as those stated by the *Canadian Copyright Act*, but only the *US Copyright Act* specifies "Derivatives."

These are the six copyrights as stated in the *US Copyright Act:*

1	Reproduction	4	Digital Transmission
2	Public Performance	5	Public Display
3	Distribution	6	Derivatives

These copyrights are the foundation and driving force of how money and rules are made in this industry. They are the rights that protect your musical work and give you control of how others use it. Whether you are an independent artist, a publisher or a record label, you are in the business of rights management. So as you can imagine, it is vital to understand what these rights are. Without properly understanding your rights it is hard to protect them and know how to negotiate deals in your best interest.

BASICS

The two fundamental and distinct copyrights apply in most instances to the use of music. As depicted in **Figure 7.1**, they are:

- The copyright in the musical work (i.e., the song or musical composition)

- The copyright in the sound recording

Figure 7.1 Basic Music Copyrights

Additionally, there is a copyright in the package design (art, photos, graphics, text) that is associated with the above.

Two symbols are recognized as the copyright notices when printed with each copy of a sound recording or attached in a digital file:

- © represents the musical work (i.e., the composition—both music and lyrics).

- ℗ stands for "phonogram" and is used to represent the sound recording. Note that another © is used for the package/design in conjunction with the ℗ symbol.

In Canada, the duration or "life of copyright," as it is called, in a musical work is the lifetime of the writer plus fifty years, or in the case of multiple writers, lifetime of the last surviving writer plus fifty years.

As this book was going to press, Canada and several other countries were in the midst of negotiating the TPP (Trans-Pacific Partnership) trade agreement, one of the proposed requirements of which was an extension of the life of copyright from life plus fifty years to life plus seventy years as applied to musical works and seventy-five years for sound recordings.

In the United States, copyrights last for life plus seventy years. As you can see, the laws are different in each country, so research is important.

It used to be not uncommon that in some instances, a recording artist who was also a songwriter signed to a record label would write a song and the record label would pay for the studio time to record it. The writer would own 100 percent of the musical composition and the label would own 100 percent of the sound recording, because the label paid for it. The songwriter could then enter into an agreement with a publisher to administer the rights to the composition. However, in many instances the publishing company was owned by the record label or shared the same parent company as the label (i.e., major labels/publishers and larger independent labels/publishers).

In today's new music industry, independent artists generally own and control 100 percent of both the "musical work" (i.e., the song or composition) and the sound recording. It's simple: if you wrote a song and paid the studio to record it, you own 100 percent of the musical composition and 100 percent of the sound recording (also known as the "studio master" or "glass master"). This means that no matter whether you are negotiating with music supervisors, publishers or labels and so on, you are the only person they will need to negotiate with (and of course in some cases your lawyer).

If another artist records a song you wrote, you still own 100 percent of the rights in the musical work (i.e., song or composition), but the other artist (or their label) will own 100 percent of the new sound recording (the master). In order to record your song and put it out on an album, they will need to obtain a mechanical licence and pay a royalty to you for each reproduction.

This brings us to the first specific copyright:

1. Reproduction

By law, no one else can reproduce a song without paying the publisher or administrator (even if they happen to also be the songwriter) a "mechanical royalty." That's it. Simple. In order to cover a song by another writer and release it, you are required by law to obtain a mechanical licence and pay a royalty to the copyright owner or their designated representative. In the United States, the government sets the minimum amount that must be paid to the songwriter(s) or their publisher (if they have one) for each reproduction. In the fall of 2013, for example, the US mechanical royalty rate was 9.1 cents per song, per copy made, for a song of five minutes or less. Each additional minute or part thereof was 1.75 cents.

It is important to understand that as an independent label and/or DIY (do-it-yourself) artist, you pay per copy made *not* per copy sold! Only the major labels pay on what they actually sell.

When it comes to mechanicals, the United States works under a "compulsory licence" regime with a fixed rate, but Canada does not. This means Canada does not have a fixed statutory rate such as the one the US government sets. In 1988 a major amendment to the *Canadian Copyright Act* eliminated the fixed rate, and now rates in Canada are set by negotiation. However, if you are manufacturing small quantities or releasing sound recordings on a one-shot or limited basis, an option called "pay-as-you-press/import" is available to you. This option has a set rate of 8.3 cents per song, per copy made, for a song of five minutes or less. Each additional minute or part thereof is 1.6 cents. The minimum number of copies for which a "pay-as-you-press" licence will be issued is five hundred.

To obtain a licence you need to contact a mechanical rights agency—such as the Canadian Musical Reproduction Rights Agency Ltd. (CMRRA) or the Society for Reproduction Rights of Authors, Composers and Publishers in Canada (SODRAC) in Canada, or The Harry Fox Agency (HFA) in the United States. If they do not represent the song, you will need to research the writer's publisher and request it directly. Depending on the writer, you might also be able to contact them directly or ask their management who to speak to. In Canada, if after pursuing all possible avenues you find it impossible to verify ownership and clear the rights, you may submit your licence to the Copyright Board of Canada pursuant to Section 70.7 of the *Canadian Copyright Act*. The licence is paid to the Copyright Board of Canada and can be collected by the original copyright owner for up to five years.

In the United States, if a song has previously been released commercially you do not require approval of the songwriter to obtain a mechanical licence. (Note that a licence is a "permission.")

For example, if you have written and commercially released a song, anyone—as long as they obtain a mechanical licence and pay mechanical royalties—can record and release the song without needing further approval (within certain guidelines). However, when you have written a song but not released it commercially, you are able to choose who releases it and negotiate any rate you want. If you choose to let someone record the song for less than the statutory rate, it is called a "reduced mechanical."

In more recent times the US government has expanded the definition of the term *reproduction* and has come up with additional mechanical royalty/licence rates. This is due to two new types of reproduction called "interactive streams." These are services like Napster, Rhapsody, Beats, Rdio and so on that charge the user a fee to listen to a song on demand, and then the ad-supported services like YouTube that don't require the user to pay a fee.

The mechanical royalties for these interactive streams are a combination of a percentage of the revenue generated by the site and a payment per subscriber. The amounts are significantly lower for sites that are non-interactive, such as Pandora, than they are for inter-active sites like Rdio.

Here are a few agencies in North America to contact regarding mechanical rights:

American Mechanical Rights Agency (AMRA)
atnmusi.ca/ch7h2

Canadian Musical Reproduction Rights Agency (CMRRA)
atnmusi.ca/ch7h3

Society for Reproduction Rights of Authors, Composers and Publishers in Canada (SODRAC)
atnmusi.ca/ch7h4

The Harry Fox Agency (HFA)
atnmusi.ca/ch7h5

2. Public Performance

As the copyright holder to your musical works, you are granted the exclusive public performance rights. Public performance is con-sidered live performances and transmissions of performances (such as radio and TV or at any business or event that plays music).

The *US Copyright Act* says to perform/display a work publicly is:

(1) to perform it at a place open to the public or at any place where a substantial number of persons outside of a normal circle of a family and its social acquaintances is gathered; or

(2) to transmit or otherwise communicate a performance or display of the work to a place specified by clause (1) or to the public, by means of any device or process, whether the members of the public capable of receiving the performance or display receive it in the same place or in separate places and at the same time or at different times. (Accessed at atnmusi.ca/ch7h6 on Nov. 6, 2013)

You have the exclusive right to publicly perform your copyrighted work! However, when you sign with a performing rights organization (PRO), you assign your performance right in the musical work exclusively to that organization (with the exception of grand rights). It will license music users on your behalf and pay royalties according to its specific distribution rules (which may differ from PRO to PRO) for those performances.

Initially you, and only you, have the right to perform your music live at a venue (club, festival, etc.). If a radio station or a TV show wants to play your music, or if an advertiser or a film company, for example, wants to feature your copyrighted music, they need to have an agreement in place with you. This is where PROs come in. Although (in theory) you could try to license radio, TV or other music users directly, this would be impractical for you and these music users as well.

For this reason, as a copyright holder you can affiliate with a performing rights organization (e.g., SOCAN, ASCAP, BMI, SESAC, PRS or SGAE). These copyright collectives are either member-owned or private companies and represent their songwriter and publisher members' repertoire as well as the music catalogues of their international affiliates via reciprocal agreements.They issue licences to those that want to use music and ensure that the songwriter and publisher get paid. This makes the whole performance rights licensing process a lot easier and more efficient.

If you are a songwriter in the United States, you need to be signed up with a PRO as a writer and as a publisher. In the United States, if you do not have a publishing company you might not be able to collect the publisher's share.

In Canada, according to the rules of the Society of Composers, Authors and Music Publishers of Canada (SOCAN), a songwriter who does not have a publishing company is able to collect both the writer's share and publisher's share (although it would be an undivided 100-percent share without a publisher assignment) by just being signed up as a songwriter with SOCAN. Songwriters who live outside

Canada need to find out what the rules are with the PRO in their respective country.

The reason you are able to perform covers in clubs is because the club owners pay annual blanket licence fees that grant them access to the world's repertoire of copyrighted music.

PROs monitor radio and TV to determine which works are being performed. You need to be signed up with a PRO and register your songs to ensure you are collecting royalties.

Depending on the radio format you are aiming for, you can encrypt your music with digital audio identification (DAI) technology to better your chances of being paid accurately (see Chapter 9, "Radio Promotion").

If your music fits the format of the top commercial radio stations (whether pop, rock, country, hot AC or urban), Canadians should upload an MP3 to Nielsen Broadcast Data Systems (BDS), which is used in Canada by SOCAN to log the radio performances from the top commercial radio stations in the major advertising markets (i.e., large cities). As well, other stations that were formerly logged under the survey method of collecting can now be included in the DAI census method if they submit their playlists electronically to SOCAN. In the United States, ASCAP uses Mediabase and Media Monitors to monitor radio plays, and also uses third-party companies to survey the stations and to cross-reference with Mediabase data. BMI does not use BDS or Mediabase, but instead uses the logs from radio stations that are sent to it three times a year. SESAC uses BDS to monitor radio performances, but is always looking for new technology to provide the most accurate data. Unlike ASCAP and BMI, SESAC looks to work with songwriters who already have a track record with their songs and are not just starting out. For this reason, you can't just sign up to be a member—you need to get in touch and talk with their writer and publisher contact. So my recommendation, when it comes to getting your radio plays monitored correctly, is to submit your music to Mediabase and Media Monitors as well as BDS. Some PROs will suggest that you submit your music to BDS, Mediabase and so on through them so that if they change services they can resubmit your music on your behalf to the new company. I suggest you contact your local PRO and ask for advice. (See more on this topic in Chapter 9.)

As for ensuring you collect royalties from a placement on a TV show, in a movie, and so on, you want to get a cue sheet when possible from the production company and submit it to your PRO. Chances are the production company will have already submitted it, but you can never be too safe. Again, ask your PRO how it collects the data and what you can do to help the process and ensure you get paid.

When it comes to public performance royalties of the composition, it doesn't matter who the performer is on the recording, or who performs onstage or is broadcast on TV; it is the songwriter and publisher (i.e., the copyright holder for the musical composition) who collect(s) the royalties.

I highly recommend checking into the distribution rules of your particular PRO to understand better the policies and procedures of how you get paid. These should be easily found on the PRO's website once you log into your account page. (Note: Tariffs are accessible on SOCAN's site, and distribution rules are available to members via their online accounts.) It might even be worth picking up the phone.

You can be proactive and not only register your songs but also submit your set lists, and other related documentation, to your PRO to collect royalties for your live performances.

See neighbouring rights further on in this chapter to find out how featured musicians and singers who perform an audio contribution on a recording are also able to collect royalties for public performance.

3. Distribution

You get the exclusive right to distribute your music. Your copyrights are exclusive to you.

This means that if you want someone to distribute your music physically or digitally you have to enter into an agreement with the distributor. Without an agreement no one can sell, rent, or lease copies of your music.

Have you ever wondered how it is that a second-hand music store is able to buy your music from you and sell it? Or how it is that you are allowed to sell your old CD collection on eBay? Considering you are not the copyright owner and you are not breaking any laws, how does it work?

This type of sale is known as the "first sale doctrine." Once you buy a copyrighted work you are allowed to resell, rent or lend it. Selling, lending or renting a physical product like a CD or DVD is actually handing over—distributing—the copy you bought. You are not making and selling copies. However, the US Digital Millennium Copyright Act (DMCA) was passed in order to address the "first sale doctrine" in the digital age as you can see where it might cause problems. Because a digital download requires burning to a CD or making a copy in order to share, sell, and so on, it actually classifies as reproducing. For this reason the DMCA states that while you can purchase a digital download you are not able to distribute it digitally the same way you might with a physical album you purchase.

When it comes to synchronizations, the right to distribute also comes into play. This refers to the licensing of music for TV and film (see Chapter 8, "Music Licensing," for more detail on this topic.). Essentially, in order to place your music in, say, a TV show, ad or movie, the music supervisor, producer or someone similar has to obtain a "synchronization licence" and a "master usage" licence. This means that they have to get permission from both the songwriter and the owner of the master recording. So if they want to use a recording of your song performed by another artist, you would be paid for the use of the song and the other artist would be paid for the use of their recording of it (the master). Unlike mechanical licences there is no set statutory rate for synchronization and master licences. This means what you get paid will vary depending on the project and on how established you are.

4. Digital Transmission

With the advent of the internet, satellite radio, cable and digital TV, not only do we have "terrestrial" broadcasting but we now also have "digital transmission."

As covered in right number 2 (public performance), by law, when music is played on the radio (AM/FM), the songwriter(s) and publisher(s) are to be paid a royalty that is generally distributed by their PRO, according to specific distribution rules of that organization.

The US 1995 *Digital Performance Right in Sound Recordings Act* (DPRSRA) and 1998 *Digital Millennium Copyright Act* (DMCA) stated that when music is played via "digital audio transmission" the rights holder of the musical composition and the rights holder to the sound recording must be paid. The DPRSRA and DMCA are both US copyright laws. Other countries may have their own laws and provisions to accomplish the same goal (mostly via World Intellectual Property Organization agreements). For this reason, and once again, I suggest researching the laws pertinent to your country.

The DPRSRA was enacted due to the absence of a performance right for sound recordings in the *US Copyright Act* of 1976. A contributing factor was the fear that digital technology would stand in for sales of physical records.

This meant that for the first time in the United States, the labels that controlled the master rights (sound recording rights) would also receive a royalty. The government sets the amount of this royalty. So if you have been played via internet radio, whether you are the songwriter or performer you are owed money.

Just like the PROs that monitor and collect your public performance royalties, there is a not-for-profit company called SoundExchange that collects and distributes royalties to the rights holders of a sound recording when it is used via digital transmission. In order to receive these royalties you need to sign up with SoundExchange, which you can do here:

SoundExchange
atnmusi.ca/ch7h7

The best part is that you can collect royalties dating all the way back to 1996, when SoundExchange first began collecting.

5. Public Display

When you create an original work you get the exclusive right to display it in public. Although this is perhaps more pertinent to painters, photographers, sculptors, graphic designers and so on, it does serve a purpose in the world of musical works copyright holders.

The *US Copyright Act* says:

> To "display" a work means to show a copy of it, either directly or by means of a film, slide, television image, or any other device or process or, in the case of a motion picture or other audiovisual work, to show individual images nonsequentially. (Accessed at atnmusi.ca/ch7h6 on Nov. 6, 2013)

Public display includes putting lyrics on websites, merch and so on.

In terms of the act, "public" includes displaying (1) at a place open to the public, (2) at a place with a group of people larger than a gathering of family or the normal circle of friends, (3) when transmitted to a place open to the public or a group of people larger than a gathering of family or the normal circle of friends, or (4) where transmitted to the public (i.e., television and radio broadcasts). (See also "2. Public Performance," earlier in the chapter.)

Without the copyright holder granting the right to display their work, it is illegal to display song lyrics on a website, in a book, on a piece of merch (such as a T-shirt or mug) and so on. The same right needs to be negotiated for anyone who wants to distribute or reproduce sheet music. The same goes for album art, logos and so on.

6. Derivatives

The *Canadian Copyright Act* does not explicitly define derivative works. The *US Copyright Act*, however, states that a derivative work is this:

> A "derivative work" is a work based upon one or more preexisting works, such as a translation, musical arrangement, dramatization, fictionalization, motion picture version, sound recording, art reproduction, abridgment, condensation, or any other form in which a work may be recast, transformed, or adapted. A work consisting of editorial revisions, annotations, elaborations, or other modifications, which, as a whole, represent an original work of authorship, is a "derivative work." (Accessed at atnmusi.ca/ch7h6 on Nov. 6, 2013)

As with the other rights, the holder of the copyright of the original work has the exclusive right to create or grant the rights for a derivative work to be created.

Translations are considered a derivative. As discussed under "1. Reproduction," in the United States as long as you pay a mechanical royalty you can cover any song that has been publicly released without getting the songwriter's permission as long as you don't make substantive changes to the lyrics or melody. A translation, however, is considered a substantial change and therefore a derivative work. This means that the exclusive rights holder of the copyright needs to grant permission and can say no.

As quoted above from the *US Copyright Act*, you can see that it is not just translations that are considered derivatives. Probably the most relevant—and something I constantly deal with in the world of music licensing for TV and film—involves sampling.

Sampling combines an existing copyrighted work with a new work. This is obviously a substantial change to the original work. In order to sample someone else's copyrighted work you need their express permission.

Just like the example of placements in TV and film that require a synchronization licence agreement with the songwriter and a master rights agreement with the owner of the sound recording, in order to sample somebody's music you need permission from the copyright holders of the musical work and the sound recording. Depending on the success of the artist, you would negotiate with the artist's publisher regarding the musical work rights and the artist's label for the sound recording rights. Either party can refuse to grant you permission.

If you are able to get the permission from the holder of the musical work rights but not the holder of the sound recording rights, you could re-record the sampled section (e.g., a guitar riff or vocal hook) yourself and consequently own the rights to your master/sound recording. This is known as a "replay."

There seems to be a grey area in the understanding of how much anyone can sample somebody else's musical work in a song without asking permission. Let's clear that up and just say there is no amount allowed for sampling without permission.

OTHER RIGHTS

The rights covered so far are the rights granted to the songwriter once a song has been recorded in a tangible format. They are the rights that pertain to the musical composition. However, in select countries (ninety-one at last count, to be exact), including Canada but excluding the United States, there is another type of rights called neighbouring rights.

Neighbouring Rights

These rights make it possible for performers—including session musicians and featured performers—as well as producers and record labels in the countries signatory to the Rome Convention to collect royalties for broadcasting and public performance.

On October 26, 1961, the *International Convention for the Protection of Performers, Producers of Phonograms and Broadcasting Organizations*—commonly referred to as the Rome Convention—was passed.

The essence of the Rome Convention is this:

(1) Performers (actors, singers, musicians, dancers and other persons who perform literary or artistic works) are protected against certain acts they have not consented to. Such acts are: the broadcasting and the communication to the public of their live performance; the fixation of their live performance; the reproduction of such a fixation if the original fixation was made without their consent or if the reproduction is made for purposes different from those for which they gave their consent.

(2) Producers of phonograms enjoy the right to authorize or prohibit the direct or indirect reproduction of their phonograms. Phonograms are defined in the Rome Convention as meaning any exclusively aural fixation of sounds of a performance or of other sounds. When a phonogram published for commercial purposes gives rise to secondary uses (such as broadcasting or communication to the public in any form), a single equitable remuneration must be paid by the user to the performers, or to the producers of phonograms, or to both; contracting States are free, however, not to apply this rule or to limit its application.

(3) Broadcasting organizations enjoy the right to authorize or prohibit certain acts, namely: the rebroadcasting of their broadcasts; the fixation of their broadcasts; the reproduction of such fixations; the communication to the public of their television broadcasts if such communication is made in places accessible to the public against payment of an entrance fee. (Accessed at atnmusi.ca/ch7h8 on Nov. 6, 2013)

When sound makers and performers are citizens or permanent residents of a signatory country, or the maker's corporation is head-quartered in a signatory country, or if all the fixations for the sound recording occurred in a signatory country, then the sound makers and performers are eligible for neighbouring rights.

In Canada, neighbouring rights were enacted as part of the 1997 amendments to the *Canadian Copyright Act*. In that same year, a not-for-profit umbrella collective was created to administer neighbouring rights in Canada. This collective was originally called the Neighbouring Rights Collective of Canada (NRCC) and has since become Re:Sound.

Much like the PROs that collect on behalf of the writers, composers and publishers, Re:Sound collects the royalties on behalf of the Canadian performers and makers of sound recordings and then distributes royalties to them via the agencies listed below. (If you are not Canadian, I suggest looking into the equivalent agencies relevant to you. A quick search online can provide the detailed information.)

Performers need to be a member of one of the following in order to collect on neighbouring rights royalties:

ACTRA Recording Artists' Collecting Society
atnmusi.ca/ch7h9

ARTISTI
atnmusi.ca/ch7h10

Musicians' Rights Organization Canada (MROC)
atnmusi.ca/ch7h11

The owners or controllers of the sound recording's copyrights (traditionally record companies) need to be a member of one of the following in order to collect these same royalties:

Audio-Video Licensing Agency (AVLA)
atnmusi.ca/ch7h12

Société de gestion collective des droits des producteurs de phono-grammes et de vidéogrammes du Québec (SOPROQ)
atnmusi.ca/ch7h13

To recap, neighbouring rights are eligible only to the sound makers (the *Canadian Copyright Act* defines a sound maker as "the person by whom the arrangements necessary for the first fixation of the sounds are undertaken") and performers of the countries that signed the Rome Convention treaty. So, for example, a Canadian performer whose music is broadcast in England (a signatory country of the Rome Convention) is eligible to collect neighbouring rights. This works quid pro quo for an English performer whose music is broadcast in Canada.

However, if you are a Canadian whose music is broadcast in the United States (not a signatory country to the Rome Convention) you are not eligible for neighbouring rights and neither is an American performer or sound maker whose music is broadcast in Canada—or any other signatory country of the Rome Convention, for that matter!

By signing up to one of the collecting agencies previously mentioned, you are able to retroactively collect royalties due all the way back to 1998.

PRIVATE COPYING LEVY

In Canada there is a liability for manufactures of blank audio recording media to pay a levy to collecting agencies. *The Canadian Copyright Act* states:

> 82. (1) Every person who, for the purpose of trade, manufactures a blank audio recording medium in Canada or imports a blank audio recording medium into Canada
>
> (a) is liable, subject to subsection (2) and section 86, to pay a levy to the collecting body on selling or otherwise disposing of those blank audio recording media in Canada; and
>
> (b) shall, in accordance with subsection 83(8), keep statements of account of the activities referred to in paragraph (a), as well as of exports of those blank audio recording media, and shall furnish those statements to the collecting body. ...
>
> 84. As soon as practicable after receiving the levies paid to it, the collecting body shall distribute the levies to the collective societies representing eligible authors, eligible performers and eligible makers, in the proportions fixed by the Board. (Accessed at atnmusi.ca/ch7h14 on Nov. 6, 2013)

In Canada the money is collected by the Canadian Private Copying Collective and distributed through its member collectives. The money is paid to songwriters and publishers, as well as the performers and record labels. Consequently these monies are distributed as indicated below. (For an overview, see the Canadian Private Copying Collective website, atnmusi.ca/ch7h15)

Songwriters and music publishers: CMRRA, SOCAN and SODRAC (see URLs under "1. Reproduction" earlier in this chapter).

Recording artists and record labels:
Re:Sound—atnmusi.ca/ch7h16.

Private copying levies are collected in many countries, including the United States; I recommend looking into the laws and collection agencies relevant to your country of residence.

PUBLISHING

> "Music publishing is the owning and exploiting of songs in the form of musical copyrights." —Randall D. Wixen

As indicated at the start of this chapter, any serious musician is advised to do more research into publishing. Randall Wixen's *The Plain and Simple Guide to Music Publishing*, quoted from immediately above, is a good place to start if you are looking for a book dedicated to the topic.

The basic premise of having a publishing deal is that as a songwriter you assign part or all of your music copyrights to the publisher in exchange for the publisher exploiting the copyrights commercially. Traditionally the income generated is split 50:50 between publisher and songwriter, although there are different types of publishing agreements with different share splits, as noted further on regarding a single song, an exclusive songwriter, co-publishing, sub-publishing and administration.

The first source of income from music publishing, and before the advent of recordings, was the printing (at first by hand) and selling of sheet music. This is likely what you might first think of when you think of the term *publishing*. However, over time—like everything else about the music industry—it has evolved.

Before 1960 it was rarely the songwriter who popularized a song. The writers wrote the songs and the publishers plugged them to the performing or recording artists and they would be the ones to popularize them. After 1960, though, it became more and more common for artists to write and perform their own songs. With the publisher's traditional role no longer what it was, many writers who performed their own music started their own publishing companies. This allowed those writers more control and meant the share that they kept was proportional to their efforts. By hiring knowledgeable people and companies to run their publishing business, the artist/writer was able to make more money as they no longer were giving away all of the publisher share.

However, the 50:50 publisher and writer splits have never changed, in that a publisher can never claim more than 50 percent (the so-called "publisher share"). Songwriters with publishing companies sign up with their PROs as writers and sign up their publishing companies separately. Generally, unless directed otherwise by the share split in a work registration, a PRO pays out the 50-percent writer's royalties and the 50-percent publisher's royalties separately to the appropriate accounts.

The self-published songwriter ultimately receives 100 percent, but gets it via two payments on two separate statements. (Most PROs function on the 100-percent value system, but in the case of BMI in the United States, the system runs on a 200-percent value system made up of 100 percent of the writer's share and 100 percent of the publisher's share). This leads to some confusing mathematical equations, but it is the only way to understand and assign copyright splits. (See **Figure 7.2.**) Because it is the case that publishing is split 50:50 between writer and publisher, it is vitally important that you register your songs correctly with a PRO. As stated previously, a publisher can never collect more than 50 percent. Let's put it this way: if you don't register your songs properly, it's possible that you will lose money.

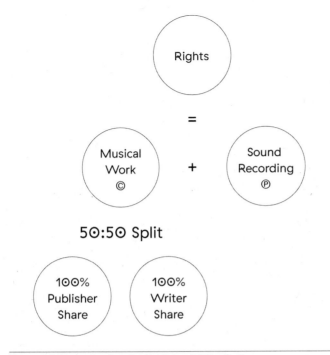

Figure 7.2 Understanding the Publisher / Writer Splits

SOCAN contacts its members for verifications and adjustments, when necessary, as probably many PROs do. However, it will always be the writer's and publisher's responsibility to monitor the various royalty accounts involved, check or review and verify statements, seek distribution queries when necessary and in general stay on top of the business accounting. These are all part of the rights management job. Once earnings begin to become regular and substantial, as one's career develops, it can be worth looking into hiring a rights administration service or accountant. A writer or publisher might also seek a co-publishing deal with a larger publisher that has more resources, knowledge and reach.

There is a lot of information available on the topic of music publishing and I recommend you look into your local sources. A good place to start is your PRO. When I have contacted my PRO with questions, it has been extremely helpful and provided a lot of answers and as well pointed me in the right direction to find more.

Songwriters and Singers

Good publishers have developed contacts with musicians, songwriters, labels, managers, movie directors, music supervisors and so on. They are experts at marketing and promoting songs as well as developing artists through co-writes, for example. They know both how to find out who needs a song and how to provide it to them. Some artists have all the connections and all the talent, and take on both the songwriter and publisher role themselves.

Nashville is a good example of a music centre that still has publishers pushing songs from their catalogue to recording artists. There are many established artists who simply do not write their own music and need songs to record. I doubt that will ever change. In fact, music mogul Clive Davis suggests that singers should not feel pressured to write their own songs and that they look for hits elsewhere. His reasoning is that no matter how many hits singers have written, or not as the case might be, it is about the next hit they record. When considering songs for a new album, why would an artist select anything but the best songs possible?

The greatest results come from a combination of talents—a great writer and a great performer (although sometimes they are one and the same).

Frank Sinatra, Billie Holiday, Ella Fitzgerald, Celine Dion, Barbra Streisand and Whitney Houston are examples of singers who haven't written the hits they are known for. Of course, other variations of talent pairing exist in songwriting—for example, since 1967 Elton John has maintained a writing relationship with Bernie Taupin. The two have collaborated on more than thirty albums and sold more than 250 million records, consequently becoming one of the most successful writing partnerships of all time (with John writing the music and Taupin the words).

Then there are the Milli Vanillis of the world, who it turns out neither wrote the songs nor performed them! Although not a unique situation,

Milli Vanilli just became the biggest scandal. The producer-created "fake/manufactured group/performer" model has had a long history in the popular music business, from the 1950s and '60s up to and including the present day. If you don't know who I am talking about, a quick search online will reveal all. In their case, the songwriters would still have collected the pertinent royalties.

The fact is that many of the greatest hits have been written by multiple songwriters with multiple publishers representing the copyrights. Understanding how copyrights are divided brings us to learning how to do the splits.

Co-Writing and Doing the Splits

Upon entering an agreement with a publisher, you (the songwriter) traditionally assign the publisher the copyright ownership of your musical work(s) in return for 50 percent of the potential earnings (the "writer's share").

Usually this is an equal 50:50 split of all money generated from publishing. Generally it doesn't matter who creates the business; whether the publisher finds the work or you do, the money is collected by the publisher and split 50:50 (variations on this can be negotiated, though, by knowledgeable parties when the contract is under consideration). The exception is performance royalties—the publisher collects only the publisher's share and the writer's PRO pays the writer their share separately. All other publishing revenue is collected by the publisher and distributed according to the terms set out in the publishing contract.

Traditionally the publisher, in return for part of the ownership in the copyrights, might pay an advance to the writer. The publisher then keeps 100 percent of all publishing royalties until the advance has been recouped. Once the advance has been recouped, all royalties moving forward are divided as per agreement (50:50, 80:20, or whatever the agreement may be). If we look at a publisher like a bank, you could see the advance as a mortgage loan except that when you pay off the loan the bank still owns half of your house! (This analogy might be even better suited to sound recordings and recording artist deals, only the label owns the whole "property" once it has recouped.) While negotiating the terms and conditions of a publishing deal, you can have reversion clauses for unexploited works after a period of time or a buyback of the contract for 125 percent of the outstanding unrecouped balance, and so on. Publishing will also be a part of modern multi-rights deals (sometimes called "360 deals") with labels and production companies, so artist-songwriters must be knowledgeable and have capable legal representation in any contract negotiations.

In today's new music industry most songwriters own and control their publishing, either by choice or by default. They register their songs with their PROs as both the songwriter and publisher, if they have a publisher membership account. Whether a songwriter is signed with a publishing company or is a self-publisher, the royalties are collected via two streams, songwriter and publisher as noted previously.

From this point onwards we need to address the 50:50 split as being an equal split between the publisher's share and the songwriter's share of the musical work (not the sound recording).

As we well know, a song can be written by multiple songwriters and represented by multiple publishers. In order to make sense of how the rights are split we need to address the 50-percent publisher's share of a song as 100 percent of the publisher's share and the 50-percent songwriter's share as 100 percent of the writer's share. That way, once we start dividing the publisher's share and writer's share with other writers and publishers on a co-written song, the splits on either side are out of 100.

As an example, let's say Oliver is a singer-songwriter with his own publishing company called Great Music Publishing (GMP). When he writes a song he registers it with his PRO. The writer's share is registered to his name and the publishing share is registered to GMP. **Figure 7.3** shows what that looks like.

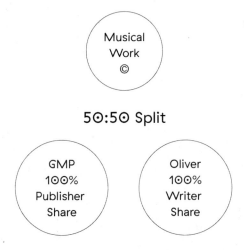

5☺:5☺ Split

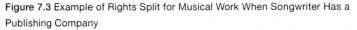

Figure 7.3 Example of Rights Split for Musical Work When Songwriter Has a Publishing Company

Let's say Oliver goes to Nashville and writes a song with Laura and they each have their own publisher. Oliver is still signed to Great Music Publishing (GMP) and Laura is signed to Awesome Songs Publishing (ASP). **Figure 7.4** shows what the song splits would look like.

It is generally considered in Nashville that the song splits are equal among all writers participating in a writing session. However, to avoid any future issues it is best to agree in writing how the writer splits are to be assigned at the conclusion of the writing session.

Entertainment lawyer Paul Sanderson describes in his book *Musicians and the Law in Canada* that "perhaps the best that can be said is that songs are protected, with the form of protection depending on the process leading to their creation." A song written by one songwriter would be subject to copyright as a musical work; a song written by two writers whose contributions are indivisible would qualify as a musical work of joint authorship; and a song written by a lyricist and a composer might possibly be the subject of two copyrights—one in the lyrics (a literary one), and one in the music (a musical work).

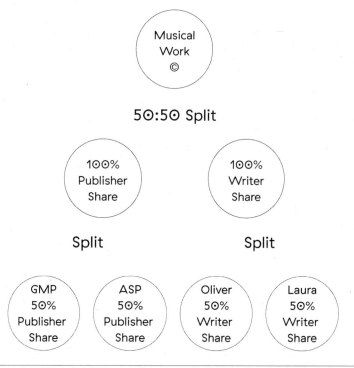

Figure 7.4 Example of Two-Way Splits for Publisher and Writer Shares of a Song

Terry O'Brien, education and outreach manager for the West Coast division of SOCAN, tells writers to analyze their writing process and how they get from nothing to something. He points out the importance of understanding the difference between composition and arrangement. Copyright should reflect creation!

One of the many benefits to co-writing a song is that both writers benefit from each other's publishing company pushing the song. The simple fact of co-writing the song can result in the other songwriter's publisher placing it, for example, on an album or in a movie or video game and you get to collect your share. If you are not signed to a publishing deal and you are your own publisher, the proactive marketing and song-plugging of the other writer's publisher makes the deal even sweeter!

Apart from the fact that you stand to benefit from any pushing that your co-writer's publisher does for your song, co-writing advances you as a songwriter by allowing you to improve your writing, expand your catalogue, build your network, learn new techniques and ultimately increase your chances of making money. Think about how this process multiplies when you write a song with more than one other writer ...

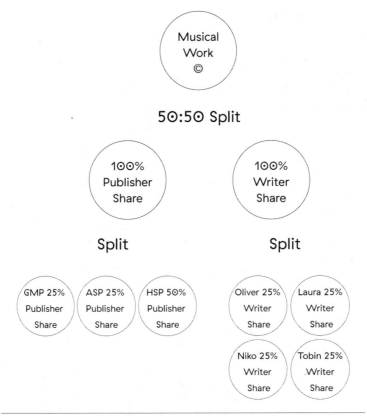

Figure 7.5 Example of Multi-Splits for Publisher and Writer Shares of a Song

Let's say Oliver writes a song with Laura, Niko and Tobin, and that for the sake of the example Niko and Tobin are both signed to Hook Sonic Publishing (HSP). **Figure 7.5** shows how the splits would look.

Billboard stated that songwriter The Dream made $15 million US from co-writing Rihanna's "Umbrella," and he wrote only a quarter of it! It is estimated that only 1 percent of the money came from the mechanicals of the six million album sales. This means that the other 99 percent came from other sources of publishing income. So having a great publisher and co-writing with successful writers can have very lucrative outcomes.

MEETING WRITERS

So how do you get to write with established songwriters? Like every other part of the business, you could find ways to build relationships with people who can introduce you to them.

The benefit of being signed to prominent publishers is that they will organize co-writes and often cover the expenses of travel and so on. (Keep in mind that writing with a hit writer these days may require travelling to Sweden!) Of course, if you are signed to a publishing deal, your advance will factor in these types of expenses (so at the end of the day you are paying to fly to Sweden).

There are of course many other ways to meet established songwriters. You can meet them at music schmoozes, especially those put on by PROs (SOCAN, ASCAP, etc.) and your local music industry associations.

You can look into workshops organized by PROs. Sign up with organizations like the Songwriters' Association of Canada (S.A.C.), Nashville Songwriters Association International (NSAI), International Songwriters Association (ISA), and/or the many others local to you, and attend their events.

Don't overlook social media. It's all about starting a conversation online and following up in person. If there are any writers you want to work with, see if they are active on social media and then find ways to start a conversation.

Now more than ever, there are many ways to make the online experience build into real-world lucrative business relationships. Using the different search tools available on the social media platforms (or using HootSuite to generate streams), you can find songwriters online as well as artists and record labels looking for songs. (See Chapter 5, "Social Media," for more ideas.)

These days, with the advent of Skype and Google Hangouts, there are a number of new ways to co-write songs. Still, there is something very special about being in the same room as another songwriter when creating music. Technology simply can't replace face-to-face, one-on-one time. So many nuances that are present when you're in the same room as another writer just don't translate through a computer screen.

Co-writing in person can be easier said than done. The majority of songwriters don't have the financial ability to get on a plane and meet with other songwriters around the world. For that reason, there are many grants available through local, national and international music associations that you should look into. At the time this book is being written, SOCAN has a house in Nashville and one in Los Angeles that members are able to stay in for free when doing writing sessions in these music centres. It tends to be a lack of initiative, not resources, that prevents artists from taking opportunities!

DEAL OR NO DEAL?

When I speak with songwriters about publishing, they either want to know how to get a publishing deal or if I think it is a good idea to set up their own publishing company. The answer is: pursue both, although it may be more a matter of when than if! SOCAN's Terry O'Brien tells writers that as their songwriting career develops, the job of a music publisher needs to be done (rights administration and exploitation or catalogue promotion), whether they have created a formal publishing entity or not. You need to learn as much as you can about what a publisher does before you create your publishing business (the first step is to do a name check with your PRO). However, eventually you may seek an established music publisher in order to move to the next level. Mike James, owner of Milk Music Co., emphasizes that the most important feature of a publisher is the contacts and resources they have (and you don't have) to collect all your nickels, including your Bulgarian mechanicals!

It should be a natural progression. Focus on the songwriting primarily because it really is all about the songs, then set yourself up as a publisher. Most publishers are not usually looking to develop potential, and are more interested in working with songwriters who already have the "goods." As Terry O'Brien puts it, "Every publisher will approach their writer/catalogue acquisition policy in their own way. Safe to say they all want 'hits,' however that might be defined these days!"

Great songs can make a lot of money for a lot of people. If you write great songs and get them the right exposure, people come to you. However, if your songwriting skills are not honed, it doesn't matter how many doors you knock on, no one's going to want to represent the material. You have to get the income started.

Learning about publishing hands-on is an important experience. You'd be amazed at how many songwriters with publishing deals don't know the difference between mechanical royalties and public performance royalties. This is concerning and it's yet another reason why it's important to do research into the process.

Like most deals in this industry, publishing deals come from publishers hearing about writers and artists through the industry grapevine. This can be through managers, labels, lawyers, friends, family, radio, songwriting competitions and so on. It is a combination of having great songs, knowing the right people and getting timely exposure.

It usually takes writing many fillers before you can write the hits, meeting a lot of people before you make the right connections, and getting your music heard by a lot of people before the right person hears it.

Going back to the ten-thousand-hour rule (see Chapter 1), with a little research you will find that almost all the greatest songs you can think of were written by songwriters at least ten years into their craft. The ones you've been told were "written in five minutes" usually had at least ten thousand practice hours in lead-up time! So the more you write, the better you get. The better the songs, the more valuable the assets you have. The more valuable the assets, the more people will come knocking on your door.

RELEVANT PUBLISHING DEALS

Co-Publishing

A co-publishing deal is typically the type of deal that a songwriter who has his or her own publishing company might enter into with an established third-party publishing company, such as a major publisher or large independent. In return for exploiting the writer's copyrights, the publishing company takes part ownership in the copyrights and becomes the administrator of the catalogue as well. Much like the situation with a traditional publishing agreement ("exclusive songwriter agreement"), the publisher will likely offer an advance upfront for a stake in the copyrights. A co-publishing deal is generally 75:25 in the writer's favour. The writer keeps 100 percent of the writer's share and 50 percent of the publisher's share—in other words, 75 percent of the rights to the musical work.

If Oliver was to write a song published by GMP and in a co-publishing deal with Humpty Dumpty Publishing (HDP), the splits would look like those in **Figure 7.6**.

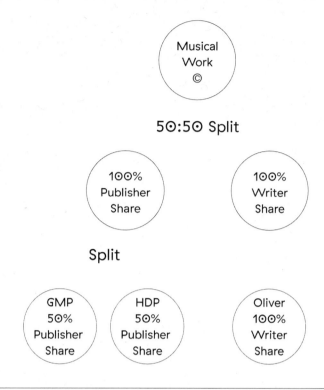

Figure 7.6 Example of Rights Split in a Co-Publishing Deal

Sub-Publishing

You may have all the savvy, connections and experience for music publishing in North America, but if you are trying to get into the Japanese market you will need to find a local publisher with established connections and local business savvy (not to mention the language and cultural skills) to represent your catalogue in that territory. The type of deal you would want to pursue in this case is called a "sub-publishing deal."

Sub-publishers are third parties representing publishing catalogues in foreign territories. Unlike publishing or co-publishing, sub-publishing deals are usually with an initial term of three years and renewed on a yearly basis after that. The split on the publisher's share ranges from 90:10 to 75:25, to your benefit. Sub-publishers do not generally share in ownership of copyrights and the terms of the agreement will stipulate what the sub-publisher can and cannot do without the publisher's permission.

By strategically obtaining sub-publishing deals in different territories of the world, you increase your international business opportunities and ability to collect publishing more efficiently in the countries within those territories. This doesn't mean that you should have a different sub-publisher in every country; it means that you should have sub-publishers that take care of specific regions of the world (encompassing multiple countries).

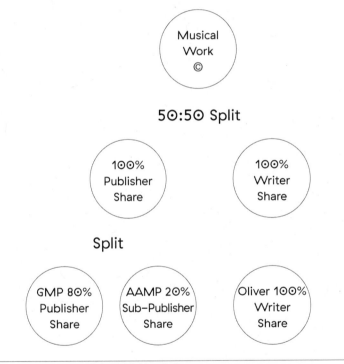

Figure 7.7 Example of Sub-Publishing Split

Continuing the earlier example of Oliver writing a song published by GMP, let's see what that would look like if Oliver has a sub-publishing deal with Awesome Australian Music Publishing (AAMP) and it generates publishing revenue—see **Figure 7.7**. Oliver's deal with AAMP is an 80:20 split, to the benefit of Oliver's publishing company, GMP.

Let's look at a similar example, only now it is with a song that Laura co-wrote with Oliver in Nashville. Oliver's publisher is GMP and Laura's publisher is ASP. The sub-publisher for GMP—AAMP—places the song in Australia. **Figure 7.8** shows what the splits would look like.

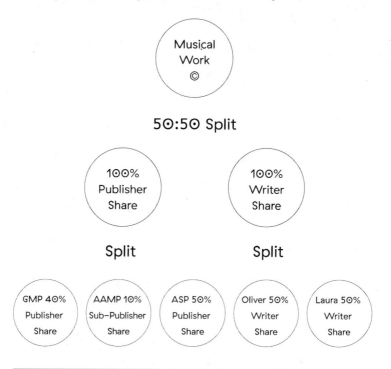

Figure 7.8 Example of Multi-Splits When One Sub-Publisher Places a Co-Written Song in Australia

Administration Deal

Another type of deal is an administration deal in which the day-to-day duties of administering the copyrights to your musical works are carried out by a third-party company.

Figure 7.9 Example of Splits on a Song with a Single Songwriter and a Publishing Administration Deal

Admin fees are generally 10 to 15 percent. All rights are retained by the songwriter and publisher and the duration of the deal is generally two or three years, with the option to renew. That is certainly a lot more appealing than sharing the ownership of your songs with a publisher for the life of the copyright. However, admin deals are generally what they sound like—mostly about administering licences, registering copyrights and carrying out the day-to-day duties of a publisher. This type of deal does not usually cover writer development, including organizing co-writes and so on. Some admin deals are a little more of a crossover, however. Kobalt Music Group is a good example of a company with admin publishing deals that offer some of the benefits that a traditional songwriting publishing deal offers (for more on their model, see their website, atnmusi.ca/ch7h17.

For an example of the splits in an admin deal situation, see **Figure 7.9**, which presupposes that Oliver's publisher, Great Music Publishing (GMP), has an admin deal with Uncle Rob Music (URM); Oliver has written a song and URM as the administrator takes care of publishing duties.

Now let's look at what happens when the song Oliver has written with Laura in Nashville generates income with URM administering Oliver's copyrights. Remember that Laura's publisher is Awesome Songs Publishing (ASP) and that she doesn't have an admin deal. **Figure 7.10** (opposite) shows how the splits would look.

This can be a great option if you have your own publisher, as it allows you to focus on your music while having the publishing duties taken care of by a third party. It goes without saying that it is only a "great option" if you cut a deal with a company that knows what it's doing. An admin deal is generally for a limited period of time, and you retain all your rights, so fortunately you are not risking as much as you are in a publishing deal or a co-publishing deal.

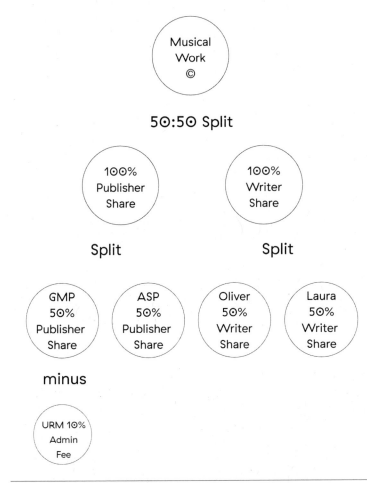

Figure 7.10 Example of Splits When Only One Party Has a Publishing Administrator on a Co-Written Song

Work for Hire

This type of deal is what it sounds like. You get hired as a songwriter for a publishing company or music library in return for a salary or fixed rate. The company that is hiring you will actually own 100 percent of the rights to the song's composition and legally does not have to acknowledge you as the songwriter or author of the work.

Work for hire is an American term; in Canada, the closest alternative is called *works made in the course of employment*. Unlike in the United States, where the writer does not have to be credited, a Canadian still retains the moral right to be credited as the author of the musical work. However, there is a lot more to it than that. For example, as defined under the *US Copyright Act*, media producers that hire a composer to create musical works for a motion picture as a "work for hire" are entitled to own all the soundtrack and score rights as if they were the author. That said, producers will often grant back to the composer the right to receive only the composer's share of back-end royalties. This is not the law, but rather part of the negotiations of the business deal. In Canada, composers pre-assign their performing rights exclusively to their PRO, which means that subsequently they cannot assign those same rights to a producer.

It is easy to assume that *work for hire* and *works made in the course of employment* are parallel terms, but there is much discussion as to the legal differences between the two. Many Canadian composers and songwriters are working with and for American companies and agreeing to the terms of their contracts. However, there are some major grey areas between the different laws that are worth looking into. Note, though, that I have not seen any film or TV score composed in Canada that qualifies as "Work made in the course of employment." Many songwriters and composers are happy to have the work and exposure and don't always look into their rights. Once again we have a conflict of laws, which gives yet another reason to look into what the laws are in your country.

"Work for hire" is fairly common in the TV, film, video game, jingles and audio-branding industry because it means that the songwriter is paid out and no longer part of future negotiations or royalty payments. Music libraries that pitch music to TV, film, video games and so on will hire songwriters and pay set rates per song or a salary in order to own the copyrights of the songs created. The libraries build their music catalogues for sync deals and collect on 100 percent of the copyrights. They may record the songs using in-house studios and consequently own the sound recordings too. This means they own 100 percent of the songs' copyrights and collect the publishing and the master sync. Libraries that don't own studios will often hire songwriters who are paid for each song and finished master, which the artist is required to produce. In today's industry, with all the available software, most composers have home studios and are able to produce finished tracks.

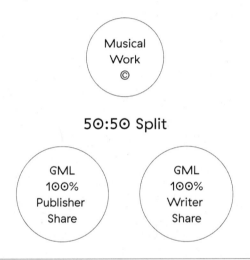

50:50 Split

Figure 7.11 Example of Splits of a Work-for-Hire Deal with a Music Library

Work for hire can be a way of making money, but in the long run you stand to lose the most. Keep this in mind before you agree to this type of work!

Let's imagine Oliver gets a call from Goose Music Library (GML), which wants him to write a song for which it will pay him a set fee in return for ownership of the song's copyrights. The deal Oliver has with GML is that of a work for hire and it would look like the scenario in **Figure 7.11**.

Meeting Publishers

So, assuming you have a catalogue of potential hit songs, how do you meet publishers and cut deals? A great way to connect with music publishers is to attend music conferences. Midem (Marché international du disque et de l'édition musicale) in France is an especially good one for connecting with international music industry folk. I have even heard about people from the same city ending up meeting and making deals in France. Whether you need a sub-publisher for Australia or a distributer for Germany, Midem is the place to make it happen. You set the meetings up ahead of time and go prepared accordingly. However, as mentioned in Chapter 4 ("Music PR"), some of the greatest connections are made in the hotel lobby bars after the day is done, so be ready for that too!

ADDITIONAL THOUGHTS

As discussed throughout this book, it is important to line up as many ducks as possible so as to have as much value as possible at your end of the deal. Never plead for a deal, but instead offer the publisher the opportunity to be a part of something exciting while you are still on the way up!

If you are not sure when to look for a publisher, keep in mind that if you are spending more time on the administration side of the music than the writing of it, it is probably time to look for a publisher. Ideally you want to focus on your innate talent to write music while somebody else with business talent can focus on making your songs generate income.

Copyrights are a songwriter's assets and building a large catalogue of musical works is in your best interest. Not everybody becomes a financially successful songwriter, but for those who do, it is generally due to just a few great songs rather than the entire catalogue. However, the success of a song differs depending on the format it is being promoted in; radio "hits" are not always usable in TV, film, video games and so on as they can take away from the action happening on screen. You will notice that songs used for this type of licensing can lack traditional radio song structures and even be fairly monotonous at times. What I am saying is that you can monetize your music catalogue by promoting different songs for different purposes. I recommend that you take your vocal songs and create instrumental-only versions as well as create edits of fifteen seconds, thirty seconds, sixty seconds and so on. You can creatively choose segments of the songs that can be pitched for the different licensing purposes. All of a sudden your twelve-song album can turn into ten more instrumental tracks and many more short edits with and without vocals.

Keep in mind that the reason why Sir Paul McCartney and John Lennon made so much more money than the other Beatles is that they wrote the songs. It's that simple. Publishing is a major part of a long-term career in music.

Enhance Your Publishing Income

Once you know where publishing income comes from, you can be proactive about generating more. The first thing to do is go and sign up with the pertinent collection agencies. Chances are you have some retroactive payments owed to you!

Controlled Composition Clause

This might seem unusual to add at this point, but a fundamental way to enhance your publishing income is to know your rights and ensure you are collecting what you are entitled to! Major American and Canadian record label contracts will often include a "controlled composition clause" in their agreements.

The controlled composition clause is used to lower the mechanical royalties they have to pay you. By agreeing to the clause, you will receive less than the legal statutory rate on every album or compilation the record label puts out now, and in the future. Quite often the clause states that you will be paid 50 percent of the statutory rate. This is only one reason why an entertainment lawyer should review your contracts. Even then it may be hard to negotiate that clause out of a deal. If you do agree to this clause, the least you can do is ensure that the amount is always kept relevant to the going statutory rate when the album is manufactured and not the going rate at the time of the first release.

Black Box

In some territories of the world, unclaimed royalties for a songwriter or publisher who is named but cannot be traced by a collection society go into what is called a "black box." These royalties are mostly mechanicals (and broadcast mechanicals) and neighbouring rights. Songtrust, a global royalty collection service, points out in its blog:

> Writers who are owed royalties but cannot be found are often referred to as "lost" writers. Many US songwriters who sell their music internationally, but are not signed to a publishing company with representation abroad, often become "lost" writers and lose their mechanical royalties. (Accessed at atnmusi.ca/ch7h18 on Nov. 9, 2013)

(Keep in mind that as the United States does not have a neighbouring rights regime, the US songwriters just mentioned would not be eligible for the corresponding royalties, just the mechanicals.)

Once a given amount of time has elapsed—and this time differs from country to country—the money in the black box is distributed to the PROs, which in turn pass that money on to the publishers, who then pay the songwriters. In Europe, PROs are both reproduction rights agencies and performing rights organizations (GEMA in Germany is an example).

The first thing you can do is ensure that your PRO has an affiliate agreement with a local PRO in the countries where your music is distributed and being played. Your PRO collects your foreign royalties for you. For example, SOCAN collects black box money, then distributes it to its members after a set amount of time. SOCAN's Terry O'Brien explains that if SOCAN receives money from a foreign territory that doesn't correlate to one of its member's works, then usually the money (over $50) is returned to the originating PRO (after SOCAN has done research and contacted the member to see if the work is theirs and just wasn't registered, for instance).

TV and radio black box royalties are released after three years, and those for live performances after one year.

Signing a deal with a sub-publisher in the foreign territories where your music is playing can be a smart move. By representing your catalogue, the sub-publisher is able to collect royalties on your behalf. Depending on your clout as an artist, you can also ask the sub-publishers to give you a percentage of the black box money that they receive.

YouTube

With over a trillion users on YouTube, you have a huge audience to tap into. By generating traffic and monetizing views of your original song videos, you can collect not only advertising revenue but also royalties. You can monetize the videos of fans playing covers of your songs or using your original compositions as background music to their videos. Why not set up a contest for fans to record a cover version of your latest single and post it on YouTube?

You need to set up your YouTube account to monetize your own videos, as well as use the available tools to find other people's videos using your compositions and monetize them. There are multiple ways to collect revenue from YouTube as well as ensure your content is identified properly—here are a few:

Audiam
atnmusi.ca/ch7h19

RightsFlow
atnmusi.ca/ch7h20

TuneSat (digital fingerprinting)
atnmusi.ca/ch7h21

YouTube content identification application
atnmusi.ca/ch7h22

YouTube partner program
atnmusi.ca/ch7h23

One way to ensure your videos come up in searches and get the most plays is to make sure they are tagged properly. Here is a great tool to help you create relevant tags:

YouTube Keyword Tool
atnmusi.ca/ch7h24

Live Concerts

In the case of performances in places such as bars, nightclubs, coffee shops, and basically any business whose main operation is something other than presenting music concerts (e.g., serving booze or coffee), PROs generally set a minimum ticket price to be in place before you can earn live concert performance royalties of your original music.

At the time of writing this, the minimum ticket price in order for SOCAN to pay you for these types of performances (Tariff 3A) is $6 or more.

The $6 requirement does not apply to Tariff 4-type music events — that is, where the main purpose of the event is solely presenting live music, such as a concert or music festival.

So make sure you agree with the booker, agent or promoter that your ticket cost be at least $6 at the gigs that require that minimum ticket price!

There is a special form to complete for your PRO — at SOCAN it's a Notification of Live Music Performance Form (NLMP). SOCAN members have up to a year after a gig to submit their live-performance form, including documentation, such as an e-flyer, contract and/or poster, and their set list.

BMI, ASCAP and SESAC have only just recently, in the last year or two, started paying for smaller performances. Before that they paid only on the two hundred (BMI) or three hundred (ASCAP) top-grossing concerts of the year (other than serious, a.k.a. classical, music).

Once again, as you can see, the rules can vary, so be sure to verify the procedure and requirements with your local PRO.

Radio

Find out how your PRO logs radio stations. If need be, ask for the radio playlist when you perform live on a show. Send it in to your PRO. This can both help ensure you get paid royalties and put you on the radar.

SOCAN logs the radio stations, so if a recording of your song is played or a live performance takes place, it will be logged according to the method and pool that the radio station belongs to (DAI, survey or CBC).

While this is not technically publishing income, make sure you are signed up with SoundExchange for performances of your sound recordings on US satellite radio or internet radio stations. If you are wondering where to direct your efforts for satellite and online radio, here is a list of services that SoundExchange collects from:

Who Pays SoundExchange?
atnmusi.ca/ch7h25

Also, don't forget about neighbouring rights. As we discussed earlier in this chapter. Re:Sound in Canada collect these royalties on behalf of the performers and makers of sound; they are then distributed to the artists via ACTRA, MROC and ARTISTI, and to the labels via AVLA and

SOPROQ. If you are not signed up with one of these agencies, you won't be able to collect these royalties.

Be Friendly, Be Professional

It makes a big difference to be somebody who is professional and easy to deal with. People like to help out people they like. Psychologists talk about the rule of reciprocity—the idea that we are all bound, even driven, to return all kinds of debts. If someone says great things about you, it's likely you will have good things to say about them. Applying the rule of reciprocity to your career, get to know your publishers, get to know their staff and be friendly—ultimately, help make their jobs easier and when the time comes they'll be sure to help you!

ADDITIONAL RESOURCES

Canadian Copyright Act
atnmusi.ca/ch7h26

Canadian Intellectual Property Office
atnmusi.ca/ch7h27

Glossary of music publishing terms
atnmusi.ca/ch7h28

List of international copyright collection agencies
atnmusi.ca/ch7h29

Mechanical Licensing and Other Mysteries
atnmusi.ca/ch7h30

Songtrust
atnmusi.ca/ch7h31

US copyright law
atnmusi.ca/ch7h32

United States Copyright Office
atnmusi.ca/ch7h33

CHAPTER EIGHT

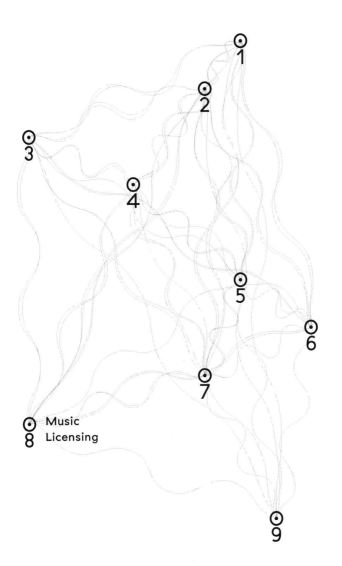

8 Music
Licensing

Music Licensing

Have you ever become a fan of artists after hearing their music on a movie, TV show, commercial or video game? Do you want to place your music, expand your fan base and get paid for it?

When it comes to discovering and breaking new artists, many people regard music supervisors ("music sups" or "supers") for specific types of shows as the new A&Rs in today's music industry. (A&R, of course, stands for Artist & Repertoire and has traditionally referred to the people who find and develop talent for labels.) Having your music licensed can not only benefit your wallet and your fan base, but can help with getting tour opportunities, radio play, publishing and distribution deals, endorsement deals, and so on.

It is no secret that some shows serve as a music industry barometer, and if you want to get your music on these shows you're going to need to know how the world of music licensing works. (Of course, defunct bands are used on many occasions in order to create the right vibe and it is not always about showcasing new artists.)

This chapter aims to help you (1) find out about projects that need new music, (2) know how to approach and connect with music supervisors, and (3) go over real examples of licensing briefs. When you have finished reading the chapter, I highly recommend that you dig deeper and educate yourselves further on music licensing by making use of all the other resources available, including the websites I recommend at the end of the chapter.

THE LINGO

What follows is an explanation of some of the publishing terminology pertinent to the music licensing world (which by and large picks up where Chapter 7, "Music Copyrights & Publishing," left off).

1. Music licensing

For the most part, the term *music licensing* means that the owner of a song gives permission for part or all of a song to be used in or on a TV show, film, ad, video game, website, greeting card, ringtone, YouTube video, corporate presentation, trailer or suchlike. The process involves clearing rights to use a musical work that either already exists or will be written and recorded for the opportunity at hand!

2. Master licence

A master licence grants the licensee the right to use a master recording with a locked moving image or other audiovisual work. This right is issued by the owner of the master. As discussed in Chapter 7, this used to be the record label, but now it is essentially whoever owns the sound recording—often the person or entity that paid for it.

3. Sync (synchronization) licence

A sync licence grants the right to use a composition locked with a moving image or other audiovisual work. It is issued by the holder of the copyright to the musical work. As we have seen in Chapter 7, this historically has been the publisher, although these days independent songwriters are often self-published.

4. Mechanical licence

In case you skipped Chapter 7 ... a mechanical right is the right to reproduce a song in a physical format as on a CD, or in a digital format via download. In the United States, the mechanical right is subject to a compulsory licence. This means that you can record a cover of any existing song and put it on your CD, and the copyright holders to the song (historically the publishers) can't do anything about it as long as you pay them as provided under the statute. You would need to ask the copyright holder for permission if the song either had never been recorded before or was recorded but not officially released. We will not be dealing with these types of licences in this chapter. A mechanical licence is needed, however, for a song to be placed on a soundtrack album or compilation. For more on mechanicals please refer back to Chapter 7.

Master licence vs. sync licence

Licensing music requires clearing the master rights and the publishing rights to a pre-recorded piece of music. It is commonly referred to as clearing the "two sides." A master licence encompasses the recorded material and the sync licence covers the musical work (also known as the song composition). A master licence is issued by the owner of the master recording—this could be the record label or the performing artist, songwriter or whoever has paid for the recording. The master licensor grants the right to use the sound from the original recording. A sync licence is issued by the music publisher or self-published songwriter and gives the person or company requesting a licence the right to record a song for use in sync with the visual project. Whoever controls each component of the song is the party that issues the appropriate licence.

As you can imagine, when an independent artist controls "both sides" (the master and the rights to the musical work), the process of licensing the music can be much faster. This is what we call a "one-stop shop." Between the quick processing and the lower licensing costs, independent artists' music is a first choice for many music supervisors—not to mention that music supervisors enjoy the role of discovering and breaking new artists!

The fees you negotiate are for the use of your master and its composition in synchronization with a locked moving image or other audiovisual work. In other words, it is the use of a specific piece of your music (often just a short segment) at a specific moment in the TV show, movie, video game, advertising, technology, new media ... The sound and image are integrated. If your music was to be used in another section of the audiovisual work, then a new licence would be required.

Here's a link to what the American Society of Composers, Authors and Publishers (ASCAP) has to say about music licensing:

American Society of Composers, Authors and Publishers (ASCAP)
atnmusi.ca/ch8h1

THE PLAYERS

Music supervisors are the focus of this chapter, but the fact is that they are not the only people who deal with musical needs. The people you need to approach will differ depending on where you are trying to license your music (e.g., TV, film, ads, videos games). The following people deal with the music on projects—these are the players you need to know:

Production companies, trailer houses, TV networks
- Music director
- Music producer
- In-house music supervisor
- Freelance music supervisor

Movies
Music supervisors are generally your target, but in indie films directors often play a major role in the music selection due to budget constraints. These directors are always looking for musicians who can help them out. The hope is that when they move up in the world, they will take you with them! I have a friend who went from scoring an indie movie for free to scoring a Kevin Spacey movie with the same director. You can meet these directors at film schools, film festivals and so on.

Advertising agencies
- Ad agency music producer
- Freelance music producer
- Music supervisor

There will be times when someone like an art director, agency producer or film editor influences the music that gets used. Editors are always the first to put music to images and create temp tracks; sometimes these tracks are kept.

Video games
- Music director
- Music supervisor

THE MUSIC SUPS SAY ...

Immediately below and sprinkled through the rest of this chapter are excerpts from interviews I have conducted with music supervisors to give you the information right from the source. The complete interviews are online at atnmusi.ca/ch8h2

Michael Perlmutter

Music Supervisor: *Bliss, Degrassi, Queer as Folk,*
Canada's Next Top Model ...

Aaron Bethune:
In your own words, what is licensing and what is its process?

Michael Perlmutter:
When a music supervisor licenses a song, there are two rights: there is a master recording right and there's a publishing right—most of the time called the "sync" right. So, we're synchronizing your song to picture, whether it's film, TV, commercial, video game or documentary. The owners of certain rights may be different people. If you're an independent artist—you wrote all the songs yourself, recorded the songs, and paid for it yourself—you own the master recording and the sync rights. So, if I'd like to license a song, I ask the artist: Do you own the master recording?—"Yes I own the master recording; I made this record by myself." Did you write the songs?—"Yes, I own the song, I wrote it so I'm the writer and I own the publishing." Then, I send you a one-page "deal memo" that states we're going to use this song in a scene, it's going to be for the world, it's going to be on a TV show, it plays for about a minute, and the scene is in a bar, and we're going to give you $1,000. For a TV show, that would include all TV media (all cable, pay, video-on-demand, any specialty TV, a bus, on a train, on a plane), non-theatrical, which means hotel rooms and educational videos and all that kind of stuff, and also DVD and internet downloads. The only money the artist gets upfront is the $1,000. The artist decides whether he wants to do it, hopefully he says yes, we send the artist a deal memo with all these points on it, he signs and gives it back to us. Subsequently, we create two contracts, one for the master and one for the publishing. It's a fairly standard three- or four-page contract,

which has all those rights with some legalese in there. Then you sign that, and we pay you. That's basically a licensing deal.

Alex Hackford
Music Supervisor: Sony PlayStation

Aaron Bethune:
How can licensing a song in a game affect a band—why is it so important?

Alex Hackford:
The fact that today labels are signing less and less content, based on records selling less and less, you have to be able to diversify your portfolio as a band, and from a band management perspective, the ability to be able to put a song in a game is huge.

With PlayStation's Major League Baseball game, I take at least one band per year that has no publisher, no label, no booking agent, no nothing, and put it in that game. It's a game that's only released in the US and Canada, so it's a local litmus test, a focus test. The best way to do a focus test is to restrict the territory so you're able to get a real sense of the effect that you are having. Baseball has a very distinct fan-gradient, and obviously the soundtrack somewhat reflects that.

Having your song in a video game is just one tiny piece of a much larger structural puzzle, a strategic game plan of how to get your message heard by the right types of people. When I've put a band in a game, we've seen their touring radius broaden, they get radio ads, record deals ... it's been a visually quantifiable effect.

I like to think I'm choosing awesome bands, but the other part of it is the climate over the past fifteen years has become DIY—both from recording, mixing and mastering a record to marketing it, getting it to the right types of people and creating a business. I work with bands that have that DIY attitude, as opposed to sitting back and saying, "Make this happen for me."

GETTING READY

After Chapter 7, it goes without saying that before you start trying to license your music make sure you are signed up with a performing rights organization (PRO). If you haven't already, take the time now to educate yourself on the different organizations available to you and what they have to offer. (If you skipped Chapter 7, I recommend going back and reading it! You need to be able to collect public performance royalties from licensing your music, performing live, having your music on the radio, and so on.)

Performing Rights Organizations
atnmusi.ca/ch8h3

I suggest that you have in place a website, your social media platforms, tour dates, merchandise and so on before you try to license your music. You want to maximize the beneficial results that music licensing can have on all aspects of your career.

Music licensing should be a part of your marketing strategy. It can help promote your next single, build a fan base, secure tour dates, build your story for radio and so on. So before you start sending out your music, make sure it is part of a plan.

A lot of music supervisors like placing music before it is released, so keep that in mind when it comes to building a timeline.

THE MUSIC SUPS SAY ...

Once you are set up and ready to reap the benefits of music licensing, the next thing is to start finding places and opportunities to license your music. Keep in mind it may be that your music is more suited to one medium than another. But first, the question is, are there any differences between licensing to TV, film, ads, video games, and so on? The following are the opinions of my good friends, the music supervisors.

Stacey Horricks

Music Supervisor: *The Bang Bang Club*, *Textuality*, Corona …

Aaron Bethune:
What would be the biggest difference between TV commercials, TV shows, movies, video games, etc.?

Stacey Horricks:
If I were to break it down, there are different styles that really appeal to different mediums. Ads usually require a definite hook, something to grab attention sonically in addition to the visuals. And with thirty seconds to do so, everything needs to happen fast.

With film and TV, you have much more freedom. Placements are longer, often mixed differently and not really genre-specific. I remember back in 2009 we had a month straight of death metal requests and it wasn't just for one TV show.

With games, I've noticed that pace is really important—there needs to be a momentum when it comes to music in games. Games, as visually stunning as they are, face the big problem that they can't use live actors in their projects, so the music has to be a little bit more dramatic to compensate for the lack of emotion they're unable to bring to their animated characters. Energy is so important to game developers. A driving rock song—yes. A meandering singer-songwriter ballad—not so much. The exciting news is that things are drastically changing in the video game world, and it won't be too long before games will require the same music you see in film. In fact, you're already seeing this with Red Dead Redemption, Braid and LA Noir.

AB:
Which mediums gain the most exposure for bands?

SH:
That's a tough question. I would probably side with ads and promotional trailers, just because of the circulation. You see the spot and hear the song maybe five times a week. A film— you might only see

it once; same goes with a television episode (unless it's the show's theme song).

AB:
How do you give economic value to songs that are being placed in these different mediums?

SH:
Songs in ads should always be paid the highest. You're selling a brand, not someone's personal story or expression. As for video games, I view them as art and believe they should be on the same scale system as film and TV. Large-budget games should pay more than the indie games.

David Hnatiuk
Music Supervisor: NBC Sports, Harley-Davidson, Fox News Channel ...

Aaron Bethune:
Are there any differences that stand out for supervising for film, TV, advertising and new media?

David Hnatiuk:
Yes and no. Let's compare breaking news and scripted content. Breaking news is reality. Scripted TV is make-believe, even though it's sometimes based on true events. What's the difference music-supervising a natural disaster in reality—such as an earthquake in Indonesia, for instance—versus music-supervising the same type of tragedy, but in scripted format? What's the difference? Well, in the scripted format, you're driving a storyline, that is guided by a director and a team of writers and producers. But if you're dealing with a tragedy like an earthquake, even in a scripted format, I would say most times it's going to be considered very serious. You're going to have to music-supervise the reality of the situation even in the scripted way. You're most likely going to have original score pieces to fill in gaps where commercial music isn't appropriate. The score pieces are often going to be representative of the tone of the moment, and the moments leading up to

the natural disaster: the human drama of the event, the tension, the hysteria ...

But then you're also going to have source music, which will most likely be commercially released music. For instance, you've got the family driving down the street in their station wagon unaware of any danger. What are they listening to on the radio before the earthquake starts? And then you've got the crew of locals hanging at the local corner sports bar—they're all watching the game and there's music on the TV they're watching, and there's music in the background from the jukebox. Then you cut out of the bar scene, and you'd do an aerial wide shot of a fault line beginning to flex, then your score comes back in to re-establish dramatic tension. So you've got a bunch of different pieces of music and musical inspiration to tell the story of this earthquake, a natural disaster.

Now in a breaking news environment, the difference is that you're actually documenting something that's happening in real time. There's no need for any commercial music anywhere. You're not going to license "Another One Bites the Dust" by Queen for a real earthquake in California, or anywhere for that matter. You'd be fired instantly, and probably have death threats from the general public. So you're going to go more along the lines of score—possibly pounding authoritative drums with a sense of urgency or emergency, some strings to build a feeling of importance, and even some tension if you will, but nothing insulting or disrespectful to those suffering from the tragedy. There's a fine line to ride there.

When you're dealing with reality, you're dealing with human lives and the politics of whoever it is you are working for, whereas in scripted content, you have a little bit more freedom because people know it's not reality.

Sarah Gavigan
Music Supervisor: Adidas, Nike, Old Navy, Hummer, Microsoft ...

Aaron Bethune:
What are some of the differences in licensing between different media—for example, TV and film versus commercials?

Sarah Gavigan:
One big difference in ads is they don't want anything polarizing. This is why you don't often hear much pop music in ads. Take the show *Entourage*: you would never hear any music from that show on an ad. You can take more creative licence in TV shows, especially cable shows. For song structure, it's the thirty seconds of an ad versus the full song at the opening credits of a show. The thirty-second format is universal for ads, and the format for TV shows and films is flexible.

Greg Debonne
Music Supervisor: MTV, VH1, Bravo, Spike, A&E ...

Aaron Bethune:
Is there any difference in the musical needs for reality–based TV shows to, say, film or TV sitcoms?

Greg Debonne:
Oh yeah, and on a number of levels too. First of all, you have to understand that you are working with different sets of production values depending on the level of programming. If you're comparing a major-network prime-time drama with really good production value to a reality-TV series, there are certain things you can get away with in programming that has higher production values that you cannot get away with in shows with lower production values—that is, reality programming. For example, if you watch reality shows, you will notice that with the field audio there is a lot of extraneous noise. When it comes to the post-audio mix, they try and rectify the problem; they try to fix these problems, ameliorate them, but it's still a lower production value.

So, if you're working on a motion picture or a major-network prime-time drama with good production values, you could have a sound recording, a piece of music in there with drums and vocals, but because you're dealing with better production values and more ability to have separation of elements, there is more time and wherewithal to get it right as applied to picture and the goal of complementing the scene. You can have a piece of music along those lines that nonetheless doesn't conflict with the content.

But in a reality program, to give a prime example, there will be pieces of music whereby the arrangement and orchestration have to be a little more minimal, particularly with regard to rhythmic phrasing, so as not to step on the content because the production values are cheaper. For example, if there are drums—which tend to eat up a lot of mid-range, and dialogue also is in the mid-range because that's where it tends to sit—the dialogue audio can be so shoddy in reality programming that there are going to be a lot of times when you can't exactly have too obtrusive of a snare, otherwise it's going to step on the content. You need all the mid-range you can get for your dialogue because of the bad audio on tape, so you're often working within a tighter set of parameters as to what you can get away with applying to the scene in a musical sense and still have that music complement the content as opposed to compromise it. There's just a certain set of criteria with respect to what's going to work well on a program with cheaper production values, that's all.

Ever notice how when you watch a film, and there are two people sitting in the car and they're talking and there's a song on the radio, somehow the song is complementing the scene and it's not stepping on the dialogue? Well, in reality programming you most often couldn't get away with that. Why? It's the production value with which you're dealing.

Michael Perlmutter

Aaron Bethune:
Is there any difference between film and TV?

Michael Perlmutter:
There is a big difference, absolutely. The main difference is the time frame. TV is weekly, so it's like working on a mini-film every week. When we worked for five years on *Queer as Folk*, it always felt like we were working on it year in and year out—mind you there's a little bit of break between each season, but an extraordinary amount of paperwork all year round. It was a very intensive music show, and we had eighteen to twenty-three episodes a year and each show had ten to twelve songs in it. Every week

we were supervising a "film." We would give the editors tons of music to work with and, luckily, we had a really great budget with Showtime and the producers, Temple Street—we could use almost any song we wanted to. But with that kind of workload, and song choice, and negotiation every two weeks, it was insane. With some of these songs, you have to deal with three publishers or record labels. You've got to make sure everyone's happy and within budget. So over five years, we used a thousand songs, and spent seven million bucks. *Degrassi* is similar, yet uses mainly independent songs. They made forty-six episodes this past season, and sometimes it was two episodes every ten days. Once you get into the routine, it doesn't feel like a lot, but from the outside, people think you're nuts.

With a film, you might have twelve months. I worked on a hip-hop film called [*You Got Served :*] *Beat the World* that was just finished, locked, delivered in December 2010. We began in March 2009. It was a good eighteen to twenty months of work. Interestingly enough, budgets changed, and when the budgets changed some of our choices had to change. So we were down to the wire in the last couple of weeks before the mix, choosing a couple of songs as replacements. We produced a few original recordings—K'naan was featured on one with KRS-One—but that was all done in the last few months. You've got time to be creative, and you can change your mind a little bit if you need to, or come up with new ideas, but for the most part TV is just a treadmill, and it doesn't stop for six to seven months at all.

THE VALUE OF MUSIC

The value of music has really never changed—it is how we experience it and how we pay for those experiences that have seen changes over the years. Music enhances the overall experience that goes with viewing moving pictures.

THE MUSIC SUPS SAY

Music licensing is one of the most lucrative areas of the music industry. However, how does a music supervisor value your music in dollars? No matter what, not all music can have the same value, right? Is there a way to add value to your music?

The monetary value assigned to each piece of music will vary based on a number of components. Let's ask the music supervisors:

David Hnatiuk

Aaron Bethune:
How do you value music?

David Hnatiuk:
Basically, the easiest way to do that is the traditional way, which in my opinion is based on exposure or outreach, and record sales. I put value in artists by how many friends they have on MySpace, how many views they have on YouTube, how many followers they have on Twitter, and how many downloads or song sales they had this past year. A great way to value music is on the success of the artist. If the artist has limited outreach, limited success, well, it's very hard to pose an argument for the financial worth of that music. Sure, if you're comparing Pearl Jam to Led Zeppelin, for instance— well, they're two very successful bands there. But if you look at their history, it could be argued that the value of Led Zeppelin is far greater because they have been around for longer and throughout the stance of their career, they sold more units. That makes Led Zeppelin more valuable. Now you throw in a recently successful major-label rock band—let's say, Kings of Leon. As well as they've done as of late, their catalogue is not yet as valuable as Pearl Jam's is, and clearly not as valuable as Led Zeppelin, therefore you price them accordingly when comparing them to those bands that have had more success over a longer period of time.

I look at it from the perspective of units sold and public outreach. Outreach is something we are able to measure more effectively than ever right now because of MySpace, YouTube, Facebook and Twitter. You can measure the marketing and promotional success of any band or artist through social-networking sites. These things are right there for you to measure. Finding out how many song sales there are in that year ... all that information is out there.

For me, that's how I start, as far as valuing music, bands and writers … their actual success, and of course, the obvious — is it good? Is it produced well? Is it written well? Is it a good arrangement? Is the singer in key? Are the musicians qualified, do they execute their performances well? Is it a good melody? Is it a catchy melody? All those basic measurements of quality of music add to the value as well.

Michael Perlmutter

Aaron Bethune:
How do you give value to music?

Michael Perlmutter:
That's an excellent question. There is an idea that the value is not necessarily a dollar figure but a marketing tool and long-run benefit. We could say you'll get a lot of exposure — and the old adage is, "you could die of exposure." But, you know what? Not necessarily in this day and age. There is so much competition. I try to make the best argument that I can, but if it is going in a show, and if nobody's ever heard of you, then the value is that people are going to hear your music. If an artist doesn't want to take $500, there is another artist who will say yes.

We all think there's only one song for a scene and I would agree in a lot of cases. We've had to replace songs because we weren't able to strike deals, and it's sometimes better in the eyes of the producer or myself.

AB:
Do you take into consideration more than just the music?

MP:
One concern I would have is that I wouldn't necessarily put an eighty-two-year-old artist in a youth show. We'd like the youth who are watching a show like *Degrassi* to connect with the artists. I mean, yes, if it's an old Frank Sinatra tune and it is really cool, then yes, but it doesn't happen very often; we're not using a lot of speed metal on *Degrassi*.

Our concern is: Does it feel right? Is it lyrically good? Is it good production? Does it say something? Does it have a heart? A lot of "feel" goes on with respect to how we choose tunes, as opposed to if the artist has sold records or not.

Kyle Merkley

Music Supervisor: *From Spain With Love*; Music Co-ordinator: *Flashpoint, The Listener, Bomb Girls* ...

Aaron Bethune:
How do you give music a monetary value?

Kyle Merkley:
Part of that comes with the clout the artist is bringing with them, which is why so much of our business is based on finding sound-alike indie replacements. For example, a producer ideally might want to have ... Arcade Fire, but the money to license them is not available in the music budget. That's when we would come in and say, "There's this really cool artist that hasn't broken yet, that really sounds like Arcade Fire, and we can get them for $1,000 to $2,000." The way we operate is much more about finding what would work for the money we have versus trying to determine what something is worth.

Alex Hackford

Aaron Bethune:
When it comes to budgets, how do you value music?

Alex Hackford:
It's relative. There is definitely perceived rates within games at this point, just as with film and TV, which have been around for a lot longer than video games have. There is a perceived value to songs in games and if we're talking about licensing as opposed to paying for original content, I generally value licensees based on a band's

cultural cache and relevance at the time, as well as record sales and things like that, and make my assessments from there.

The argument I always come up against is: profit-and-loss issue. When the bean-counters here are looking at my balance sheet and saying, "Is this song going to sell more copies of the game or not?" that's unquantifiable unless it's a music-based game like SingStar, Guitar Hero or Rock Band, where the game couldn't exist without the music. If it's a first-person shooter, or an action game, or a sports game, it's a hard question to answer.

I try to keep my reach within a certain field and obviously want to be able to justify it by the band's current marketplace value. If the band is writing original music for the game, and we're going to own it, which is generally how we do these things, then the rates are significantly higher because the band or label or both are giving up percentages of the copyright.

At PlayStation, we have a pretty significant catalogue of original music that we have amassed over the years. Everything from 8-bit to 16-bit music and full orchestral scores—by people like Jim Dooley—as well as songs by people like Rakim and a bunch of other big bands.

HOW TO SUBMIT MUSIC

Make sure you do your research before sending music to a music supervisor. You need to know you are sending it to the right person and that they accept unsolicited music. You might want to write first and ask if they are accepting new music and how you should send it. My experience is that it can really vary person to person—one music sup might want an MP3 in an email attachment, another might want a link so as to stream the music, and another might want a physical album with the artwork … The more you know the more likely you are going to get their attention.

THE MUSIC SUPS SAY ...

Here are a few opinions from the music supervisors:

Greg Debonne

Aaron Bethune:
What is the best way to submit music—CDs, MP3s, links, etc.?

Greg Debonne:
It really depends on the music supervisor. I know people who don't
want CDs. They don't want clutter. They would prefer to have it
sent as a YouSendIt [now called Hightail] folder, and so on and so
forth. I also know other people that only want to accept music on
CDs. It really varies. One thing you should find out from the music
super is what format they prefer to have it sent in . Because if
some potential licensors solicit me, I will tell them how I prefer it
be sent. Not on a prima donna level or anything, but rather, "Hey,
can you send a CD and make sure they're AIFF [audio interchange
file format] source files at 48k [kilohertz] because that's broadcast standard? And can you send me a disc because it acts as a
physical reminder of your music."

Sometimes ... it will be, "Well, we don't really want to do that"
because maybe they're too cheap to pay for postage—I have no
idea. They might insist on sending it to me online via a YouSendIt
folder, which is fine if the particular music is applicable to the project I'm doing at that time. If it's not, I may listen to it, I may like it,
I may save it to one of my drives with all the best intentions of getting back to it. However, because it's not in a physical format, I may
forget all about it. I may forget that I stashed it on my drive. That's
why, personally, I really do like to receive either a custom drive or
a disc of some kind—something physical, tangible—although not
every music supervisor feels the same way.

Regardless of whether it's sent on a disc or a drive, I prefer high-
quality files, source files. Anyone can up-convert an MP3 to an
AIFF in iTunes, but then you're degrading the file. For example, TV
broadcast standard is AIFF at 48k. Those are large files. By the

274   MUSICPRENEUR

way, a CD-quality audio file is AIFF at 44.1k. I always prefer licensors to send me broadcast-standard AIFF at 48k, or even WAV at 48k. If they send me CD-quality—meaning it's at 44.1, where I have to up-convert—that's okay, no big deal, but it is nice to receive an already broadcast-standard source file from the licensor. I do know of a couple of production companies whereby, for whatever reason, the music supers there want MP3s. MP3s are fine for previewing, but they're a compressed file format that's going to be applied to programming that gets even more compressed for air. Either send me a drive, or a DVD-R or CD-R. The more material you're sending me, the more advantageous it is to receive it on a drive. If it's a relatively smaller cache of music that will fit on a DVD-R or two, well, then it's okay and fine to send me a disc. Again, I like the physical reminder.

AB:
What catches your attention when you receive a new submission?

GB:
As much as I want to be a purist who doesn't really care what the presentation is like provided the music is right, because ultimately I don't care, I must say that receiving something with a professional label on it makes a difference in catching the attention. That means it's not a CD-R with Sharpie writing on it and an 8½-by-11 piece of paper in there with typewritten track titles, a sheet I'm probably going to lose. A professional label has more definition by nature, and it's more concise on the eye and mind.

What captures my attention doesn't have to be a big, fancy presentation, but it should be sent professionally and cleanly. That will get my attention because I know the potential licensor has taken their time to do it right. Quite often, it's usually reflective of the attention to detail that they've put into what counts the most: the music itself.

Ultimately, what captures my attention in a submission is the artistry and craftsmanship of the music being presented from every angle. That means composition, arrangement, orchestration, production, engineering, etc., and of course the soul of it. All of that captures my attention and adds up to an aggregate impression.

Alex Hackford

Aaron Bethune:
If a band is sending music, how do you like to receive the submissions?

Alex Hackford:
Ideally, I prefer a link to a site like box.com, or SendSpace—something that allows me to stream and preview the song before I download it. A MySpace page works for that, although I prefer a site with high-res download options.

AB:
Does that mean you like to receive WAV-file options?

AH:
Absolutely. Downloading a WAV file is always the quickest, easiest way to do it.

AB:
Do you need the instrumental track for the song?

AH:
We'll always ask for high-res instrumental and high-res a cappella, if it's available.

David Hayman
Music Supervisor: *Rookie Blue*, Telus, Shaun White Skateboarding, *The Whistleblower* ...

Aaron Bethune:
What catches your attention when you receive a new submission?

David Hayman:
I love artwork. When people send me music and there's no artwork, I'll often find it myself and take a few minutes to search it out to get a vibe. Interesting song titles, interesting things that are different production values, exciting collaborations. I mean, it is very hard to get a music supervisor excited, but I think glossiness doesn't win the day. I think that direct simple emails are better from trusted names. If bloggers in the community, or people that represent music that I respect, tell me something is good I'm going to give it a listen. You really have to have a good song first. We can tell hype from crap. If you're in the same city as a music supervisor it's a really good idea to offer to take them out to lunch, or go for a coffee or something. The face-to-face value is just huge. We have hearts and we love to work with people. When you are one-on-one, it takes a relationship to a whole different level. So, if you are in Toronto, come see me. All the major cities are not full of music supervisors, but there are a handful of them and you should be meeting with them if you're an artist.

AB:
Are MP3s what you're looking for, or is the physical copy still the best way to submit?

DH:
It's Earth Day, so I should be slapping myself on the wrist, but I want physical copies. I miss CDs, I miss artwork, I miss care, I miss branding, I miss images of artists. I can remember great CDs that I used to pore over as a kid; now, when I get these discs, the ones with good packaging really stand out to me. Of course, I love an MP3 if at the heart of it the song is good. That's the bottom line. It doesn't matter how you bring it to me, as long as it is well labelled with all your contact information, everything I need to know about who owns the track, I can put it into the system. The edge does go to the person that can bring me a compact disc, because like I said the image, the look, the photos add to the value of the band and their position in the market.

Ron Proulx
Music Supervisor: *The Listener, The Man in the Mirror, Due South* ...

Aaron Bethune:
What catches your attention when you receive a new submission?

Ron Proulx:
Something that sounds passionate, different or rather unique, because it is very hard to capture my attention if you sound like Madonna or you sound like any band that I know. But, when someone sounds truly different, it's like back in the day when you first heard Massive Attack—you went "Wow, what's that?"—or the first time you heard Portishead and went "What's that?" or the first time you heard Loreena McKennitt and you went "What's that?" That's what gets you—it's when you say "What's that?" as opposed to "That's just like so-and-so, yeah, yeah, I've heard that before ... " For me that doesn't do it so much. There is so much music out there that it is hard to make it unique these days.

Sarah Gavigan

Aaron Bethune:
What does a perfect email from an artist look like from a music supervisor's point of view?

Sarah Gavigan:
Short and sweet. I'm not looking for your bio, tour dates or the brag sheet; none of that matters. Quick descriptions and the song is all I'm looking for, and if the song has the attributes we need for commercials, we go from there. A link to the song where I can choose to either stream or download is preferable and 128k quality is fine for the initial step; if we are interested and want more, we will contact you and get a higher-quality file or the WAV file. I prefer Box.net.

NEGOTIATING

When it comes to licensing your music, there is no set rate like there is with a mechanical licence. There is room for negotiating. There is usually an overall budget per project that can sometimes be flexible.

THE MUSIC SUPS SAY ...

Before you can negotiate, you need to know where you can negotiate. Let's ask the music sups!

Kyle Merkley

Aaron Bethune:
What are things people should keep in mind while negotiating?

Kyle Merkley:
Make sure you're not getting taken advantage of, and look at any
clauses that involve trailer or promotional uses. Sometimes there
are deals where you'll be providing in- and out-of-context promotional uses, and typically a lot of production companies will go out
and get both. But if you're really looking at a low amount of money,
one thing you can limit back is the trailer or promotional rights. And
you can limit that to in-context only. Further to that, you can look at
term—how long this deal's lasting.

Once again, most production companies we work for are asking
for perpetuity, which means forever. So you can try and scale that
back. The norm really is world for all media, which covers all production for anything that they want to do. However, to be truthful,
when you're in a band starting out you should probably agree to
whatever deal you can get.

When a music supervisor comes to you with a deal, it's typically the
best thing we can do. There's really little room to exceed past that.
So, when we're coming to you with a fee and the required rights for
the deal, that's likely the best deal we can do. Anything beyond that
becomes difficult. I think that's something to understand—that the
music supervisor, at least in my experience, is not holding back any
money from you.

Negotiating is often for the bands with the clout. If you're an
indie band, it's either you want it or you don't. When we have an

independent band, or a licensor working with independent bands looking to negotiate, it's fine to ask if there is any more money, but it shouldn't be expected.

Sarah Gavigan

Aaron Bethune:
Is there any room for negotiation regarding budget once a supervisor has contacted a band or group and said "We want to use your song"?

Sarah Gavigan:
I think it's important to ask why you want to negotiate. One of the most important things musicians need to know is what their music is worth; once you know what it's worth, you may not need to negotiate! Some artists are willing to give away their music for almost nothing in order to create that buzz. Other musicians aren't because it isn't about the buzz for them at that point, it's about selling a proven product, and they won't go below a certain number. If you get an offer and you aren't sure, ask around and get some comparable licensing fees. Know what the licences are worth before you start negotiating! For example, something I tell my students is that if you get approached by a music supervisor, find out how far along in completion their project is; that alone will tell you how badly they need your music. In this sense it's a bit of a chess game, and it's important to know how to play if you want to be successful in negotiating. It's in the artist's best interest to ask questions, and not just blindly agree and say yes.

HOW DO YOU FIND OUT ABOUT PROJECTS?

When approaching music supervisors with your music, it certainly helps to know who is looking for music in the first place and what kind of music it is they need. But how do you find that information?

Music is generally licensed in post-production. IMDb Pro is a good way to find out which movies are currently in post-production, who the music supervisor is and their contact information. You can also use IMDb (Internet Movie Database) to find out who the music supervisor was in a project that you feel featured music similar to yours.

Before reaching out, be familiar with the music supervisor's previous work. Have an idea of their taste. You would be surprised at how much information you can find. Have they been interviewed or written articles online? Do they have a website? If they're on Twitter, which bands or artists do they follow? All the information that you can gather can help you determine the right person to approach and how you approach them.

If you want to get a feel for the work and "sound" of a music supervisor, you can use YouTube to research scenes featuring music in projects they have worked on. Keep in mind there is a difference between underscore, the featured tracks, and source music. The featured songs are likely going to be a better representation of the music sup's personal "sound." You can also use the following sites to find music used in commercials and then research who the music supervisor was:

Adtunes
atnmusi.ca/ch8h4

AllMusic
atnmusi.ca/ch8h5

TuneFind
atnmusi.ca/ch8h6

In order to know how and when to approach a music supervisor, not only should you know about the projects being worked on but also the time frames involved. Time frames will vary quite drastically from a TV show to a movie, to an ad, to a video game. Some have months to find music and some have literally days to hours!

As well as knowing about specific needs and projects to pitch to, you want to be on their radar. Music supervisors are always keeping their ears open for new music and although it might not fit a current project they will keep it on file for future reference.

Getting on the radar and making it into folders "for future reference" comes from working every aspect of your career. Are you playing live? Do you have an online presence? Are you networking with the right people? Are you causing people to talk about your music and spread it virally? Do you have videos getting attention? Are you making a name for yourself on your local scene? Are you working your PR to traditional media? You want to make it easy for a music supervisor to "stumble" upon your music or for the right person to talk about it!

I share new music in my newsletters and compilations; where suitable, I make personal recommendations of bands to look out for. I have built relationships over time, so when I suggest listening to a band it is coming from a peer instead of a stranger. You need to find ways to build relationships and create conversations. Many music supervisors are on social media platforms and a relationship can be initiated that way. With an understanding of past projects they have worked on, a feel for their musical interests and a knowledge of the current projects they are working on, not only do you have a conversation starter but you are able to present music that has a strong chance of interesting them.

Here are a few other sources for discovering what is cooking:

- *Film Music Magazine* (atnmusi.ca/ch8h7)

- *Songwriter's Market* (atnmusi.ca/ch8h8)

- *The Hollywood Reporter* (atnmusi.ca/ch8h9) comes out every Tuesday and provides production lists of everything in development, in current production or in post- production.

- The Music Business Registry (atnmusi.ca/ch8h10)

- Twitter and HootSuite searches to find out who is talking about music needed and movies in post-production.

- *Variety* (atnmusi.ca/ch8h11) comes out both daily and weekly. This Los Angeles–based magazine is, along with *The Hollywood Reporter*, the bible of American film and television production information.

THE MUSIC SUPS SAY ...

Ron Proulx

Aaron Bethune:
How can artists find out about new projects and their related music supervisors?

Ron Proulx:
That begets the question of how should artists be looking to get their music in film and TV. It used to be that an artist, because there weren't so many trying to do this, could get heard above the noise. Now I think the best way to find out about stuff is getting someone to work on your behalf rather than you yourself trying to find it. I just don't buy into one artist with five songs or fifteen songs spending time trying to get their music into TV shows. It's too competitive, too many people doing it now. I'd leave it up to the people that make it their job to find out what shows are looking for music. I have people send me two songs and I tell them, "You're kidding me, you can't be sending two songs to people—you're killing yourself."

Putting in the time before you contact a music sup to research can be the difference between licensing your music and getting blacklisted.

Kyle Merkley

Aaron Bethune:
What are some ways to go about finding out about these projects and gigs?

Kyle Merkley:
One would be looking into production listings. You could be looking

into things like *Variety*, *The Hollywood Reporter*, etc., seeing what's in production and tracking down that production company. If it's any kind of reputable production company, reach out to them and say, "Who is your music supervisor on the show? I'd love to reach out to them."

Ideally for us, you own the masters and the publishing 100 percent, because that makes it one-stop and really easy. From there just offer to submit your music and say you'll love to get involved and hear more about any opportunities that may be involved in making that production.

You want to monitor what's going on, and once you reach out to the music supervisors, keep in touch with them, and be accommodating to what their needs might be. It really goes back to following up with music, and making sure that you're conveying to the music supervisor that you understand the ownership of your music.

I think I might have mentioned that briefly before. It's just that when you are reaching out to a music supervisor, my favourite emails are: "Hey here's a link to my music, I own it 100 percent masters and publishing." That's a big thing for me—immediate explanation as to the ownership of your music.

David Hayman

Aaron Bethune:
How can artists find out about new projects and their related music supervisors?

David Hayman:
I'd say the onus is on the artist more than ever. Five years ago we were seeing websites where people would post projects saying, "I'm working on this please send your music." I used to do blast-outs, which means an email to all of my network to try and find ideas for certain commercials. Often I'd send the video along with it or the script. Nowadays it has become a lot tighter. Confidentiality rules the day. There's a sort of culture of fear in the advertising industry and in the marketing industries. Everybody is keeping

things very close to the chest, whether it be to protect ideas or actual products. It's been harder for me to inform the musical world of what's going on and have people send me music. What I have to do now is rely on artists just to bug me—really, literally, bug me—by email. I hate to be bugged by phone and I am sure most supervisors are the same. We don't mind getting an email saying "Hey what's up, what's going on?" because stuff is always going on whether you hear from us or not. That's your opportunity to be kept in mind, if they see your emails pop into their inbox every couple of weeks. It's so easy to forget musicians; you can only imagine how much music we get. So I think the onus is on the artist—don't rely on your record label, publisher or whoever is pushing your music. It isn't a bad thing to make connections directly with music supervisors—at the heart of it, music supervisors are fans of the music and musicians, not managers. We love musicians, so we do welcome calls; I know I do, and I'm always looking to connect and collaborate with new, young and exciting artists.

Sarah Gavigan

Aaron Bethune:
How can an artist find out about a project that needs music?

Sarah Gavigan:
That's not really the best way of going about getting your music licensed—that's more of the second step. The first step is making connections and relationships with the right people. It's almost impossible for an individual or artist to get in on a project blindly. You have to earn the trust of a music supervisor first. Build a relationship, and then dig in for the specific projects. When a music supervisor hears something we might use, we drop it into our database for another search. The band or individual might not get the call right away, but you are in the database.

HOW DO THE SUPS FIND NEW MUSIC?

Music supervisors usually have reliable sources or filters among:

- Labels
- Publishers

- Managers
- Online
- Friends
- Independent artists

I have heard time and time again that good music always permeates to the top. If something is good, word will spread. A lot of music supervisors attend live shows. They are part of the music community and know who's making the noise. If you want to have your music exposed to music supervisors, the best place to start is by building relationships and networking.

THE MUSIC SUPS SAY ...

Stacey Horricks

Aaron Bethune:
How do you find new music?

Stacey Horricks:
Seventy percent of the time it's from the labels, publishers and music licensors who send their latest releases via email. I also go out a lot in New York, so live music shows, cafés, bars, lounges and restaurants are also prime resources. When it comes to online, I don't visit blogs as much as I used to, but I do check out the music my friends are posting on their Facebook and Twitter feeds.

David Hnatiuk

Aaron Bethune:
How do you find out about new music?

David Hnatiuk:
At this point, being a music supervisor for well over a decade, I'm on most of the major and independent mailing lists, so I'm constantly getting CDs and MP3s, web links, sound files from music-production entities, libraries, record labels, publishers and individuals on a daily basis. I'm always being invited to shows in the greater metro area—the New York, New Jersey area. Being in

the New York City area, you couldn't ask for a better place to be exposed to every genre of music and arguably the highest level of quality in the world at any given time.

So the live music scene is constantly happening. And I love the internet. I really do. Even MySpace, to this day, as antiquated as some people might think it is when comparing it to Twitter and Facebook. MySpace is still a useful platform for exposing new music and being exposed to new music. I also love Broadjam [a music community website]. It is an amazing tool for music supervisors to link up with artists, bands and composers who are eager to place their music in media. Believe it or not, iTunes is also a great tool for experiencing new music too.

Greg Debonne

Aaron Bethune:
How do you find new music?

Greg Debonne:
When I am hired to do a particular series, I look at the needs of that show. I have a conversation with producers and then I set about putting together a music project for that series that's solid from the outset even though I know I'm going to be adding to it and there are going to be needs that come up throughout the post-production process, which is what music supervision usually is. It's in the post-production process. After a series has been shot and it's being edited, that's when the music is being applied.

I have a lot of go-to sources. I also look for new sources as well because, especially with a lot of reality programming, which is wall-to-wall music, you can really wring sources dry that you like. You can't keep using the same material over and over again even if it will work; you need to keep it fresh. Producers can want their show to have its own definitive sound. You need to keep bringing in new music, so you look for that new material according to the stylistic parameters of the programming. That's how I would say I go about finding new music.

Alex Hackford

Aaron Bethune:
How do you find new music?

Alex Hackford:
I get pitched so much music. I probably get twenty-five to thirty CDs a day and then constant links and blogs and different bits and pieces. I know there are some music supervisors who like to have the act of discovery themselves— "I want to dig for it and find that nugget, I don't want it to be handed to me by the person who represents the music." I'm less precious, partly because we have a big-volume business, but also because I have a very small department here who would do specific song-based placements, so I need to avail myself of all the people I have.

We all have trusted filters in any aspect of our lives. There are those types of filters that I have—other musicians, specific publishers, some label reps and other music supervisors.

I have some really good friends who are big DJs all over the world and I lean a lot on those guys because tonally—from a song and not score-based perspective—a lot of the music in our games is up-tempo. There are calls sometimes for slower, down-tempo, ballady stuff, but that's not the norm. My friends know what reacts, what's new and what's not. They have a visual representation of that stuff. So I lean heavily on those types of people as well as people in touring and established bands, a lot of sort of nerdy blog searching and then a couple of shows on KCRW [a US National Public Radio station]. But for the most part, I'm digging on my computer. Not so much radio, but Little Steven's radio show in NY was one I always found really cool stuff on.

WHAT KIND OF MONEY IS IN MUSIC LICENSING?

It always comes down to what people are willing to pay and what you're willing to accept. Let's see what the people paying have to say.

Greg Debonne

Aaron Bethune:
What sort of money can be made these days with placements?
Has the value of music changed?

Greg Debonne:
Yes, actually it has. To answer your first question, back-end royalties paid from your performing rights society can be lucrative from the usage in TV. As you know, each country has one. In America, there are three: ASCAP, BMI and SESAC. You want to be affiliated with a rights society in the country in which your music is being played. If you are with the society in England, PRS, but now live in the States yet are still with PRS, what you want to do is switch to ASCAP, BMI or SESAC, or at least have a sub-publisher of some kind in the country where you're getting most of your action.

You need to actively make sure that your compositions are registered with that performance rights society [also known as performing rights organization], making sure that your name, your publishing entity and the titles of your compositions are accurately noted on their website. Whenever your music is played, the use of your music in a program goes on the cue sheet. Subsequently, that music cue sheet goes to the performance rights society, who in turn will track the use. If your composition is registered, then you will get paid on the back end.

Vocal uses pay more than instrumental uses. The longer the use, the more you are paid. Other factors come into play, that is, whether the program is on a network or cable channel, number of re-airs ... There are several factors that affect how much you're being paid. In a nutshell, the more your music is being played, the more royalties add up. It's always good to look at your royalties as an aggregate because all those little $10 payments—$40 here, $30 here—add up. If as the licensor you're actively pushing a catalogue, the larger catalogue you have, the more money you stand to make on the back end from your performance rights society for those uses relative to royalties.

The other way that a licensor makes money is by upfront sync fees, meaning that when a music supervisor wants to license your music, there is an upfront fee that can be negotiated.

Now as far as the value of music is concerned, which was the other part of your question, keep in mind that music is a medium that, for whatever reason, is constantly being devalued. Because we work in entertainment, we know that the entertainment industry is set to try to devalue whatever they can on a certain level. In a realistic sense, you have to strategize and structure your business model as a licensor to adapt to certain realities in the business, depending on who the licensee is and what level of programming or entertainment it is for which the licensee is interested in using your music.

Music is something that everybody thinks they know about, so sometimes there is a cavalier attitude about it. A recording artist friend of mine, Chris Darrow, once pointed out that music is the most abstract of all the art forms out there because it is intangible. You can't see it; you can't touch it. You can only hear it. Therefore it makes it that much easier for people to overlook its actual value.

So, music is constantly trying to be devalued. It's becoming increasingly hard for the independent licensor to get a fair upfront fee for using their music in a program. That doesn't always have to do with the music supervisor being a weasel and trying to get the music for free. The reality is that when you're the music supervisor, you have a certain budget with which to work for that programming and it isn't always ideal. If it's lower budget programming, you still have to make that show work.

There have been many times on cable programming that I don't license something because I simply don't have the budget or I can't justify the expense for their catalogue. If I can offer that licensor an upfront sync fee and justify the dollars, then I do.

That is one area where it can be beneficial for a licensor to have a publishing deal because the publisher's job is to maintain and maximize the value of the catalogue. The other side of the coin is you can always forgo placements in that way as well. There are certain licensing opportunities where if the money is too little, the publisher might say "absolutely not." It's not really the licensee's decision or even position to tell the publisher what they should or shouldn't quote. A publisher or publishing administrator can give an artist or composer some leverage. They can also make it difficult to get as many placements for that licensor as well, depending upon the situation.

Ron Proulx

Aaron Bethune:
How much money can indie artists expect to make from licensing music into TV and film?

Ron Proulx:
The fees are coming way down real fast. Supply and demand, which any business has: supplies go down, fees go up; supplies go up, fees go down. There is an endless supply of music now. It is so easy to find music, it is ridiculous. So the fees have gone through the floor. When people used to say things like, "We've got $20,000," they're lucky to get $3,000 in that same environment. People are much more aware, producers are much more aware of the whole music licensing thing. And people have been competing on a cost basis, which is always bad for any business—to compete with cost. That is how Walmart competes with other businesses, on cost. They keep the cost going down, down, down because they have pure volume. We even get people trying to give us music for free. I have no expectation that our producers will go that low, but they won't pay a lot for it. Music traditionally has been something people don't want to pay a lot for, like live music at the bottom end of the barrel.

David Hayman

Aaron Bethune:
What sort of money can be made these days with placements and has the value of music changed?

David Hayman:
It depends who you are and what product you are selling. If you are selling me a piece of thirty-second instrumental stock music, then you will be getting stock prices. In Canada, 250 bucks for a background cue, maybe if are lucky $1,000 for part of a commercial. It's really tough because a lot of the middle-of-the-road music and the instrumental stuff is competing with the stock music houses, and the stock music houses have become so saturated that they are now competing with each other, going lower on the prices that are already ridiculously low. So that's a big issue.

For an American spot compared to a Canadian spot, you are going to get ten times the amount, so it is great to get on big brands because they may be adapted for other countries. You could be starting off with something as low as $10,000 for a national Canadian television commercial, but after renewals, and different aspects and different terms and different ways that they want to promote it, you are going to see that doubled, tripled, just have a life beyond that single initial licence. For one-offs, let's say for a commercial, you are seeing anywhere between $5,000 and $25,000 depending on the band. Every once in a while they will spend $100,000 on a big sound. We've done licences that for the Canadian market have gone over a hundred grand. That's something to note, but those are hits that have value and assets beyond managers pushing music to supervisors, the Ray Charles of the world. It is hard to gauge fees because fees are based on terms. So you have got to be able to negotiate and remember that every single piece of the placement can be negotiated whether that may be the term, the way that they are using it out of context or in context, the duration. The bigger balls you have, the better negotiating hooks you have, the better you will do.

Alex Hackford

Aaron Bethune:
What is the average amount of money that an indie band can make from a placement in a video game?

Alex Hackford:
Our fees are competitive. For an unsigned band, we'll pay anywhere between $5,000 and $8,000.

CONSIDER BUILDING A CATALOGUE WITH OTHER MUSICIANS

You might find yourself suited to representing not only your own music but that of others too. It is regularly the lack of business skills that gets in the way of artists developing a career in music. If you possess the skills, then adding the music of others to your existing catalogue will put you in a position to solve the needs of busy music sups and help other artists to license their music. Everybody's careers and bank accounts benefit. Companies like LicenseQuote (atnmusi.ca/ch8h12) and YouLicense (atnmusi.ca/ch8h13) provide a service that makes the licensing process of your music easy. With their self-automated set-up, your music can even be licensed while you sleep!

ENSURE YOU ARE COLLECTING ALL REVENUE

Look into the different companies that provide "digital fingerprinting" and tracking of your music. A career in today's music industry is sustained by ensuring that you are collecting from as many revenue streams as possible. You would be surprised at how often music is used and goes unpaid to the copyright owners.

Signing up with a company like TuneSat (atnmusi.ca/ch8h14) and Songtrust (atnmusi.ca/ch8h15) can help ensure you are collecting what you are owed.

The importance of timing when you connect with a music supervisor and submit your music is huge. Once again, I am turning to the music supervisors to elaborate:

Alex Hackford

Aaron Bethune:
Game production is generally a long process, so how much do you try to coincide the timing of the release with the music you are giving the exposure to?

Alex Hackford:
From a production timeline perspective, our games take roughly fourteen to sixteen months from the point we get involved to the point that they actually come out. I'm dealing a lot with managers or artists themselves because if I'm nine months from the release of my game — most people don't even have stuff recorded that's going to coincide with the release.

I love to make opportunities that are larger than just the opportunity in the game. To do that the band has got to have the record out, and be touring on the back of it, and people aren't generally touring on the back of something they've had ready nine months before its coming out. It's a delicate and fun juggling process.

The game audience are more nitpicky and critical than any other audience ... definitely more than TV and as much if not more so than film. If you buy a $60 video game and spend fifty hours playing it, then you are going to be hypercritical just by virtue of the time investment and the time–monetary investment. That breeds a certain type of microscopic deconstructionism. "I heard that song on *Grey's Anatomy* two months before this game came out, how could they use it ... ?" Believe or not, that stuff happens, and it happens frequently.

A lot of times games come out at a certain time every year. You can research their release cycle and figure that nine months before the game is supposed to be released is when I'm going to be working on it. This type of information is easily obtainable with a little bit of legwork. There are sites like Kotaku and Game Informer, as well as just going into stores like EB Games or GameStop, looking at their release schedule and asking, "What do you have coming out?"

If you are a band, artist, manager or publisher, those are the type of approaches I would make. It would really take no more than an hour of your time, and would greatly, greatly increase the odds of somebody like myself, or like Steve [Schnur] at EA [Electronic Arts] or the people at Activision or Harmonix checking out your material.

SUBMISSIONS

Musicians face choices about whether to submit music directly to music supervisors or to catalogues or libraries or via third parties.

Is it worth submitting to a music library? Will music supervisors want to hear directly from artists? Let's find out!

THE MUSIC SUPS SAY ...

Stacey Horricks

Aaron Bethune:
Do you need to have relationships with publishers, labels and libraries, or are the chances of an artist contacting you directly just as good as going through a library or publisher?

Stacey Horricks:
The chances aren't quite as good and it heavily relies in the presentation. We get so many emails from music labels, publishers, licensors and artists in one day, we're not able to hear everything. So if you want to get noticed, know how to market your song in an email. Visually it needs to catch my eye, whether it's with a smart subject line, promo shot or an intro that draws me in. For instance, the artist might know what projects I am working on and has hand-selected a few songs they think will work. Letting me know this within the first five to eight seconds of reading will hold my

attention longer than "Hey, I just wrote a couple of songs, are you looking for anything?"

David Hayman

Aaron Bethune:
Is it realistic to think that artists can approach music supervisors directly or are their chances higher going through a company or library, etc.?

David Hayman:
The question is, how are you valuing your music? If you're going through a stock service, you've devalued your music immediately. As soon as your music hits some sort of online database it's old— it's like driving your car off a lot. It becomes stock, however way you want to spin it. Stock music gets stale once it sits. What we're looking for is unique stuff. Contact a music supervisor directly, get a relationship, say, "What's new? What's coming out? What are you working on?" If you're a good artist, we'll keep talking to you. Talent really shines through—so does charm. A lot of times we will dismiss song pluggers, people that are pushing their specific agendas. I'd rather focus on a blog to tell me what's hot. I'm not going to listen to the major labels or any hype they send me; I'd rather see those six blogs to see what they're saying about them. I'd much rather see you focus as an artist on making good with music supervisors on a collaborative level. Forget album sales and that stuff, get your music reviewed and get it hyped. That will get the attention of music supervisors. Good music always permeates to the top and that's true no matter what genre it might be. We'll find you!

David Hnatiuk

Aaron Bethune:
Do you prefer working with libraries, or directly with artists?

David Hnatiuk:
I have great relationships at major record labels, independent record labels, major publishers, independent publishers, production

music libraries, as well as with independent artists, independent producers and independent songwriters. They all have their ups and downs, positives and negatives that can be listed. But I will continue to do business with all of those types of entities, because limiting my potential to place a song, or fulfill the needs of my clients, is the last thing I want to do.

It's easier to go to an independent single person because, frankly, you're dealing with less people. The more people you take out of the mix, the easier the situation is to deal with. Time is money, and the less time you spend on the phone, email, text, or fax, the better … as long as you get the deal done! But generally the smaller the entity, the more specialized they become. I accept that as a reality of what I do, and I embrace it.

Whatever the placement opportunity is—whether it's a commercial or a scene in a film—ultimately, it's never going to be just one song or two songs that I'm trying to put in the scene. So, often, I'll have a song from a major label, a song from an independent producer, a song from a guy in my apartment building or a song from a major music publisher. So everyone in every level of success will often get a shot at the same scene because ultimately it expands the possibilities, and basically narrows down the chances of failure. My ultimate goal is success for every scene that I music-supervise. Failure is never an option.

So, generally, I try to spread myself out in every possible relevant creative direction and to every possible musical provider who's relevant to whatever I'm working on. If that ends up being a library or an individual person, then so be it. I don't care as long as it's good. If I have a low budget, I'm not going to deal with a very large publisher or record label necessarily, because the chances are I'm not going to get something for really cheap. Maybe then, if I knew I only have a few hundred dollars to deal with, that would influence me to deal with an individual over a big company.

I will say that given the suffering state of our general economy, major publishers and record labels have become more willing to

lower their prices to accommodate the growingly more common
modest production budgets of TV and film.

Michael Perlmutter

Aaron Bethune:
Is it more likely you will pay more attention to artists sending
their music to you directly or is it in their best interest to go
through a library or company?

Michael Perlmutter:
To each his own: if an independent artist has the time to make
connections, then that's great. We get a lot of submissions from
the artists themselves or their managers. But I love pitch companies; they have great taste. Remember, if you're going to be
represented by a pitch company, that they may have three hundred
bands on their roster—what kind of attention are you going to get?
I would suggest you speak to the pitch company and see where
you're going to sit on their roster. Maybe have a four-month tryout.
Granted, they might not get you a gig or placement in four months,
as it's really hard, but you want somebody to work hard for you and
not just be another artist on the shelf.

AB:
Does this mean you don't need to look for music if you're getting
this many submissions?

MP:
We're always looking for music. We're always seeing who is out
there. We look into unknown bands, email them or go to see them
play live. We like to expand our network monthly, so we listen to the
artist that we do work with and will continue to work with, but we
also want new music. We all know that TV shows and films would
love to get an artist before anybody's ever heard of them. That's
happened in *Grey's Anatomy* and EA [Electronic Arts] Games and
all that.

For example, an artist sent me a link to her music. It was five
o'clock and I wanted to listen to some music at the end of the

day—we pitched one of her songs for *Degrassi*. I didn't know her from a hole in the wall. The song went on *Degrassi*—she was thrilled and had an amazing amount of feedback after it aired. Facebook, MySpace, people buying her stuff, the whole thing. That makes us proud, and the TV shows love that stuff, because it adds credibility to what they're doing.

These artists have to be their own marketing department: they have to understand the business. Even if you get a manager, you need to understand the business. I don't think anybody understands everything, but at least understand different parts of deals or contracts and create your own PR and marketing tools.

Greg Debonne

Aaron Bethune:
Is it realistic to think that artists can approach music supervisors directly or are their chances higher going through a company or library or publisher, etc.?

Greg Debonne:
I can only speak for myself, as well as from the standpoint of what I gather from certain key licensors that have been doing this for a long time. You can contact a music supervisor directly, especially if that music supervisor is smart and into constantly improving their cache of music. I think the music supervisor needs the licensors, meaning the music super needs the artist/composer or whatever as much as the artist/composer needs the music supervisor. If that music supervisor is smart, they will look into what that person soliciting them has to offer. If it's fine, then they'll accept it for criteria they may have at the moment relative to their day-to-day needs. I don't turn people away; however, I do know certain licensors who have told me that when they have approached certain music supervisors, the answer they get back is, "Oh, I don't accept submissions, except by an agent, a library or a publisher, etc., etc."

Do I think that artists have a better chance of having their music licensed if it is with a library or a non-exclusive sync house? Again I can only speak for myself. No, actually. It comes down to the actual music and the quality of it and how applicable and/or viable it is to the current needs of a program. It makes no difference to me whether it's being pitched to me by a non-exclusive sync house, a library, an agent, or whatever. It's either right or it isn't.

Ron Proulx

Aaron Bethune:
Is it realistic to think that artists can approach music supervisors directly or are their chances higher going through a company or library, etc.?

Ron Proulx:
I can only speak from our point of view. I think that life has changed and therefore the latter is the better method now. We used to deal with artists directly all the time and really enjoyed it. In fact, we have made some really good friends with certain artists that we've licensed from a lot. But it would be very difficult now, in this environment, to get our attention as a single artist — not impossible, just far more difficult because there is just so much other noise happening and so many other people with a lot of recordings. You can only talk to one person at one time and if I'm going to talk to you for only ten minutes and hear about your ten songs I should spend my ten minutes talking to you if you have a thousand songs. So it's a better idea these days for artists to deal with people that do this for a living. They are much more plugged in. Or if you're an artist, here's another way of doing it: go find ten other artists that will let you do it for you and them, then you're becoming the guy that is doing it for a living.

Alex Hackford

Aaron Bethune:
Can artists approach you directly?

Alex Hackford: Absolutely. I'm listening to most of the A&R registries that Pulsar [the collective] puts out and music supervisor directories that come out. Sony has particular rules about unsolicited content, so an email with a public streaming link is always better than somebody sending an MP3. If you're sending an MP3, odds are I don't know you, odds are I'm not going to download it — I've had to replace two or three computers because of corrupted files or viruses. I'm very wary of people sending me stuff unsolicited.

At the same time, I try to put as many unsigned bands into our games as possible because I'm a musician, I've been in bands and managed small bands and know how hard it is to get your foot in the door — and so I try to make sure that door stays open.

WHAT MAKES A SONG LICENSABLE?

What makes a song radio-friendly or a potential chart-topper does not necessarily make it licensable for TV, film, ads and so on. So what does make a song licensable?

THE MUSIC SUPS SAY ...

Alex Hackford

Aaron Bethune:
What characteristics make a song licensable for the video game format?

Alex Hackford:
It depends on the game. We don't make a lot of M-rated games. There is a rating system called the ESRB [Entertainment Software Rating Board] that rates video games which is very similar to the MPAA [Motion Picture Association of America], the rating system for film. Ultimately the primary issues that we have with M-rated songs are brand mentions like somebody's rapping about my Nike boots or whatever else. That becomes an issue because we have to clear the use of a brand name — the tertiary major brand.

Lyrical content: if somebody's talking about murdering somebody violently, that becomes an issue as well. Although sometimes it doesn't — in God of War, a multimillion-selling game, the main character is running around eviscerating people and we used music with a bunch of heavy bands: Trivium, and Dream Theater and Kills-witch Engage, all of which were incredibly violent.

With Major League Baseball, which I'm working on right now, I have to clear the rights and practices of major-league baseball itself, as well as with the MLB Players Association and the ESRB [Entertainment Software Rating Board].

AB:
So how are songs chosen for games?

AH:
Music supervision for games is very similar to the process for music supervision for film or anything else. I work very closely with game directors, game producers and first-party developers—the people who are actually making the games.

We go through the process and each game has a different process. It becomes trial and error, plugging things into the game and seeing how they work, pulling them out, going from there.

We have a game here called SingStar, which is one of the first and largest selling music-based games. It's a competitive singing game, and we've just released our dance version featuring a bunch of big artists. In that instance, the process for song selection is very different than for games like Gran Turismo, Twisted Metal, God of War, because it's about the songs and wanting to perform them.

The funny part about that process is that sometimes a great song is not fun to sing—if there is a twenty-five-minute guitar solo or lots of screaming for instance. It's fun because we take the songs and put them into test code for the game, sit down, crack open a couple of beers and see how they play.

With other games, it's a luxury to put things into an SDK [software development kit] and really have a sense of how it's going to sound, how it's going to play. There a certain instances, like cutscenes [where the player watches] in games that are scored statically— meaning there is no adaptive element to the music. So if I'm playing

Heavy Rain, there are lots of cutscene cinematics that are static—
they stay the same no matter what happens in the game.

In that instance, cue placement—just like there would be in a
film—is very important because you know when a cue starts, how
it starts, where it starts, what elements of the cue are used, and
it really ties into the emotional arc of the scene. But a lot of times
in game play, the user is prescribing the discovery elements or
emotional elements within a game, so it's hard to dictate cue placements based on an independent user's actions.

From a musician's perspective, it's fascinating. It forces you to see
the amount of creative control of how your music is going to be
interpreted because different scenes get made from larger scenes.

Unlike a film, which is two hours of static visual material, a game is
up to sixty to seventy hours of content. Composers for games that
have sixty or seventy hours of content are generally composing
maybe four hours of music. So that music then has to be adapted
through the rest of the game play in such a way that a lot of times
it doesn't come up the way that a composer intended. So there is a
lot of trust and collaboration that goes into that process.

SAMPLE BRIEFS

When you pitch music for a particular project, you are generally given
specific information as a guideline to help you understand the needs
of the project in detail. Here are some unedited sample requests from
music supervisors to give you a feel for what you get to work with.
Sometimes for ads you will be given the actual spot without music.

Wine Commercial

Client & Product: *Wine Company* [company name withheld]

Medium & Time: TV & Internet (*Wine Company* corporate site
only) / 0:30 spots with 0:15 cut-downs

Territory: Canada Only (excluding Quebec)

Term & Language: 3 months / English

Budget: 1OK per side = 2OK per song placement (this includes both master and sync)

Deadline: Tuesday, Sept 6th (end of day)

Creative: Target Demographic: 3O—5O year old women

Spot #1—LIGHTS

Keywords: Moody, effortless, cool, contemporary, indie-pop

Reference songs/styles: "Threads"—This Will Destroy You http://www.youtube.com/watch?v=YdqT3MDAG2w&feature=related

"Feeding Line"—Boy & Bear http://www.youtube.com/watch?v=NAjKNsLgvAU

Attached: .mov file of a rough mockup/demo for "Lights."

Lyrics, vocals or instrumentation: It doesn't matter. If you are looking at vocal tracks, we welcome lyrics that are both on point and non-related to the content. Mood, theme and reference styles are what you should pay the closest attention to.

Spot #2—SHOES

Keywords: Upbeat, playful, fun, catchy, indie-pop

Reference songs/styles: "In the Twilight"—Alex Ebert http://www.youtube.com/watch?v=PvM2R7ir2a8

"Shut Up and Let Me Go"—The Ting Tings http://www.youtube.com/watch?v=tolm-O7if3c&ob=av2e

"The Hat Song" http://www.youtube.com/watch?v=p-GD8-irj3sE

There is no demo footage for "Shoes," but here's a rough idea on what it will look like:

This commercial will have a great energy to it. The music and the pace of the edit will make you feel good. One after another, we'll see different feet wearing different things in their surrounding environments. Each image has a way of expressing a different mood/occasion: Brogues on office carpet. Flip-flops on sidewalk. Ski boots with skis attached, looking down from chairlift. Bare feet in the sand. Converse on a concrete floor. Heels, red carpet. Slippers on hardwood floor. Flippers on pool deck. Birkenstocks on grass. Snowshoes on snow. Hiking boots on trail. Wool socks in front of fire. Cut to multiple bottles of *Wine*. The camera selects one by pushing in on it.

Lyrics, vocals or instrumentation: They're not tied to lyrics, though it does help establish the playful and upbeat mood of the spot.

Please tag all submissions with your company info (preferably MP3s)

Thanks & have fun!

TV Show

Season 2 of *TV Show* [show name withheld] (that'll start up next year but I collect tunes early as long as they're in the $1—2k all in range. Sometimes we have a little more and sometimes a little less depending on how many songs in any given episode. We only have 10K all in [$10,000 to cover synchronization and master licences] per episode and use a lot of music. Here's the brief.)

Here are the main genres:

1 Singer-songwriter (not young) mostly but not limited to male vocals for characters 35—44 age range. Check out tunefind. com to see the tunes we've used for season 1 to get an idea.

2 Non-production-sounding hip hop for dance clubs and for football workout scenes.

3 Rockin' or retro rock for action scenes/sports football scenes (all tempos). We use a lot of this for the show, especially for opening scenes and football games.

4 Rock for younger demo graphic (19–25 year old). No teeny bop or pop.

5 This show likes to use current-sounding singer-songwriter-type easy-going-feel artists for background restaurant scenes with our older main characters. (Brett Dennen may be a good template.) As these scenes have heavy dialogue, vocals can't be too overpowering.

Of course you can send links for me or zip drives. Whatever is easiest.

Thanks again and look forward to perusing your hand-selected tunes for this.

Beer Commercial

The Client: *Beer Company* [company name withheld]

The Concept: On a rooftop party, we see people dancing and having a great time. The DJ turns up the volume but is suddenly interrupted by another happening party on a nearby rooftop. A girl approaches, hands him a *Beer* and now he has a great idea. He adds a vinyl to his scratch table and adds another layer to the music to create one great-sounding mashup. The two DJs raise their *Beers* to one another and continue on.

Tag Line: *Beer*. [Slogan withheld.]

The Music: It's time to be creative! We need two songs that are great individually, but when they come together create an amazing mashup. So feel free to suggest one song ... or two that will work great together. We don't want the end result to sound like a remix. We need a clear contrast.

Things we like ...

Cross-genres: Cypress Hill/Johnny Cash mashup http://www.youtube.com/watch?v=ZwJQy2BkJ-o

Old vs. New: Beatles vs. LCD Soundsystem: http://www.youtube.com/watch?v=MPtWh5XjiHO&feature=player_embedded

Songs with a great beat "Gems" ex. Mos Def's "Quiet Dog" http://www.youtube.com/watch?v=ZchVayloSDc

When searching for tracks, keep these key words in mind for at least one of the tracks:

Should feel human, aspirational, premium, optimistic, smart, urban and energetic (but not wild and too out of control = drunk people partying), inclusive, social party spirit.

Media Rights: TV/Internet—1 year, US

Budget: $150,000 US /per song. This is pending on the song/artists' popularity.

Submission Deadline: Thursday, Nov 18th (end of day)

Bring on the party tunes!

HOW TO GET THE MOST MILES FROM A MUSIC PLACEMENT

Once you get your music licensed, don't let it amount to simply bragging rights and cash—ensure that it is going to make the largest impact on all aspects of your career.

Getting your music featured in or on a TV show, ad, video game, movie and so on should give you a reason to approach your local newspaper, local TV station, local radio station, etc. You should also look into the areas where the show gets the best ratings, the region in which the ad is being aired, the market that the video game is being sold to, and so on, and approach the media in those areas, contact the local promoters so as to play shows in those markets ...

Make sure your music is for sale or that you have a special promo in place.

Post song lyrics to help people searching for your music to find it. Make sure you are including tags such as "heard on ... "

Take advantage of tools like Shazam to get your music discovered as the music is featured! You can learn to submit your music here:

Submit your music to Shazam
atnmusi.ca/ch8h16

Also be sure to learn from others—find out what other artists getting licensed are doing effectively to benefit from the exposure.

Gather as much information about the demographic being targeted as you can. Find out who the audience is, where they live, their age, any and all information you can. A good place to start is by asking the people who license your music, and if they don't know ask who would. You can also research this information online. The more you know about your audience, the better you can be at marketing to them.

Mike James, owner of Milk Music Co., says to be sure you ask for cue/air sheets from the music supervisor (or production company the super works for) or, in the case of commercials, the ad agency involved. Having these sheets to send in to your PRO is an airtight way of making sure you get paid.

MORE RESOURCES

Above the Noise Music Industry Podcast
atnmusi.ca/ch8h17

Artists House Music
atnmusi.ca/ch8h18

Guild of Music Supervisors
atnmusi.ca/ch8h19

How to License Your Music
atnmusi.ca/ch8h20

LicenseQuote
atnmusi.ca/ch8h21

Music Library Report
atnmusi.ca/ch8h22

Music Supervision Central
atnmusi.ca/ch8h23

Play It Loud Music Industry Blog
atnmusi.ca/ch8h24

Play It Loud Music Industry Newsletter
atnmusi.ca/ch8h25

Strategies for licensing the use of music in film
atnmusi.ca/ch8h26

YouLicense
atnmusi.ca/ch8h27

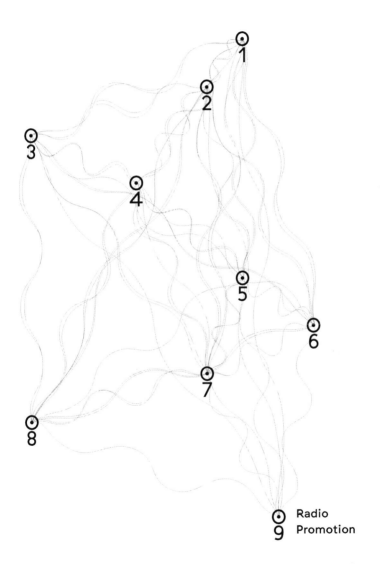

CHAPTER NINE

1

2

3

4

5

6

7

8

9 Radio Promotion

Radio Promotion

Have you ever wanted to turn on the radio and hear your own music? The idea that you would be in a store, in your car, on a bus, in a bar or in another country and hear your song come on the radio is, for many, the ultimate dream come true. Not only is it a vanity dream come true but it is a vital part of commercial success.

Having a "hit" on the radio sells albums, tickets and merch, builds fan bases and so on. Getting a hit on commercial radio as an independent artist is next to impossible. This is one area that the major labels still have a stronghold on. However, there are songs that are so undeniably good that they find a way to radio stardom. You're going to need to know how to get your "undeniably good" song to the right people in the right format and with the right follow-up. And that's what we're going to focus on!

I hear bands say all the time, "The radio has got to play our music — it's like nothing else you've ever heard!" Well, guess what, just because it sounds like nothing else is the very reason it won't get played on commercial stations. If the music is not familiar to listeners within the first few seconds, they will usually change the station, affecting the station's advertisers. And radio does not want to lose sponsors.

Radio stations work hard to develop their brand — a sound and personality their listeners recognize. It's what keeps their audience listening to their station and not another. There's a reason why, if your favourite rock station is playing in another room, from a distance the sonic quality of the songs sounds the same ... it is the station's recognizable sonic brand! If you want your music on a specific radio station your music will have to fit that station's brand.

Aside from acknowledging a station's brand, you need to start by educating yourself as to which radio format your music fits. Sending your latest metal epic to an adult contemporary station is not going to have good results.

Below are a few links that describe the different radio formats. Keep in mind that you can cross into more than one format. Artists like Taylor Swift have been very successful at appealing to multiple formats.

New York Radio Guide
atnmusi.ca/ch9h1

Radio-Locator
atnmusi.ca/ch9h2

Radio Programming Formats
atnmusi.ca/ch9h3

BEFORE STARTING A RADIO CAMPAIGN

These are a few of the things you need in place:

- **A strategy and amount of time you can dedicate to the campaign.** Follow-up is the most time-consuming and most important aspect. Just sending music is *not* enough.

- **At least three finished radio-ready singles.** The music has got to be great, from the songwriting to the production and master. When you listen to your music, does the quality match up to the other music being played? MP3s at 320 kilobits per second (Kbps) are considered broadcast quality.

- **An artist website ready to reap the benefits of radio exposure.** (It should include creative ways to spend money easily; easy sign-ups for a newsletter; tour dates; etc.)

- **If not a tour, the ability to tour** in the radio markets where potential airing will happen.

- **A story that sets you apart,** that shows the buzz surrounding you.

- **The ability to be organized** and follow through!

Renowned Canadian radio promoter Oscar Furtado recommends that, before getting started, you make the radio single available on YouTube. The video needs only to display the single's artwork, although it is worth creating a lyric video (showing the song lyrics) later on. Oscar additionally recommends creating special banners mentioning the single, which you can use for your website as well as social media platforms and of course advertising (blogs, etc.).

Before starting a radio campaign it is advisable to engage radio stations and their hosts via social media as well as at station events and fundraisers. So next time your local radio is putting on an event, be sure to go and mingle and make your presence known.

If you build a rapport with radio before you do a campaign, you greatly increase the likelihood that the station(s) will take a listen and give your single a chance.

An artist's radio campaign that is combined with a tour, new music, a great story and so on will undoubtedly be more successful than if you have not established yourself, and radio is the first medium you approach.

An important thing to do before you make your first contact with any radio program directors (PDs) or music directors (MDs) is to learn what their jobs consist of, what their average day is like, what is expected of them, how many calls they have to take, and so on. This will help you with your approach and with being respectful of their time. Mike James, of Milk Music Co., gives great advice: "Don't be confrontational if you think you are being ignored—you'll end your campaign before it starts." Most PDs and MDs know each other and if there is an artist who is causing a problem, they warn each other. Once again, being professional and friendly is the key—remember the rule of reciprocity!

GETTING YOUR MUSIC TO RADIO

Getting your music to a radio station can be done physically or digitally. Let's focus on digital delivery.

There are a number of companies that will send your music to lists of radio stations. Here are a few:

BDS Nation
atnmusi.ca/ch9h4

Digital Media Distribution System (DMDS)
atnmusi.ca/ch9h5

Radio Submit
atnmusi.ca/ch9h6

These companies offer digital delivery of your music to the inboxes of radio music directors and program directors. They notify the MDs and PDs that they have new music to review.

The MDs and PDs receive a brief summary or story and photo of the artist—and, of course, the music! They are given the option to stream or download the tracks. If you are lucky, they download your music and add it to their playlists. To give yourself the best chance of that happening, you will need to follow up! For starters, you'll want to make sure the MDs and PDs actually check out and listen to your music. Just sending the music is not enough!

Artists and labels hire a radio promoter or tracker because their job is to ensure your music gets the best chance of being listened to and added to a station's playlist. A good radio promoter or tracker will have established relationships with radio stations.

A company like DMDS (see link above) provides you with a way to digitally deliver your music and story to the radio stations and also with a way to discover if the stations have streamed and/or downloaded the track after receiving it. What is more, you can see the actual names of the people at the station who showed interest. This is key information!

What a company like DMDS will *not* provide is direct contact information (email or phone number) because of confidentiality laws. So it is your job to find that information. The best way is to search the station call numbers online and access the contact information on their websites.

Once you have a phone number for the station, you can call and ask the times that are best to reach the MD (or PD, depending on who is in charge of new music). Keep in mind that many commercial stations have the playlists delivered to them and the MDs simply select tracks from the playlists provided. This makes it next to impossible to have your tracks added, as the MDs and PDs really have no say.

Most stations, especially in Canada, will have an "indie night"-type show that features upcoming artists. Canadian content law ensures that all Canadian radio stations include a certain amount of Canadian content (CanCon) in their program's and "indie night" shows are often packed with CanCon. So, getting added to rotation might not be possible, but being featured on an "indie night" show is a lot easier and it provides great exposure to the station's audience!

If you do get featured on this type of show, be sure to let your fan base know. It is a good reason for a call to action. Get you fans to phone in, email, comment on the station's social media outlets, request your music … You want their help to show that there is an audience for your music.

Getting Organized

I have found it helpful to create spreadsheets that list radio station contact information, including names and job positions, postal addresses, email addresses and phone numbers. I also include columns for comments. This is very important for the purpose of following up, as well as for recording feedback.

If you decide to use a spreadsheet, every time you phone a radio station you can include the essence of the conversation in your comments column. It might be that the person you speak to needs another week because she hasn't had a chance to listen to the track, or the person may say that he loves the track but it's not a fit or the vocals don't work or the program doesn't have space this week and maybe you can follow up next week, or the person may be taking the music to a music meeting and need you to follow up the next day, or perhaps the person gives you the contact information of another station to be in touch with ... Any and all feedback is important.

The process of gathering contact information as well as calling up and following up with the radio stations, as you can imagine, is a time-consuming endeavour (another reason people pay a radio tracker or promoter to do it). That said, once you have done the research and have the contact information, you can certainly establish your own relationships. This is especially useful for your future campaigns.

There are websites that provide contact information for radio stations. Some are free and some sell the service. Here are a few:

National Campus and Community Radio Association (NCRA)
atnmusi.ca/ch9h7

Radio Station World
atnmusi.ca/ch9h9

Streema
atnmusi.ca/ch9h10

Radio-Locator
atnmusi.ca/ch9h8

If you are considering hiring a radio tracker or promoter, one idea is to do some of the groundwork yourself. If you succeed in getting a few stations to add you, radio trackers or promoters will quite often charge you a reduced rate as they no longer have to start from scratch.

In regards to how long you should promote a single, three months is the average duration of a campaign—but that is not to say that a single can't be pushed for as long as a year. The adds to radio stations achieved in that period of time are generally as many as you can expect to get.

With all the hard work you put in the first time around, the second time should be easier. Any amount of success at radio should be followed up with another single—once you get the ball rolling, you don't want it to stop!

With the results of the first campaign you should pay special attention to the stations that added you, featured you, showed interest and that you built a rapport with. The results should be factored into your tour routing.

Digital Music Delivery?

Let's talk about getting the music to the radio station. If you use a company like DMDS to digitally deliver it, you can either pay a set amount for a package of stations (e.g., "Country Top 100" or "North American College and Community") or you can pay a yearly membership and handpick the stations you want to send to. This is good if you only want to target radio stations in your touring market, or to gain exposure in the surrounding area of a festival you are performing at, or maybe you or your music are being featured in a TV show and you want to get airplay in the markets where it receives the best ratings ... The membership fee, however, is not cheap!

There are companies that are paid members of DMDS and that act as brokers. Many radio promoters are also paid members of DMDS and will act as brokers too. They offer, through their membership, the service of hand-selecting the stations you want to target, at a price. The price is usually an upload fee plus a set rate per radio station. Here is one of those companies:

RDR Music Group
atnmusi.ca/ch9h11

To summarize: You can use the services of companies like DMDS or brokers to send your music digitally to the inboxes of the MDs and

PDs of the radio stations that best suit your music. With the knowledge of who opened, streamed and downloaded the tracks, and after finding their contact information on the station's websites, it is your job to track and promote your music through follow-up.

Strategy

As for the strategy, like all areas of your career, don't be random! Line your ducks up, make sure all the pieces work together. Everything should feed into everything else: airplay should help with a tour; in turn a tour gives an extra reason to be played on the radio; from a PR angle, a tour and radio play add interest for interviews; interviews in the local papers of the towns and cities you tour in help with radio stations having a reason to play your music …

Pitch

When you are not an established artist, you need to build a compelling story. For example, instead of going to major commercial radio first, go to secondary-market radio and get as many adds as you can there. Get your music to college and community radio, where you can more easily do on-air interviews and performances. This helps to build your on-air experience. Use secondary markets in which you can tour and build a fan base willing to call in and request your song. If you can show the major commercial stations the success in the secondary markets, you are more likely to get interest. At the end of the day, nobody wants to miss out on a hit!

Build a story that shows you are building a buzz. A radio station is much more likely to play you if you are touring through the area rather than play a band that never leaves its hometown. You can even combine your efforts with that of the local show promoters to work together at getting interviews, on-air performances, spins and so on. Everyone stands to benefit.

Even if a station initially says no or hasn't made up its mind on a track, it is wise to keep the station up-to-date on the progress the track is making. By this I mean letting someone at the station know if other stations are adding the track, or about features, performances worthy of mention and any other type of successes that the band is having.

Getting on the Charts

Focus on reporting stations. If you get enough action in secondary markets, you will find yourself appearing on the charts. In the case of college and community radio in Canada, you will appear on *!Earshot* (atnmusi.ca/ch9h12). For the college charts in the United States, check out *CMJ* (atnmusi.ca/ch9h13).

You can request to be added, or simply sign up on the station's website, to receive the station's weekly charts and top playlists. If we go back to the concept of "Fan Profiling" (Chapter 2), this information is useful for finding bands that have similar sounds and whose fan base could be yours too.

The commercial radio stations in Canada are monitored primarily by Nielsen Broadcast Data Systems (BDS) and Mediabase. These companies monitor the reporting stations (more than 240 radio stations across Canada at the time of writing this; keep in mind that the number of radio stations can fluctuate quarterly). BDS and Mediabase input the spins that make up the charts. The higher up these charts you get, the more stations are playing your music and the more spins you are getting. This ultimately affects other opportunities, including sales and performances.

Using census data provided by BDS, in 2007 the Society of Composers, Authors and Music Publishers of Canada (SOCAN — a principal performing rights organization, or PRO, for Canadians) started to take advantage of digital audio identification (DAI) technology to provide a more complete record (census) of performances on certain types of Canadian radio stations. In order to take advantage of DAI technology and stand the best chances of charting and getting paid for radio spins by your PRO, ensure that you are signed up with BDS and Mediabase. You can do this directly with them, although DMDS also provides this option as will some PROs. I will say this is not for all genres of music and in fact is only if your songs fit the format of those stations logged under this method; in other words, if you play

Brazilian death metal–ambient polka dub, you probably aren't going to get played on a BDS/DAI-logged station!

Get your tracks encoded with BDS
atnmusi.ca/ch9h14

Get your tracks encoded with Mediabase
atnmusi.ca/ch9h15

SOCAN distributes royalties for radio play to its members based on data collected from three pools: DAI, surveys (e.g., college and community stations) and CBC. From the roughly 850 stations that SOCAN collects licence fees from, more than 65 percent of the money generated comes from the 250 or so stations (this number fluctuates from quarter to quarter) in the DAI pool. Surveys are conducted four times a year. In Canada the royalty rate for a survey station is about $4.40 a play, but with only twenty-eight days a year (or seven days every quarter for each station) of logs, you will be paid less frequently. The royalty for BDS/DAI-logged stations is about $1.50 per play (this rate fluctuates quarterly), but because it is a census, every play is logged. If you want to know which stations are monitored by BDS, here is a list:

BDS Stations Monitored
atnmusi.ca/ch9h16

Submitting Music

Radio stations have their own preferences when it comes to music submissions. Most commercial stations want digital delivery and a lot of college and community stations want physical. Sometimes you'll find that even though a station might have received a digital copy, the person you dealt with still wants a physical copy too. College and community stations like to have physical copies for their libraries, which are available for visitors and DJs to pick up copies from, to play on their shows.

When sending physical copies, make sure you highlight which tracks you want listened to. Even take off the wrapping to make getting to your music as easy as possible. Make sure you have the right information on the album's spine for shelving purposes. If you're Canadian, make sure you have specified the CanCon (Canadian content).

Send the stations you build a relationship with music and/or tickets to give away; get creative with ways to engage and reward the listeners. Be sure to build and maintain your relationship with the MDs and PDs—you never know where they will be working next! Dealing with some of your best contacts will be like dealing with friends, so sending a Christmas card or something similar is not a bad thing. Relationships are huge in this industry.

The finer details
When you are planning your radio campaign, keep in mind:

- Time zones. Very important! If it means making calls at 5 a.m., then that's what you've got to do.

- Send your music on a Monday and make your first follow-ups on the Tuesday; Wednesday is often when music meetings take place and decisions are made!

- Aside from CDs, WAV and MP3s at 320 Kbps are considered broadcast quality.

Free Music Delivery

Ultimately, although companies like DMDS have become the industry standard of music delivery, that is of course not the only way. Here is a way of using free resources to create your own digital delivery:

Use an email marketing company like MailChimp or Mad Mimi to create a "newsletter." You want to essentially recreate what a company like DMDS sends. So, you need to make sure you have a photo, a brief description or story of the artist, as well as a way to stream and download the music. For this you can use companies like SoundCloud or Bandcamp to embed a music player for the single you are promoting. You can then use a company like Hightail, Dropbox or Box.net, or even Google Drive or Microsoft SkyDrive to create a file for the download. Then you just create a link on the newsletter or promo to the file.

Email marketing companies like MailChimp and Mad Mimi allow you to see who opens what you send, as well as the links they click on. This means that you can see which station's MDs and PDs have opened your email and whether or not they have downloaded the tracks. You can also use the analytical tools of SoundCloud or Bandcamp and so on to see the numbers of streams and downloads.

Companies like DMDS provide you with a list on their website of stations that they deliver to. You can research the stations' contact info online and in a phone call find out the names of who you should send your music to as well as their email address and extension number.

CONSIDERATIONS

If you want to make things happen, you'll find a way—everything else is just an excuse!

Aside from terrestrial radio stations, don't forget internet and satellite radio.

A number of companies offer their expertise in creating specific playlists for businesses (such as restaurants, shopping malls, hair salons, etc.) that create the perfect atmosphere and sonic architecture for the business's brand. They are paid for their services and the artists whose music they use are paid through their PRO as public performance. Research who these companies are and send them your music.

Mood Media is the big one and is the parent company for Muzak and DMX. I suggest researching online how to get your music to them. There are smaller companies that are always looking to add quality music to the playlists they offer their clients, including Canadian ones such as:

Music Direction
atnmusi.ca/ch9h17

There are companies, such as Westwood One, that provide broadcast programming and radio content to hundreds of stations. And then you have companies like The Lund Consultants, Inc. that are radio and programming consultants for many stations. Their expertise is to inform the stations through market research which music and content is going to give a station higher ratings. There's nothing wrong with being on their radar either!

If you are able to write a Christmas track, that is a great time to go to radio. Stations of all formats play Christmas music. It is a time to expose your name to the masses. Back it up with a Christmas tour. You'll be able to promote yourself to all stations in the towns and cities you tour through!

MORE RESOURCES

Canadian content requirements for music on Canadian Radio
atnmusi.ca/ch9h18

Interview with Director of Music Programming at Sirius XM Radio Canada, Jeff Leake
atnmusi.ca/ch9h19

Interview with Radio Promoter Oscar Furtado
atnmusi.ca/ch9h20

Play MPE: Secure Media Delivery System
atnmusi.ca/ch9h21

Lund Consultants, Inc.
atnmusi.ca/ch9h22

Westwood One
atnmusi.ca/ch9h23

Epilogue

Music has been a part of my life since I can first remember. I used to lie under my grandfather's grand piano and listen as he played. Sometimes he would have a friend over for piano duets or be accompanied by a violinist. Lying beneath the piano, I'd watch his feet on the pedals and listen to the sounds resonating and blending together in harmonic bliss. It was such a powerful experience that I am transported back as I write these lines.

When I was four my grandfather started teaching me to play the piano, and then at the age of seven I picked up my stepfather's guitar … and I haven't put it down since.

Music has never been an option but rather a necessity. Aside from my family, it is what gives me a sense of belonging. I cannot imagine my life without music.

I realize that this is how many people feel. And like many, I wanted to make music my life. However, in order to be a career musician I realized it would take more moving parts than just "talent." At that moment I decided to turn my attention to the business of music.

What started as trying to help my own career turned into helping others with theirs. It fulfills me to see others thrive in this industry and I have been fortunate to be a part of many success stories.

I try to approach everything with a curious mind, to get as much information as I possibly can so as to have a deep understanding and be able to form an opinion. The contents of this book have allowed me to share what I am most curious about and what engages me on a daily basis, and that is the music industry.

Writing this book has been a liberating experience as well as a way of giving clarity to my own thoughts. I have put in as much as I can and left out as little as possible. My hope is always that the student surpasses the teacher, and that can only happen when you share all that you know.

I started this book by urging you, before anything else, to make incredible music. It always comes back to that: make great music and believe in being yourself, in making *your* incredible music.

From climbing a mountain in the Andes to climbing the music charts, success means taking one step at a time and never losing site of your goals.

It is hard to tell just what the future holds, but one thing is for sure: there will always be music. I hope this book enables you to be a part of the soundtrack to many people's lives ...

—Aaron Bethune

The End

Acknowledgments

I have to thank my beautiful wife, Laura, for being my biggest supporter and for putting up with me while I was becoming an author. My son, Oliver, for being a reminder of the importance of completing this project and setting an example.

My dad for believing in me and what is now my mantra, that your thoughts create your future; my mom for giving me the books that helped set the bar high for my own writing. Both my parents for being entrepreneurial and showing me you can do whatever you put your mind to. Doug for the encouragement and for giving me a place to write this. I also have to acknowledge my mom and stepdad for supporting me in my early mountaineering adventures. Mike and Fern for their unwavering support.

I need to thank the mountain in this book, Cerro Aconcagua, for opening my eyes and giving me a new view on life. My grandfather and dad for introducing me to the piano and my stepdad for introducing me to the guitar. Life has never been the same since.

Thanks go to my Above the Noise music industry class for setting the wheels in motion for what would become this book. To my friends Dan, Carl, Niko and Zack and producer Rick Salt for giving me some of the experiences I needed for writing *Musicpreneur*. My friend and editor Cheryl for guiding me on my journey to being an author and for putting so much love into this project. It really is as good as it is because of her. My friend Josh for understanding my vision and giving his interpretation in the design of this book. I am very grateful to Josh for writing the introduction to what I feel is one of the most important chapters of this book. I was delighted and humbled to have Marty Frascogna read the book and write the foreword in support of my vision. To Mark Hall for being a mentor and role model of authenticity. I am immensely grateful to Terry O'Brien at SOCAN, who went above and beyond to ensure that the chapters on copyrights, publishing and radio promotion were accurate, well-written and Canadian-friendly. For taking the time to read over the original manuscript and give me their feedback—all of which has made it into the pages of this book—I want to acknowledge Eric Alper, Steve Azar, Cameo Carlson, Rob Feduk, Oscar Furtado, Bill Girdwood, Robbie Grayson, David Hayman, Mike James, Steve Jones, Karen Kang, Chris Keaton, Steve Keller, Pelle Lidell, Brett Manning, Mark Montgomery, Marty Neumeier, Lee Parsons, Andrew Roberts, Luke Ronsse and Jonathan Rosner. I am very grateful and am always a call away to return the favour! Thank you to Arbutus Music for providing space when needed and Jamie Penner for all the support, including technical.

There are many more people I am thankful to as I finish up my first book. You know who you are.

Select Bibliography

The following are some of the books and articles that are referenced or quoted in Musicpreneur *and/or that helped shape the thoughts for the writing of this book.*

Adams, Ramsay, David Hnatiuk, and David Weiss. *Music Supervision: The Complete Guide to Selecting Music for Movies, TV, Games, & New Media*. New York: Schirmer Trade Books, 2005.

Avalon, Moses. *Confessions of a Record Producer: How to Survive the Scams and Shams of the Music Business*. San Francisco: Backbeat Books, 2006.

Brabec, Jeffrey, and Todd Brabec. *Music Money and Success: The Insider's Guide to Making Money in the Music Business*, 7th ed. New York: Schirmer Trade Books, 2011.

Bunzeck, Nico, et al. "Absolute Coding of Stimulus Novelty in the Human Substantia Nigra/VTA." *Neuron* 51, 369–379 (2006).

Byrne, David. *How Music Works*. San Francisco: McSweeney's, 2012.

D'Agostino, Ryan. *Rich Like Them: My Door-to-Door Search for the Secrets of Wealth in America's Richest Neighborhoods*. New York: Little, Brown, 2009.

Dutton, Kevin. *Split Second Persuasion: The Ancient Art and New Science of Changing Minds*. Toronto: Anchor Canada, 2011.

———. *The Wisdom of Psychopaths: What Saints, Spies, and Serial Killers Can Teach Us about Success*. Toronto: Anchor Canada, 2013.

Fisher, Rodger, and William Ury. With Bruce Patton. *Getting to Yes: Negotiating Agreement without Giving In*, 3rd ed. New York: Penguin Group, 2011.

Frank, Jay. *Future Hit DNA: How the Digital Revolution Is Changing Top 10 Songs*. Nashville: Futurehit, 2009.

———. *Hack Your Hit: Free and Cheap Marketing Tips for Musicians*. Nashville: Futurehit, 2012.

Frascogna, Xavier M., and H. Lee Hetherington. *This Business of Artist Management: The Standard Reference to All Phases of Managing a Musician's Career from Both the Artist's and Manager's Point of View*. New York: Billboard Books, 2004.

Gladwell, Malcolm. *Blink: The Power of Thinking without Thinking*. New York: Little, Brown, 2005.

———. *Outliers: The Story of Success*. New York: Back Bay Books, 2011.

———. *The Tipping Point: How Little Things Can Make a Big Difference*. New York: Little, Brown, 2000.

Godin, Seth. *The Icarus Deception*. New York: Penguin Group, 2012.

Heller, Steven. *Iron Fists: Branding the 20th-Century Totalitarian State*. New York: Paidon, 2008.

Jackson, Tom. *Live Music Method: All Roads Lead to the Stage*. Printed in the US: PCG Business, a division of Pilot Communications, 2012.

Jones, Steve. *Brand Like a Rock Star: Lessons from Rock 'n' Roll to Make Your Business Rich and Famous*. Austin, TX: Greenleaf Book Group Press, 2012.

Kahneman, Daniel. *Thinking, Fast and Slow*. New York: Farrar, Straus and Giroux, 2011.

Kang, Karen. *BrandingPays: The Five-Step System to Reinvent Your Personal Brand*. Palo Alto, CA: BrandingPays Media, 2013.

King, Emily, and Angus Hyland. *C/ID: Visual Identity and Branding for the Arts*. London: Laurence King, 2006.

Krasilovsky, M. William, and Sidney Shemel. With contributions by John M. Gross. *This Business of Music: The Definitive Guide to the Music Industry*, 8th ed. New York: Billboard Books, 2000.

Lathrop, Tad. *This Business of Global Music Marketing: Global Strategies for Maximizing Your Music's Popularity and Profits*. New York: Billboard Books, 2007.

Levitin, Daniel J. *This Is Your Brain on Music: The Science of a Human Obsession*. New York: Penguin Group, 2007.

Lindstrom, Martin. *Buyology: Truth and Lies about Why We Buy*. New York: Doubleday, 2008.

MailChimp. "Email Marketing Benchmarks" (Resources/Research). http://mailchimp.com/resources/research/email-marketing-benchmarks/ (Accessed November 14, 2013)

Mlodinow, Leonard. *Subliminal: How Your Unconscious Mind Rules Your Behavior*. New York: Vintage Books, 2013.

Neumeier, Marty. *The Brand Gap*. Berkeley, CA: New Riders, 2006.

———. *Metaskills: Five Talents for the Robotic Age*. Berkeley, CA: New Riders, 2013.

Passman, Donald S. *All You Need to Know about the Music Business* 6th ed. New York: Free Press, 2006.

Pink, Daniel H. *Drive: The Surprising Truth about What Motivates Us*. New York: Penguin Group, 2009.

———. *To Sell Is Human: The Surprising Truth about Moving Others*. New York: Penguin Group, 2012.

————. *A Whole New Mind: Why Right Brainers Will Rule the Future*. New York: Penguin Group, 2006.

Redfield, James. *The Celestine Prophecy: An Adventure*. New York: Grand Central, 2006.

Robinson, Ken. With Lou Aronica. *The Element: How Finding Your Passion Changes Everything*. New York: Penguin Group, 2009.

Sanderson, Paul. *Musicians and the Law in Canada: A Guide to the Law, Contracts and Practice in the Canadian Music Business*, 3rd ed. Toronto: Carswell, 2000.

Seelig, Tina. *InGenius: A Crash Course on Creativity*. New York: HarperCollins, 2012.

————. *What I Wish I Knew When I Was 20: A Crash Course on Making Your Place in the World*. New York: HarperCollins, 2009.

Shacher, Ron, et al. "Brands: The Opiate of the Nonreligious Masses?" *Marketing Science* 30(1): 92–110 (2011).

Sinek, Simon. *Start with Why: How Great Leaders Inspire Everyone to Take Action*. New York: Portfolio, 2009.

Van Praet, Douglas. *Unconscious Branding: How Neuroscience Can Empower (and Inspire) Marketing*. New York: Palgrave Macmillan, 2012.

Villoldo, Alberto. *The Four Insights*. Carlsbad, CA: Hay House, 2006.

Wentz, Brooke. *Hey, That's My Music! Music Supervision, Licensing, and Content Acquisition*. New York: Hal Leonard Books, 2007.

Werner, Kenny. *Effortless Mastery: Liberating the Master Within*. New Albany, IN: Jamey Abersold Jazz, 1996.

Wilsey, Darren. With Daylle Deanna Schwartz. *The Musician's Guide to Licensing Music: How to Get your Music into Film, TV, Advertising, Digital Media & Beyond*. New York: Billboard Books, 2010.

Wixen, Randall D. *The Plain and Simple Guide to Music Publishing*. Milwaukee, WI: Hal Leonard Corp., 2005.

Wooten, Victor L. *The Music Lesson: A Spiritual Search for Growth through Music*. New York: Penguin Group, 2006.

Zander, Rosamund Stone, and Benjamin Zander. *The Art of Possibility*. New York: Penguin Group, 2000.

About the Author

Photographer: Mark Maryanovich

Aaron Bethune was born in Montreal and grew up in England and Spain. He has played piano since the age of four and guitar since the age of seven. He studied Jazz Performance at university on Vancouver Island, on Canada's West Coast, has recorded a number of pop-rock albums and been a session player on numerous recordings. His involvement in the music business started with the world of touring and he has booked major label acts as well as independents from Spain to Japan. With his company PlayItLoudMusic he has licensed music into major TV shows, movies and commercials. He has developed, mentored and managed artists, is an in-demand music and creative consultant, and has been a part of many success stories along the way. His expertise in music, branding and marketing goes beyond the music industry and has allowed him the opportunity to work with many forward-thinking companies and individuals. He is a juror for FACTOR (The Foundation Assisting Canadian Talent on Recordings), a speaker and a music educator. He is a musicpreneur and is constantly looking for ways to break patterns through creative collaborations. He is passionate about the outdoors, with a special interest in mountaineering, and lives in Victoria, British Columbia with his wife, Laura, and son, Oliver Winter.